THE GOTHAM LIBRARY
OF THE NEW YORK UNIVERSITY PRESS

The Gotham Library is a series of original works and critical studies. Devoted to significant works and major authors and to literary topics of enduring importance, Gotham Library texts offer the best in literature and criticism.

Comparative and Foreign Language Literature:
Robert J. Clements, Editor

Comparative and English Language Literature:
James W. Tuttleton, Editor

Poetry and Truth in Robert Browning's *The Ring and the Book*

William E. Buckler

New York University Press
New York *and* London
1985

The publication of this work has been subvented in part by a grant from the Abraham and Rebecca Stein Faculty Publications Fund of New York University, Department of English.

Library of Congress Cataloging in Publication Data

Buckler, William Earl
  Poetry and truth in Robert Browning's The ring and the book.
  (The Gotham library of the New York University Press)
  Includes bibliographies and index.
  1. Browning, Robert, 1812–1889. Ring and the book.
2. Franceschini, Guido, conte, 1657–1698, in fiction,
drama, poetry, etc. 3. Franceschini, Pompilia, 1680–
1698, in fiction, drama, poetry, etc. 4. Italy in
literature. I. Title.
PR4219.B8 1985   821'.8   84-22808
ISBN 0-8147-1072-7 (alk. paper)

Clothbound editions of New York University Press
books are Smyth-sewn and printed on permanent
and durable acid-free paper.

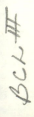

For three teachers

Sister Mary Victor Bowling, S.L.
Father Jerome Palmer, O.S.B.
Professor Royal A. Gettmann

who have been unwithdrawing presences in my consciousness

Contents

Preface

I have attempted throughout this book to look with fresh, open eyes at the chief work of one of the major poets of the nineteenth century. My focus has been on the poetry rather than the learning, on the imagination rather than the erudition, of one of the spectacular literary texts of the post-Romantic period. Like Henry James, I perceive *The Ring and the Book* as giving us what is most "ineffably . . . worth while" in our own lives, namely, a "noble exercise of our imagination"; that is the quality of the poem I have tried to capture.

In Chapter 1, I have drawn on an article previously published in the *Henry James Review*, V (Winter 1984) entitled "Rereading Henry James Rereading Robert Browning: 'The Novel in *The Ring and the Book*.' " I am grateful to the editor for permission to do so.

The text of *The Ring and the Book* used is that edited by Richard D. Altick (New Haven: Yale University Press, 1981), which, with minor corrections and a few alterations in printing style, is that of the first edition of 1868–1869. It is the basic text of the Everyman (1911), Oxford (1912), Penguin (1971), and Yale editions. All references to the poem will be given by book and line number in the text. However, quotations incorporated into my critical exposition do not observe the Penguin style of outside single quotation marks with inside double quotation marks, but the more familiar American practice of double marks outside, single marks for quotations within quotations. This slight alteration should reduce confusion and add to the comfort of reading.

The main arguments of this book were presented as a series of three lectures at the Graduate Center of the City University of New York in March–April, 1984, under the auspices of the Victorian Committee of the Graduate English Program.

For help in seeing the book through the press, I am profoundly grateful to two young nineteenth-century scholars with admirable authority of both eye and mind, Debbie Chappell and Doucet Fischer.

1.

Introduction: An Essay in Critical Redirection

On May 7, 1912, the Academic Committee of the Royal Society of Literature marked the centenary of Robert Browning's birth with an address by Henry James entitled "The Novel in *The Ring and the Book.*"[1] Though the address has become famous—"a classic of enthusiastic appreciation"[2]—it has never been accepted by commentators on *The Ring and the Book* for the value of its critical insights into how and how well the poem actually works but has been said to tell us "more about James's view of the art of the novel than it does about the poem."[3] Such benign neglect of what is probably still the most thoroughly creative and critically apt introduction to *The Ring and the Book* has been inevitable and unfortunate. It has been inevitable because academic critics regularly follow a set of interests, habits, rules quite different from those of imaginative creators and are suspicious, if polite, toward intruders on their turf; it has been unfortunate because the qualities generally lacking in traditional academic commentary on the poem are the very qualities James offers. What James emphasizes is the clarity, strength, honesty, precision, and persuasiveness with which the poet has found and released into our imaginative consciousness the "most worth while" significance of his material; he has done all that art can properly aspire to—has looked into the heart of human experience in such a way as to give us what is most "ineffably . . . worth while" in our own lives, a "noble exercise of our imagination" (p. 410). That is just the quality later commentary on *The Ring and the Book* has lacked, and as a result, the poem has suffered a steady critical decline.

"The Novel in *The Ring and the Book*" is no ordinary piece of criticism. In it, James pays Browning the highest compliment one writer can pay to another: he adopts the poet's "favourite system" and acknowledges through a strategy of dramatic resistance, finally overcome, the profound influence of Browning on his own imagination. "The Novel in *The Ring and the Book*" is a dramatic monologue in prose in which James subjects criticism to creation by converting a critical argument to an imaginative experience. Like *The Ring and the Book* itself, it is an exercise in creative-critical reading in which James shifts the focus from analytical criticism as usually practiced to creative experience and takes thereby the risky chance that his audience, estranged by his strategy of reaching the pinnacle of critical affirmation by the circuitous route of critical depreciation, will wholly misconceive his ultimate intention. Like Browning, he asks his audience to look through the substance at the thing signified and to see that, if his technique has failed, his intention has not, namely, to pay Browning the refined sort of homage that a willing and active acceptance of his imaginative influence represents.[4]

James fully recognized the monstrous aesthetic challenge (the "earthquake") that Browning accepted in undertaking to write *The Ring and the Book*. He was not the "fabulist" of the situation, its "inventor and projector," but its acceptor; not its architect and builder, but its appropriator and dismantler. With his "swoop of practised perception" and an energy, courage, and confidence perhaps never before shown to the same degree by a poet over a forgotten and defiant slice of human history, he sought, with "a curiosity almost sublime in its freedom, yet almost homely in its method" (p. 388), to transcend artistic form as traditionally apprehended.

No critical commentator on *The Ring and the Book* has ever ignored this point, of course; it is fundamental to the whole aesthetic rationale of the poem and is expansively elaborated by the poet-speaker in Book I. But James appraises it from a vantage point different from that of the other commentators, including the most recent ones. Their focus has been on the fait accompli, and their method has been explication, paraphrase, summary, and adoption or rejection. James has a different focus—that of a fellow artist intensely devoted to art—and both his skepticism and his awe are stimulated, not by prosy arguments about just what the poet meant by the ring metaphor, but by the audacity *and enthusiasm* with which an established artist—one who had already produced such fine works as " 'Men and Women,' 'Dramatic Lyrics,' 'Dramatis Personae' and sundry plays" (p. 388)—would dare to base an ambitious work of art on "a block of sense already in position and requiring not to be shaped and squared and caused any further to solidify . . ." (p. 388). For that, James saw no precedent, and in it he had no a priori faith. It was too great a break with past assumptions of artists about art to hold much promise of success. On the other hand, the "energy of appropriation" on the part of an accomplished artist was unprecedented too, and this kept James's skepticism from hardening into frozen unbelief. Thus James pointed directly at the *creator's* issue that has been too perfunctorily shuffled around by other critics: how Browning became an important founder of poetic modernism on the basis of wholly "founded" materials, or how the *poet's* story takes critical precedence over the *poem's* story, as we know that, in an important sense, Browning intended.

Analogous to the cautionary force the poet's enthusiasm for his new aesthetic adventure has on the critic is his appearance of an inordinate and relentless design upon the reader: "Browning is 'upon' us, straighter upon us always, somehow, than anyone else of his race . . ." (p. 399). And yet, there is "just the hint of one of those flaws" "glimmer[ing] through our poet's splendid hocus-pocus" that raises doubts. Is the shape he gives to things "too complete"? Is there a degree of "pretension" in his apparent determination "to impose" his subject on us (p. 393)? And is even our tendency to "recoil," to "push our chair back . . . just to see a little better" also the result of authorial calculation (p. 399)? It is an enormously interesting question, and in it there is the possibility of the poem's redemption from one of the most ambiguous reader responses to it.[5]

James hints at something very basic and imaginative—that Browning makes of himself a calculated illusion, an exaggerated metaphor, of our common if variously subtle rage for dotting i's and crossing t's and invites us, if we will, to consider at a truly radical level that one man's poetry, like his facts and his perceptions, is another man's prose. After all, why should everything be relative except aesthetics? Medieval hocus-pocus is being set against Renaissance smart-aleckness, and it can be assented to in infinitely varying degrees. The radicalism of James's suspicion is consistent with his sense that Browning is changing the rules at their very roots and opens the largest question of poetry's relationship to truth (or the poem's overall aesthetic significance) to possibilities whose radical implications later critics have not been quite willing to pursue.

Another aspect of *The Ring and the Book* that James makes positively conversional is recognized with the experienced eye and sensibility of a fellow artist—the picture, the ambience, the quantitative atmosphere of late-seventeenth-century Italy. "We have in the whole thing . . . the element of action which is at the same time constant picture, and the element of picture which is at the same time constant action," a moving "mass"—"thick," "effective," and "complete." Acclaim of this aspect of the poem is unqualified: it is so true, vivid, beautiful, and infatuating, provides such a heated bath for the senses and perceptions, that the critic surrenders to the creator in a "cloud of gold-dust" from the "Golden Isles" of poetry. In such an atmosphere, such a "temperature," he *wants* "to feel" both the "historic and aesthetic truth" of the poem, both its "pictorial" and its "moral" interest and unity.

This response of the artist in James the critic has found little correspondence in later commentators. They have been all but blind and deaf and immune to the peculiar sights and sounds and fevers to which James totally succumbed. They have made epistemological, ethical, psychological, theological, and thinly historical arguments, but they have hardly ever shown that they can immerse themselves in the medium itself, can hear and measure and smell and look and understand at a truly physical level. And yet, as James fully understood, late-seventeenth-century Italy is no mere accident of the Pompilia myth; the myth's literary character, its complexly interwoven morality-play action, loses much of its human reality, much of its life and carriage, when it is extracted from its setting and made a debate rather than a sensuously textured experience of people in a certain time and place and physical-spiritual climate. This was Browning's antidote to the common critical temptation to distill the principle out of the person, his way of "instracting" truth as a corrective to abstracting it. As the poet-speaker's recollection of his discovery of the Old Yellow Book in "Lorenzo Square" that June day is made inseparable from all the ambient circumstances in which the discovery was made (I, 33–83), so the various characters speak under the strongest sense of time, place, and circumstance, and in rendering their personal testimony—consciously or unconsciously, manipulatively or inadvertently—they create thousands of images of their temporal, spatial, and attitudinal locus in a world that, however metaphoric or representative of a timeless human state, is particularized and peculiar to their story. Each breathes an individual air, is accustomed to an individual smell, whistles individually in an individual dark. Roman and Tuscan see the world in different lights, use different body languages, are amused by tales of different textures. Everyone, including Pompilia and the Pope, shows his or her peculiar form of bravado, and everyone, like the Pope, faces a future of terrifying possibilities that, even if judged to be implicit in the human condition, have vivid peculiarities of time, place, and circumstance. *The Ring and the Book* is poetry, not history, but it is planted in historical illusion. That palpable ambience is the medium from which its feeder roots draw the nutrients, the life-force upon which the illusion, and hence the poetry, depends.

James identifies three interwoven characteristics of *The Ring and the Book* as poetry qua poetry. One is what he perceives as Browning's underlying idea of "the poetic":

> To express his inner self . . . and to express it utterly, even if no matter how, was clearly, for his own measure and consciousness of that inner self, to *be* poetic; and the solution of all the deviations and disparities or, speaking critically, monstrosities, in the mingled tissue of this work, is the fact that whether or no by such convulsions of soul and sense life got delivered for him, the garment of life (which for him was poetry and poetry alone) got disposed in its due and adequate multitudinous folds. (p. 398)

A second characteristic is the source of a "perpetual anomaly": despite the fact that Browning magnifies all the chief figures in the poem by giving to each a "copious share" of personality, an "iridescent wash . . . of temper and faculty" out of "his own great reservoir of spiritual health," they still make of the poem "a great [independent] living thing, a great objective mass" (p. 398). A third characteristic is Browning's transformation of this "great living thing," this "great objective mass," totally into language: "We move with him but in images and references and vast and far correspondences; we eat but of strange compounds and drink but of rare distillations; and very soon . . . we feel ourselves . . . in the world of Expression at any cost" (p. 398).

These active, nontheoretical, and, in a practical sense, dominant characteristics of the personality of the poem are the chief determinants of the strong physical impression it makes. The individual self-portraits express the poet's inner self "utterly" in that the creation of them wrings from him all his capacity to perceive and tell the truth, to reach the outer limits of informed, imaginative conscientiousness. Even if we should withhold from him a judgment of critical success, we can hardly deny that, as a poet, he has gone all the way. The "magnification" obvious in the self-portraits is the poet's way of declaring that his characters, too, must be given the opportunity to express their inner selves "utterly" and that, however one may feel about their individual perceptions and evaluations, they all hold true as characters even under the microscope of the poet's imagination. The conversion of everything into language is a reminder that that is the chief poetizing process of our daily lives and therefore these self-portraits are exaggerated mirrors of ourselves. Poetry *is* expression as, for better or worse, expression is poetry. We may use the term in other figurative and illuminating senses, and other arts may find analogies in poetry as poetry finds analogies in the other arts. But in the final analysis, poetry is language, at once the most common, most abused, and rarest gift to man. *The Ring and the Book* is a splendid revel of language, and it is to be measured, in one particular and crucial sense, by the masterful way in which, through language, it transforms its "particular horrid little drama," its "mere vulgar criminal anecdote" (p. 403), into an incomparable display, a "heroic vision," of the awful truth with which man, particularly modern man, must—and perhaps in his fashion will—cope. It is not a rationalization of faith, *and one may read it with deep empathy and complete detachment from traditional religious values.*

The poet's imagination has been invested in the conversion of his myth, not of his reader, except as a "noble exercise of our imagination" is conversional. What he shows with a force bordering on violence is how infinitely poorer without faith would be the lives of four fascinating people—a young woman who is forced for years to couple with a wolf and whose flesh is at last fatally torn by wolfish fangs; a restive priest compelled, after some equivocation, to follow the dictates of an inner voice, defying the dogmatic decorum he is pledged to uphold in favor of a higher morality for which he has only the most solipsistic sanction; an ancient Pope struck with both the terror of his personal recognition that Christianity may have played itself out and the triumph of a human miracle so inexplicable, so tender, and so intact that it dispels for a moment his massive gloom and fuels his will to act gladiatorially *pro Domino*, and, in a grotesque inversion, a nobleman so far gone in self-corruption that he seeks to transform every value that man, in his long wayward struggle toward nobility, has sought to institutionalize, and thus to guarantee, into a form of self-interest so base that his failure's very proximity to success casts a terrifying light not only on the fragility and corruptibility of our most sacred institutions, but also on our historically robust institutionalizing mentality.

At the climax of his essay, James defines the chief center of interest in *The Ring and the Book* as "the exhibition of the great constringent relation between man and woman at once at its maximum and as the relation most worth while in life for either party"; this, he says, is "what comes out clearest, comes out as straightest and strongest and finest, from Browning's genius . . ." (p. 409). It is brilliantly said by one creator of another. It cuts through all the substantial but secondary developments by which the poem's subject is enlarged and enriched and identifies the great *secular* subject from which all the rest draws its energy and significance. It is the subject that places Pompilia firmly at the poem's unifying center, as it is the subject that Browning triangulates through the characters of Guido, Caponsacchi, and the Pope. More than anything else—more, for example, than the eternally irresolute question of whether or not Guido finally repents and is "saved"—it is the subject that justifies, artistically as well as thematically, the presence of Book XI in the poem's architecture. In the poet's triangulation of Guido, Caponsacchi, and the Pope around Pompilia, Caponsacchi occupies the delicate middle ground between the bestial, cunning, self-centered, erotically sadistic, meanly exploitative Guido and the manly, intuitive, conscientious, spiritually detached, gloriously generous, pathetically courageous Pope. As the embodiment of *homo agonistes,* Caponsacchi struggles experimentally to find firm footing between conflicting and often lurid appearances of moral obligation—the Church of the present and the Church of the future, rule and reason, Aquinas and mysticism, external pressure and internal force, prudence and inspiration, caprice and heroism, romantic passion and moral imperative. What he discovers is that there is no perfect machinery for resolving such conflicts—that life is a grotesque marriage of good and evil and that moral man's destiny is the endless struggle to rescue good from evil guided only by conscientiousness and expectant only of ambiguous results. Thus he passes through the fiery furnace of impassioned experience, yields up his youthful, beautiful, romantic, and inadequate idealism, and achieves the sad but precious wisdom of moral maturity: "O great, just, good God! Miserable me!" (VI, 2105)

Even if readers have less enthusiasm than that shown here for the relevance and force of James's insights, they cannot fairly deny that how and how well *The Ring and the Book* actually works as a poem, where the dynamism of one of the great imaginative efforts of modern literary art actually lies, is the undivided focus of his attention. Just such a focus is, I think, what has been lacking in more recent commentary. It has represented the poem as original, ingenious, idiosyncratic, witty, intellectually intricate, morally serious, psychologically probing, literarily sophisticated, historically informed—*and static*. To use somewhat vintage terminology, *The Ring and the Book* emerges from it fairly bristling with "fancy" and almost wholly devoid of "imagination." This commentary finds a thousand apt metaphors and then seems to abandon them, failing in the end to make the conversion that will convert us, the readers; it fails to supply the motive for full co-participation in a profound moral and imaginative awakening as exciting and precarious as a morally and imaginatively engaged life itself.

Part of the problem is a holdover from the 1950s, when it was customary to overdraw distinctions between "traditional drama or narrative" or "classical narrative and dramatic poetry," on the one hand, and "modern poetry," on the other, and to assert that poems like Tennyson's *Idylls of the King*, which, it was said, take an "objective view of events," do not "meet . . . the conditions for modern intellectual and moral conviction," while poems like *The Ring and the Book*, which take a "subjective view," do meet them.[6] Few informed critics of the eighties would agree that *Idylls of the King* takes a more objective view than *The Ring and the Book* does, or than *Hamlet* does or *Faust*. Indeed, they would probably agree that *Hamlet, Faust, Idylls of the King, Empedocles on Etna*, and *The Ring and the Book* are all imaginative efforts to reexamine the very meaning of the subjective-objective dichotomy and that the case for the "classical" character of all of them is just about as strong as the case for their "modern" character.

It has been said that *The Ring and the Book* is built on two conditions, one of them wholly unprecedented and the other "unprecedented in major poetry before *Faust*." The latter or Goethean condition is "that the poem is not to derive meaning from any external standard of judgment"; the former or singularly Browningesque condition is that the poet "does not like Goethe give meaning to an old myth, but draws his meaning out of 'pure crude fact.'" The "facts themselves, all of them, unselected and as they came to hand . . . were to yield the meaning." Thus was born "a genuinely modern literature," and with its birth, the "traditional" or "classical" works of Homer, Virgil, Dante, Milton, Tennyson, and Arnold—works that do not "meet . . . the conditions for modern intellectual and moral conviction"—fell from literary grace, and a "new *ars poetica*" possessing "a virtue quite opposite" to the Sophoclean-Arnoldian wholeness and steadiness of view emerged.[7]

All of this now seems far too commodious. It has not been demonstrated that *The Ring and the Book* does not "derive meaning from an external standard of judgment" or that this is an apt critical criterion for dividing it and *Idylls of the King* into two separable categories called "traditional" or "classical" and "modern." In fact, it can be quite cogently argued that both, like life itself, have "an external [rather than internal] standard of judgment"—something like what Arnold called the power, not ourselves, that makes for righteousness—and that that is precisely what the two poems share. It is not the myth of *a* man or *an* institution or *an* age, but the myth of resilient man in all ages. It is not the "old order" "isolating truth within itself against itself"—the "dying order mak[ing] its own contribution to truth, by dying, and by summoning up its own conscience to condemn itself to death"[8]—whatever that fanciful personification may mean; it is man's enduring poetry periodically cleansing itself.

Nor has it been shown that, by seeing life "steadily" and seeing it "whole," Arnold[9] meant anything essentially different from what Browning means in *The Ring and the Book*. And if one is going to use Goethe as a way of illuminating what, in part at least, Browning is doing in his poem, one might prefer to a personal interpretation of the way *Faust* works the supreme importance Goethe saw for the writer in "control[ling] his sub-

ject-matter and keep[ing] himself beautifully objective":
"Through me," Goethe wrote, "the German poets have become aware that, as man must live from within outwards, so
the artist must work from within outwards, seeing that, make
what contortions he will, he can only bring to light his own individuality. I can clearly mark where this influence of mine has
made itself felt; there arises out of it a kind of poetry of nature, and only in this way is it possible to be original."[10] This
not only gets at the heart of the subjective-objective issue, but
also suggests a way of correlating the imaginative presence and
visual absence of the poet of the piece.

As to the "harder condition" that Browning imposed on *The
Ring and the Book* than even Goethe had imposed—namely,
forgoing "an old myth" and drawing "his meaning out of 'pure
crude fact' "—again, *non probatur* is a fair response. The myth
is clearly there. It may be in a corpse-like state, requiring the
poet to lie

> upon the corpse, dead on the couch,
> And put his mouth upon its mouth, his eyes
> Upon its eyes, his hands upon its hands,
> And stretch[] him on the flesh;
>
> (I, 765–768)

but it is there as a historical rather than a fictive configuration
of representative human experience. It is not an "old myth" in
the sense of an old familiar, but its "facts" are not "unselected," and they did not come randomly "to hand." Indeed,
they came to hand in the form of a book and quite providen-
tially. The facts were all there, but so crudely interpreted that
they had no power to live even faintly beyond one or two generations. Nor had the crude contemporary interpretation been
wrong. What the myth had lacked was an interpenetrating
imagination—an immortalizing soul—and that is what the poet,
after a lapse of almost 200 years, brought to it. Theoretically,
a poet might have done this at any time between the gathering
together of the book and the writing of *The Ring and the Book*,
but none did so because the book did not fall into the hands
of the "right man" with the "right way." Even when it did fall

into the right poet's hands, he had to talk it into life over a long period of time before he discovered how to give it human carriage and an immortal soul.[11] But what he discovered was not that the facts could speak for themselves; he discovered that, like Michelangelo's David, they lay dead within their stony silence and could speak only after release into a living shape by a profoundly conscientious, imaginative craftsman willing thus to release them and let them have an autonomous life both in themselves and in the sensitized imaginative judgment of the individual viewing them. Like Michelangelo, he "disappeared" with each stroke of his chisel-pen, "the book" becoming all in all, his presence except as art's ineradicable signature never again manifesting itself until the work was complete and could indeed speak for itself.

But even if it were true that the organizational assumptions and method of *The Ring and the Book* were in part "unprece- dented . . . before *Faust*" and in part wholly unprecedented, the mere assertion thereof—like the assertion that it "derives its meaning from the relativist ethos predominant in Western culture since the Enlightenment" or that the poet's "aim" was to put multiple "points of view" into place[12]—gives the poem only the shortest possible imaginative shrift. To say that some- thing is "modern" does not mean that it is poetically compel- ling, and that is the critic's ultimate challenge. *The Ring and the Book* embodies a larger, more poetic, more awesome power than the power that such assertions, even if accepted without de- murrer, indicate. To say that the poem "derives its meaning from the relativist ethos" may be both descriptively accurate and critically inert unless one goes on to say that this is a his- torically conceived metaphor whose *imaginative* meaning de- rives from the distress that the metaphor undergoes in the overall action (the myth, the plot) of the poem. Pompilia, for example, endures the wounds of it; Guido manipulates it; Ca- ponsacchi is torn by a conflict in part induced by it; the Pope fights his way to a full acknowledgment of it, creates out of it an adversarial personification, and beheads the object of his own personification's advocacy. Further, even so brief and unde- veloped a correlation between the historical metaphor and the imaginative myth as this suggests how explosively active rather

than inert the metaphors of the poem really are and points to
the likelihood that its so-called historicizing, though literally true,
is only the poet's way of rooting in factual or historical time
an intuition about the human condition that is perceived as
timeless. And putting multiple "points of view" into place does
not begin to describe the explosive imaginative aim of the author of *The Ring and the Book*. What the poet-speaker tell us of
his aim in Book I is that, after a serendipitous discovery so
happy that it seemed in retrospect providential, after repeated
enthusiastic but failed efforts to convert this happy discovery
into art, and after a second discovery less serendipitous but even
more solemn and inspired than the first—namely, that art is
only a clever hoax or delusion unless the artist can, like the
ancient Elisha and not like the modern Faust, make himself
wholly and sincerely the agent of the inspiration (the power,
not himself, that creates life) and have enough faith in its innate power to facilitate rather than mediate it—only then was
he sufficiently schooled in art's relationship to life to make a
ring out of a book, poetry out of history. Like the man and the
woman who make love that bears fruit, the artist is not the author of life but its agent, and what he enables, he must believe
in as both real and sacramental. The image at the center of
the concept is ultimately hermaphroditic, not in the degener-
ate modern sense, but in the ancient sense, both firm and approximative, of a metaphor on imagination's innermost fron-
tier.

But a poem as substantively rich and imaginatively challenging as *The Ring and the Book* cannot be much diminished by occasional efforts to overmodernize it; its distinctive way of regarding the tragedy and triumph inherent in human history—
in mankind's past, present, and probable future—is too robust
and penetrating, its poetic taproot too deep-reaching, to be
permanently harmed by such critical parochialism, however
appealing it may seem for a given moment. Much harder for
a poem like *The Ring and the Book*, or any poem, to throw off
are efforts of friendly critics to stereotype it—to invest it with
an authority that it is said rather than shown to have, to clothe
it in the clichés of high-mindedness. Once that happens, it is
very difficult to persuade real poetry-readers to take an inter-

est in it because people who look upon poetry as a lifeline are the ones least likely to have patience with stereotyped, authoritative high-mindedness.

It is a startling idea that a poem as imaginatively rambunctious as *The Ring and the Book* should ever be reduced to a cliché, but that in effect is what has happened; the commentators have made it an ingenious, witty, learned, intricate cliché. Its "ultimate meaning" is parochially Christian: "In human affairs the pervasive curse of doubt can be countered only by the vigorous response of a soul inspired by Christian teaching."[13] The poet of the piece is infallible: "He could not have misread the record; to do so would be to deny the infallibility of the poet's intuitive grasp of the truth."[14] The Pope is Browning's mouthpiece in the poem. Pompilia is "nothing short of a saint," and hers is an "unchanging perfection";[15] that Guido "is the devil incarnate" is beyond doubt;[16] the "meaning of Pompilia's story" is that she "could become a blazing star for those still struggling on earth";[17] Caponsacchi "represents the highest in manliness and courage" as the Pope "represents the highest moral attainment of human wisdom."[18] The Roman Martyrology is too full to require our poets to add to its lists, and if such dreary edification were the purpose of *The Ring and the Book,* it would hardly deserve to be read.

But *The Ring and the Book* is not another exercise in sanctimonious infallibility; it is an advanced course in the critical-creative reading of life, and its basic proposition is infallibility's anti-proposition. In Books I and XII, Browning has cast himself in the role of a poet undergoing the ordeal of creation in a generic sense, a poet, moreover, of a certain temper of mind whose way with ideas must be assessed in the light of that temperament. The ring metaphor (the ring-and-book metaphor, more precisely) is the poet-speaker's tentative, approximative way of trying to explain to the reader what he thinks he has discovered about art's relationship to life, and it is no more absolute than any other metaphor a poet might choose to mirror his thoughts. Despite the initial enthusiasm the poet-speaker felt for the old book, it took him three false starts and an alignment with the right role model (Elisha, not Faust) before he could see the image of life that lay in the old book's

tomb and could discover how to raise it from the dead. He has
faith in the rightness of what he has done and is hopeful that
its innate integrity will find for it a sympathetic hearing, but it
is in fact faith that he goes on. The tone of lyrical reverence
that he feels at the point of raising the curtain on the "ring"—
that is, the exhibition of dead truth brought back to life through
the fully engaged imagination—turns to sober recognition of
how "brightness . . . hastes to blend with black" (XII, 21) when
the formal curtain falls upon the living truth. In the rapid un-
raveling that life undergoes when stripped of art's clarifying
form and energizing idea, he has yet this steadying faith: if God
is true—if there truly is a God—then it is the poets and not the
priests who must find him because "This spiritual love acts not
nor can exist/Without imagination . . ." (Wordsworth, *The
Prelude*, XIV, 188–189).

   To see the Pope as the spokesman for Browning is to contradict unequivocally the whole aesthetic of *The Ring and the
Book;* to see him as representing "the highest moral attainment
of human wisdom" is to contradict the "one lesson" that the
poem's myth is meant to teach:

> This lesson, that our human speech is naught,
> Our human testimony false, our fame
> And human estimation words and wind.
>   (XII, 834–836)

The Pope of the poem is a distinctive, complex, solitary old
man discovered in an inherently conflicted role and faced with
both a particular duty that he resolves through oversimplifi-
cation and a general situation that strikes such terror into his
soul that he lashes out against it in a fury of indignation, and
his monologue's strains of pity and fear induce a catharsis that
is at once incomplete and salutary. The Pope is not only fallible but deeply faulted. His case-making is transparent, his logic
peccable, his courage real but partial, his understanding of
sexual passion severely limited, his sense of role contradictory,
his anger highly abstract, his loneliness palpable, his sympathy
largely retrospective, and his need for one last toe-to-toe confrontation both exhilarating and pathetic. His is a sincere but

besieged faith, a desperate but relentless hope, a self-indulgent and generous love, and a readiness but slowly arrived at to do symbolic battle with evil however futile it may appear in realistic terms to be. The Pope's genuine grandeur is enriched, not threatened, by his conspicuous and conspicuously human imperfection, and by learning not to be threatened by it, we may get to "Know life a little, [we] should leave so soon" (VII, 1666).

It depletes the poem's imaginative energy to see Pompilia as "nothing short of a saint," of "unchanging perfection." She is the most impressive example of human grace under human pressure that the poem reveals, and to collapse her heroic struggle with exploitative human forces into the stereotyping metaphor of a saint is to enshrine her in metaphoric blandness and de-create her. That is the temptation to which Other Half-Rome succumbs, the temptation to "unself" her that she recognizes in her well-wishers and rejects (VII, 707), and the temptation that any reader responsive to the poem's own vigor must resist. So far from being "unchanging" is Pompilia that she emerges gradually out of personal vacancy, copes passively with insurmountable odds until her strategy of martyrdom self-destructs, totters momentarily on the brink of existential despair, discovers when hardest at bay an ineradicable nucelus of the self, suddenly takes charge of a life she had been on the verge of throwing away, moves with growing clarity and vigor into contest with the forces of de-creation congregated against her, enjoys a brief but sufficient period of respite, and is at last physically destroyed by the enemies of her distinctive self only to discover, under the tutelage of a conscientious, selfless, imaginative confessor, that by seeing life steadily and seeing it whole—by a full reenactment of the hell her life has been—she can gain a worthy victory over human life and human death and return, intact and infinitely magnified, to the heaven from which she came.

But even more destructive to the imaginative engagement that *The Ring and the Book* requires than the conversion of Pompilia's life story into a mere exercise in hagiography is the implication that her monologue embodies no crucial poetic revelations against which the other monologues can be measured. If she is "unchanging perfection," she cannot provide a fair basis by which to assess the other imperfect, unstable, struggling characters in the poem. The fact is that she changes more, endures more, disciplines herself more severely, has a stronger, more concrete sense of identity, and gains greater self-knowledge than anyone else in the poem. She is at once the least judgmental and most creative person in the poem; she is the least inclined to role-play, takes the fullest close-range look at the worst life has to offer, and effects in her life's real circumstances the best consummation possible. We know all this from the way her monologue actually works, and it thus becomes the touchstone by which the actual workings of the other monologues are to be tested.

Also, much of the drama of identification and understanding is lost if one succumbs to the Pope's judgment and sees Caponsacchi as a representation of "the highest in manliness and courage," a romantic hero swashbuckling through an operatic morality play. In the poem's reality, as distinct from the critics' myth, such a reading simply rejects the many clues the poet has implanted in the monologue that such a tempting evasion of the truth of Caponsacchi is to be resisted. Though there is sound reason to qualify Altick and Loucks's characterization of Caponsacchi as *"l'homme moyen sensuel,"*[19] he is the poem's most representative man: *Caponsacchi c'est moi!* is a more centrist and credible response to his story than to anyone else's story in the poem, but few readers would say, "I am 'the highest in manliness and courage.'" Caponsacchi has to learn some very harsh truths about himself, and he learns them at a minimalist rather than at a grand level; the best that can be said of his final position is that it is satisfactory. His "heroism" is antiromantic rather than romantic in that he has, by the end of his monologue, reversed the direction of his life from a tendency toward evil to a tendency toward good, but the journey ahead is a long and joyless one, and he will have to be eternally vigilant lest he fall back into the strategies of self-delusion that have characterized his life as a priest and to which he is clearly still susceptible even at the end of his monologue.

Caponsacchi twice gives testimony before the Court, and in his second deposition, given here as his monologue, he remembers his first appearance very differently from the way it was. That is a measure of his tendency to see matters very differently from the way they were, and this tendency persists strongly throughout the first three-quarters of his monologue—up to the incident at Castelnuovo—and is brought under control but imperfectly thereafter. Moreover, as he must learn a new way of perceiving the truth about himself and his world, Caponsacchi must learn a new, more disciplined, more truthful language with which to talk about them, and in that, too, he makes but imperfect progress. Occasionally in his words we hear echoes of Other Half-Rome, Archangeli, Bottini, and Guido, and these remind us of the particles of dross in his soul. Gradually he begins to develop the simplicity, economy, and honesty of Pompilia's use of language, and this confirms us in our perception that he is slowly moving in the right direction. But none of the close textual observation necessary to a recognition of the mixed and representative character of Caponsacchi's motives, manner, and metamorphosis would be possible if we were to read his monologue as the "Papal critics" read it, making him "the highest in manliness and courage."

Finally, there is the incorrigible villain of the piece. Guido is a thoroughly nasty, incompetent, ill-natured, mean-spirited, predatory, cowardly human being with a genius for imprisoning himself in his own character's defects; but he is not "the devil incarnate," and to make him so not only does much to disqualify *The Ring and the Book* as a great poem, but even throws it back to the literary level of a one-dimensional medieval morality play. Guido is Pompilia's opposite in human character and action, and her human achievement is inverted in him. Guido is a wolfman from the savage Arcadia of Plato's *Republic,* the Arcadia of King Lycaon whose "actions so disillusioned Zeus that he decided to destroy the entire race by a deluge."[20] As a wolfman, he is the central bearer of one of the most controlling, least noticed themes of *The Ring and the Book,* namely, the theme of a virulent male sexism. Indeed, that theme is the central revelation of Book V, the basic motive of Book XI, and the decisive consideration on the issue of Guido's so-called "salvation." It runs strongly through Books II, III, IV, VIII, and IX, and it is a crucial element in both Caponsacchi's and the Pope's monologues. Only a brief confirmation of its relevance to Guido will be attempted here.

At the center of Book V, supplying its structural, interpretive, and rhetorical fulcrum, is Guido's account of the incident at the inn at Castelnuovo when the three principals in the action are brought face to face and measured (V, 1037–1162). Everything preceding flows to it, and everything following flows from it. It bridges the center of the 2,058-line monologue numerically, and at *its* center Guido is faced with the most dreadful and inevitable of charges: " 'You shrank from gallant readiness and risk,/Were coward: the thing's inexplicable else' " (V, 1090–1091). Haunted with his memories of that scene and faced with the charge thus relentlessly phrased, Guido suddenly drenches himself in a torrent of self-abasement:

> Say I stand
> Convicted of the having been afraid,
> Proved a poltroon, no lion but a lamb,—
> Does that deprive me of my right of lamb
> And give my fleece and flesh to the first wolf?
> Are eunuchs, women, children, shieldless quite
> Against attack their own timidity tempts?
> Cowardice were misfortune and no crime!
> —Take it that way, since I am fallen so low
> I scarce dare brush the fly that blows my face,
> And thank the man who simply spits not there,—
>   (V, 1094–1104)

Eunuchs, women, children—all the "shieldless" people the wolfman preys on—*and he is one of them!* Then Guido characterizes Caponsacchi's and Pompilia's contrasting behavior in the incident:

> They braved me,—he with arrogance and scorn,
> She, with a volubility of curse,
> A conversancy in the skill of tooth
> And claw to make suspicion seem absurd,
> Nay, an alacrity to put to proof
> At my own throat my own sword, teach me so
> To try conclusions better the next time,—
>   (V, 1119–1125)

Bravery, defiance, tooth and claw, alacrity, proof, teacher—all the things he liked to think of himself as—*and they are she!* For one blazing moment of recognition, Guido sees, not what Pompilia really is, but what in his wolfish manual are the marks of her nobility. He does not recover quickly even from the memory of the incident (at line 1163 he is still trying to recollect himself), and Book XI suggests that he does not recover at all. He toughs it through the rest of this monologue, but from that ghastly self-destructive moment, he vows never again to take the least chance of being like "eunuchs, women, children" again.

This brings us to Book XI and the issue of Guido's "salvation." First, it must be recognized that the Pope does not in fact prophesy Guido's last-minute conversion.[21] What the Pope says is simply that he has "no hope/Except in such a suddenness of fate" (X, 2116–2117), and the "one instant" he speaks of—"So may the truth be flashed out by one blow,/And Guido see, one instant, and be saved" (X, 2126–2127)—is not the last minute of Guido's final cowardly scream for life, but the instant that follows the "blow" that only God can know, the instant between the blade's touching of the neck and the actual death. Secondly, the speech that Professor Langbaum finds noble others may find adamantly unyielding and horrifying. Earlier in the verse-paragraph cited in evidence, Guido speaks of cheating death of its sting by the full satisfaction of his "wolf-nature":

> The last bad blow that strikes fire in at eye
> And on to brain, and so out, life and all,[22]
> How can it but be cheated of a pang
> While, fighting quietly, the jaws enjoy
> Their re-embrace in mid back-bone they break,
> After their weary work thro' the foes' flesh?
> That's the wolf-nature.
>
> (XI, 2310–2316)

That, I suggest, is the "nucleus" of himself that Guido holds "it probable" he will carry into eternity, and the death-peace ("The appropriate drunkenness of the death-hour" [XI, 2326])

in which Langbaum sees a "strange sparkle" and "signs of regeneration" is nothing more than a momentary, animal-like
surrender to physical death as imminent and inevitable. Thus
although no man can finally know whether or not Guido does
"see, one instant, and [is] saved," the overwhelming preponderance of the evidence, including the irresistible logic of the
imagination, suggests that he goes into eternity an unregener-
ate and defiant wolfman and that the buckling at the very end,
like the buckling at Castelnuovo, shows merely that, like most
private bullies/public deceivers whose very truth is a lie, Guido
is a coward at the core.

The conclusion from the foregoing is that *The Ring and the
Book,* like the epic tradition to which it gives a dramatic turning on the principle of working "from within outwards," is an
enormously problematic poem, as problematic as its subject, the
inward-outward life of man in this world. It distresses all its
metaphors, and it takes an official view of only one thing: *"Art
still has truth, take refuge there!"*[23] Its essential focus throughout
is on how we think, not on what we think, on consciousness
rather than conscience, on imagination rather than morality.
Its very complexity is a metaphor of the first importance: if in
the privileged role of poetry-readers, both engaged and detached, we lack the staying power to tough it out, to "[see] life
steadily, and [see] it whole," how can we hope to "Know life a
little, [we] should leave so soon" (VII, 1666)?

This brings us to our final issue—the dramatic monologue
form and how to see it. It is said that "the dramatic monologue . . . makes it possible for us to apprehend the speaker
totally, to subordinate what he says to what we know of him
through sympathy," and the way the dramatic monologue works
is illustrated through the Pope's monologue: "the judgments
the Pope pronounces as evolved truth are *the kind the dramatic
monologue offers*—judgments of character. The Pope does not
weigh argument against argument, fact against fact, but cuts
right through the facts to a *sympathetic apprehension* of the motives and essential moral qualities behind the deeds. He relies
not upon logic to make his judgments but upon talent, intuition, insight, the advantages of his own character gained
through a long experience of life and people" (emphases

added).[24] Thus sympathy with the speaker is offered as the basic premise of the dramatic monologue (its "essential condition . . . and final cause"[25]), and a special kind of judgment, the kind that results from seeing things from the inside and deriving meaning "from the poetic material itself," determines the dramatic monologue's *"way* of meaning."[26]

While one may welcome this encouragement to free the dramatic monologue from the dead end of formal classification and at the same time enjoy it as a very special kind of poetic experience, not allowing a freer approach to dissolve into no distinctive approach at all, one may yet find it an inadequate guide to or description of the way *The Ring and the Book* actually works for him, and that, after all, is the "effect" that this less restrictive approach to the dramatic monologue appeals to for its critical authenticity.[27]

The problem is that this newer, freer, more creative way of conceiving of the dramatic monologue suffers from the same defects as the older, more formal, more restrictive method: it tells us how, methodologically, we must read if we would read correctly, and while this may do very well as a beginning, it simply will not do as an end. Nor should it: it is a more ingratiating way of mechanizing poems than the speaker-audience-interaction formula, but it is still formulaic. It is dogmatic, systematic, and bullying, threatening us with the insufferable damnation of missing the boat.

The need for sympathy and judgment can be granted; they are cultivated qualities indispensable to a worthwhile reading of any form of poetry or to a sophisticated rapport with any product of imaginative creation—poetry, painting, music, or the "ceaseless artistries" of the "Great Foresightless."[28] But sympathy with *the poet* and what he is trying to do, not necessarily with a particular character through whom he is trying to do it: the former makes us maximally available to the poem, while the latter assumes that the form is inherent in the subject rather than the result of a critical choice the poet has made about how best to enable both himself and his readers to experience his subject. And the very best judgment we have it in our capacity to make, not the particular "kind" of judgment "the dramatic monologue offers": the former keeps our experience of the canon of poetry and of the individual poet whole, while the latter would force us to see a difference of kind between modern and traditional or classical poetry that the critic of the eighties will no longer yield to the critic of the fifties.

The discrepancy between what the character in a dramatic monologue says and what the poet from his decentralized vantage-point "says" is the locus, the imaginary point, at which the critical-creative content is customarily lodged in a dramatic monologue, and that is the imaginary point the critical reader is seeking. In that quest, many readers may find a freer critical response monitored by a conscientious watchfulness far more fruitful than the straightjacketing implicit in a rule of "sympathy" that, in many cases, they can respond to only with the utmost artificiality and a rule of "judgment" that tells them what "kind of judgment" they are expected to make. For them, the result may be a criticism whose revelations come, not from externally imposed rules that at some point in their application will almost certainly seem either too mechanical or too peremptory, but from the experience of a poetic text combined with all the other experience, poetic or otherwise, they bring to it. Laws apply to facts known or deduced, and literary criticism, like poetry itself, has as its focus, not facts, but a process of conversion with too many variables to be subject to laws except in the metaphoric and permissive sense of illumination rather than regulation.

Conscientious, experienced, critically responsive readers of *The Ring and the Book,* for example, may not find themselves regulated in any useful way by either formula of "correct" reading of the poem as a whole or of its individual monologues. They may instead find the poem's critical-creative excitement just where Browning said it was—in a fusion of fact and imagination that is at once explosive, comprehensible, and nonformulaic. They may even reach a point of critical-creative gratification in which they neither quite remember nor quite forget that they are involved in a "modern" poem composed in "an appropriate form for an empiricist and relativist age." And without much caring whether or not they have reached this state of imaginative response by extending proper "sympathy" to the various speakers and by making the "kind of judgment we get in the dramatic monologue," they may find their entire sense of reality dilated by a recognition that subjectivity and objectivity, invisible poet and visible speaker, seer and maker-see, fact historic and fact poetic have been brought into such a new and stimulating relationship that life itself appears under a new and more meaningful aspect.

Having reached such a point of critical-creative response, it may seem to them that a world view is just as inherent in the poem as a number of representative individual views; that the emergence of modernism is both conscientiously recorded and conscientiously critiqued; that alongside the drama of corrupt and exhausted authority are the drama both of the quick and ugly aftershock and of that saving remnant of the human spirit that grows sturdier in adversity and blooms when and where one least expects it; that the collapse of institutionalized truth, including the institutional Pope and the institutional poet, is not to be equated with the collapse of religious truth or poetic truth, but is a reminder that the human search for objectifying guarantees is, in this life at least, an inevitable and futile search that falls apart at the moment of keenest expectation and recalls us to the reality that we must work "from within outwards," discovering such truth of the macrocosm as is accessible to us in the microcosm of our "own individuality": "there arises out of it a kind of poetry of nature, and only in this way is it possible to be original." Such a way of working does not constitute a modernist rejection of objective truth and a retreat into a concept of truth as purely subjective and "relativist." It is a reworking of the Apollonian principle that the most dependable way to an understanding of the truth of one's world is an understanding of the truth of oneself, terms like *objective* and *subjective* being stripped of the content they are customarily assumed to possess.

And this, I suggest, is also the way *The Ring and the Book* works and what, ultimately, it means. The poet offers it to us as a course in critical-creative reading, and that is its basic poetic function. Behind it is the poet of *Men and Women, Dramatis Personae,* and all the earlier work through which Browning had honed his art and his ideas. But as *The Ring and the Book* itself makes every effort to tell us, something quite new, exciting, and conversional had happened to the poet in the struggle to take charge of his providential subject. It had at first been something of an interesting sleeper; then it had become an irresistibly fascinating but recalcitrant, seemingly unmanageable mass; it had ended by helping him to a new, more inclusive reading of human life's complex truth and of the indispensability to it of the poetic imagination. The real excitement, then, lay in the imaginative or critical-creative reading itself, not in a set of derivative conclusions that, like all derivative conclusions, must eventually self-destruct. So it is the reading process itself that he has given us. He does not in that sense create a new poetry; every significant poet since Homer has been doing essentially the same thing. What he does create is a new poetic "voice" in which we hear the "evidence" of a chorus of "voices" together bearing fresh witness, some of them in spite of themselves, that however seemingly infinite, unprecedented, and discouraging our problems may seem, art (poetry, critical-creative reading) still has truth, and though it may not have the power to defeat the enemies congregated against us on their own terms, it may yet deny them victory over us and enable us to save our souls.

Notes

1. The address was published as an essay in the *Quarterly Review* (1912) and later collected in *Notes on Novelists* (New York: Scribners, 1914). References to the essay are to the New York edition and are given in parentheses in the text.
2. Richard D. Altick and James F. Loucks II, *Browning's Roman Murder Story: A Reading of "The Ring and the Book"* (Chicago: University of Chicago Press, 1968), p. 364.
3. Altick and Loucks, p. 364.
4. I have developed this analysis of the essay in considerable detail in an article entitled "Rereading Henry James Rereading Robert Browning: 'The Novel in *The Ring and the Book*,'" *Henry James Review*, V (Winter 1984), 135–145.
5. In his chapter on *The Ring and the Book* in *The Poetry of Experience: The Dramatic Monologue in Modern Literary Tradition* (New York: Random House, 1957), p. 135, Robert Langbaum attempts to resolve the ambi-

guity inherent in the discrepancy between Books I and XII and II through XI by falling back on a distinction between "facts" and "poetry," but that is the very distinction that gives rise to the ambiguity. Langbaum also, like most of the commentators, takes the narrow, simple, and unsatisfactory view that the Pope speaks for Browning, but this only tries to wink the ambiguity away.

6. Langbaum, p. 135 and passim.
7. Langbaum, p. 136 and passim.
8. Langbaum, p. 128.
9. *To a Friend*, l. 12.
10. As quoted by Matthew Arnold in "Heinrich Heine," *Essays in Criticism, First Series, The Complete Prose Works of Matthew Arnold*, ed. R. H. Super (Ann Arbor: University of Michigan Press, 1962), III, 110. Henry James appears to have had this passage in mind when he was writing "The Novel in *The Ring and the Book*."
11. One can take one of two views of this matter. He can hold that the poet-speaker has misrepresented Browning's four-year neglect of the Old Yellow Book; or, as here, he can read this period of gestation as an imaginative, but not necessarily false, explanation of why the poet talked to several people about the poetic and novelistic possibilities inherent in the Old Yellow Book before he himself discovered the will and the way to understand the poem we have.
12. Langbaum, pp. 133–135 and passim.
13. Altick and Loucks, p. 361.
14. Mary Rose Sullivan, *Browning's Voices in "The Ring and the Book": A Study of Method and Meaning* (Toronto: University of Toronto Press, 1969), p. 212.
15. Langbaum, pp. 110, 111.
16. Altick and Loucks, p. 52.
17. Sullivan, p. 210.
18. Langbaum, p. 112.
19. Altick and Loucks, p. 55.
20. Philip Mayerson, *Classical Mythology in Literature, Art, and Music* (Waltham, Mass.: Xerox College Publishing, 1971), p. 153.
21. In an article entitled "Is Guido Saved? The Meaning of Browning's Conclusion to *The Ring and the Book*" in *Victorian Poetry*, 10 (1972), 289–305, Langbaum argues essentially that the Pope accurately predicts Guido's salvation and that Book XI is ultimately Guido's true recognition scene and would be "superfluous if its only function is to elaborate what is sufficiently established without it—that Guido is utterly evil."
22. The Pope's "one instant."
23. Words given to Goethe by Matthew Arnold in his poem "Memorial Verses," l. 28.
24. Langbaum, *The Poetry of Experience*, p. 121.
25. M. W. MacCallum, "The Dramatic Monologue in the Victorian Period,"

Proceedings of the British Academy 1924–1925, p. 276, as quoted by Langbaum, *The Poetry of Experience,* p. 78.

26. This is Langbaum's particular point of view in Chapter 2, "The Dramatic Monologue: Sympathy versus Judgment," *The Poetry of Experience,* pp. 75–108. Of course, it is not true that the Pope does not weigh arguments or rely on logic. He does both rather extensively, badly, and futilely.

27. Langbaum, *The Poetry of Experience,* pp. 134–135.

28. Thomas Hardy's metaphor for the Immanent Will in *The Dynasts,* which is as close as he is willing to get to "God."

2.

A Credible Feat:
Books I and XII Revisited

The critics of *The Ring and the Book* seem to have decided long since that the opening and closing books of the poem are, if not quite perfunctory, too obvious in their general import to require much further critical engagement. That Browning speaks there "in his own voice" is accepted as a fact admitting little if any question,[1] and it is said that, "in the main," these require "little discussion" and are given little.[2] Even after one has admitted that the ring-and-book metaphor that is the particular focus of one verse paragraph in Book I (679–697) has generally been talked to death by too many commentators, their literalizing of upwards of ten percent of *The Ring and the Book* is curious. It implies that the author of one of the most conscientiously imaginative poems in English—that is, a poem in which the idea of the imagination is the object of very disciplined honing and the function of the imagination is a subject of profoundest importance—saw no need to apply the imaginative principle to himself. If Books I and XII are verse, therefore, and not poetry (being mediated entirely by Robert

Browning *in propria persona*, they "tell [no] truth/Obliquely," "do [no thing] shall breed the thought" that outruns the obvious statement they appear to contain) then far better, one might think, had they been in prose, not seeming to be the very thing they are not!

That such literalizing of Books I and XII can lead to pernicious results should be sufficient justification for reopening the question. In the closing, perorative pages of her "Study of Method and Meaning," Mary Rose Sullivan summarizes her perception of the "Larger Design" of the poem as follows. The poet, she says,

> is doing God's work, completing the incomplete, saving the good from oblivion. . . . As the poet mirrors God, doing His work on earth and making Him apprehensible to man, he stands as the connecting link between time and eternity, drawing the finite and the infinite ever more closely together. . . . He could not have misread the record; to do so would be to deny the infallibility of the poet's intuitive grasp of the truth. . . . the process merely involves a willingness on his part to stoop to the level of ordinary man. . . .[3]

Is this the new morality we are meant to admire? the poetcraft for which we are asked to sacrifice the priestcraft? the infallibility of poetic intuition for which we are to give up the infallibility of the Pope? Then perhaps we should let His Holiness speak for Browning since he seems so little qualified to speak for himself. As the poet-speaker in Book XII laments,

here's the plague

That all this trouble comes of telling truth,
Which truth, by when it reaches him, looks false,
Seems to be just the thing it would supplant,
Nor recognizable by whom it left—
While falsehood would have done the work of truth.

(XII, 848–853)

Nor can the critical problem be salvaged by the claim that Professor Sullivan's is a basic misreading of the text. Such misreadings are, as the poet-speaker says, inherent in mediated texts because they assert what many will inevitably either misread or counter, and art's solution, he also says, is to create, not an adversary through assertion, but an ally through involvement. The possibility of such a happy aesthetic result makes it worthwhile, I suggest, to explore Books I and XII as "sample-speeches" of a poet-speaker who is role-playing in a way we can identify with in the imperfect but sufficient way in which imaginative writing customarily works.

The proper place to begin in a poem as organically evolved as *The Ring and the Book* is at the center,[4] and the following crucial passage occurs at the center of Book I:

> I find first
> Writ down for very A. B. C. of fact,
> 'In the beginning God made heaven and earth;'
> From which, no matter with what lisp, I spell
> And speak you out a consequence—that man,
> Man,—as befits the made, the inferior thing,—
> Purposed, since made, to grow, not make in turn,
> Yet forced to try and make, else fail to grow,—
> Formed to rise, reach at, if not grasp and gain
> The good beyond him,—which attempt is growth,—
> Repeats God's process in man's due degree,
> Attaining man's proportionate result,—
> Creates, no, but resuscitates, perhaps.
> Inalienable, the arch-prerogative
> Which turns thought, act—conceives, expresses too!
> No less, man, bounded, yearning to be free,
> May so project his surplusage of soul
> In search of body, so add self to self
> By owning what lay ownerless before,—
> So find, so fill full, so appropriate forms—
> That, although nothing which had never life
> Shall get life from him, be, not having been,
> Yet, something dead may get to live again,
> Something with too much life or not enough,
> Which, either way imperfect, ended once:
> An end whereat man's impulse intervenes,

Makes new beginning, starts the dead alive,
Completes the incomplete and saves the thing.
Man's breath were vain to light a virgin wick,—
Half-burned-out, all but quite-quenched wicks o' the lamp
Stationed for temple-service on this earth,
These indeed let him breathe on and relume!
For such man's feat is, in the due degree,
—Mimic creation, galvanism for life,
But still a glory portioned in the scale.

(I, 707–741)

Not only is the subject of the passage thoroughly generalized; the poet-speaker insists unmistakably through repetition that his central emphasis is on "man/Man." It is *man's* "Inalienable" right and "arch-prerogative" to grow, and he does this by imitating the Creator of "heaven and earth," that is, by trying to create. Being only man and not "God," he cannot create in the pure originating sense, but he cannot even fulfill the law of his being *as man* unless he tries "to rise, reach at, if not grasp and gain/The good beyond him." He does this through *imitation* of "God's" creative act. He mimics "God" by finding, filling up, appropriating *forms* so that what once had life can have life again. Thus man, "the inferior thing," though he can never *be* "God" or even "God-like" in the pure sense, yet can in his "due degree" and on his finite "scale" collaborate with "God" through an analogous victory over death, an impulse continually realized to "Complete[] the incomplete."[5]

Having made man the general agent of such creativity as humanness offers, such reaching beyond itself as we have evidence of, the poet-speaker distinguishes between two broad types of "mimic" creators belonging to the genus *man* (I, 742–772). One is the Faust-type, who has the customary "feeling . . . /For truth," but stops "midway short of truth" and rests on "a lie." Faust's failure as a model for man is an overweening faith in himself (a sort of arrogant Pelagianism) and a quite inadequate faith (indeed, a disbelief) in the not-self. Hence, he disproportionately stresses " 'a special gift, an art of arts,/More insight and more outsight and much more/Will to use both of these than boast my mates,' " while at the same time revealing that he has faith only in his gift's illusionary result: " 'What shall be mistily seen, murmuringly heard,/Mistakenly felt. . . .' " The other is the Elisha-type. Coming upon someone dead, Elisha

> went in
> Therefore, and shut the door upon them twain,
> And prayed unto the Lord: and he went up
> And lay upon the corpse, dead on the couch,
> And put his mouth upon its mouth, his eyes
> Upon its eyes, his hands upon its hands,
> And stretched him on the flesh; the flesh waxed warm:
> And he returned, walked to and fro the house,
> And went up, stretched him on the flesh again,
> And the eyes opened.
>
> (I, 762–771)

Elisha, like Faust, also had faith in his gift, but it was a silent faith. He saw himself, not as a mage or magician with a talent for hocus-pocus, but as an agent of "the Lord" doing, in his humbler fashion, the Lord's service. Giving himself entirely to the work in a spirit of methodical completeness, reverence, and faith in the result, he did what he could the first time and then, nothing daunted, did it again. In consequence, the wonderful thing happened: "the eyes opened," and life was renewed.

This, I suggest, is the crucial internal metaphor, the touchstone, of Books I and XII and even of *The Ring and the Book* as a whole. What the poet-speaker has done from beginning to end, despite its autobiographical, subjective, ad hoc, freewheeling, so-called modern appearance, is to be measured against a specific internal criterion modeled after an objective, ancient, *external* example. Man is the genus, the poet the species, and though the poet may have " 'a special gift,' " it is a gift we all have in our "due degree." The poet, like us, is not infallible, and the idea of his "stoop[ing] to the level of ordinary man" is just as offensive to our sense of moral propriety as the idea of anyone else's "stooping." He is no more God-like than we are and no more of a "link between time and eternity" or between "the finite and the infinite." Like Faust, the poet is vulnerable to his gift; like Elisha, he must lend his gift out in the spirit of a humble, faithful, affirmative agent of a power, a "Creator," different in kind from himself as he is *like,* in kind, to the rest of us. Otherwise, while the poet might fill the happy (or unhappy) few with a sense of high glamour, he could not touch us where we actually live or help us "to rise, reach at . . . /The good beyond. . . ."[6] What we need is that degree of faith in our own gift that will enable it to work, and to help us find that faith is the poet's role.

Viewed from this perspective, the poet-speaker in Books I and XII is nothing so literal as Robert Browning. He is a species of man, a poet, who begins in a state of high excitement over a specialized but representative experience of having achieved a victory over death, of having "Complet[ed] the [long-since] incomplete," and a strong sense, therefore, of how it is done; he ends with a far soberer recognition[7] that life very quickly reverts to the most discouraging level of shabbiness once its suspension in "form and idea" has been brought to a close. Thus his final defense of "the artistic way" is not the ebullient assertion of a self-satisfied poet star-struck with his nearness to God; it is, as the context and tone say it is, a statement of the minimalist creed of a besieged but unyielding, creative stoic—Christian perhaps—that art is truth's only real worldly refuge. He had begun with the exultant realization that he was indeed and at last an artist, a poet, the possessor of an Apollonian gift; he ends with both a knowledge of that gift's severe price and the recognition that he has no choice but to pay it—"If precious be the soul of man to man" (XII, 830).

Being somewhat deferential over self-exposure at such an intensely personal level, he disguises it lightly as a dogma ardently if only personally held ("to mouths like mine, at least"), but it is clearly the result of two empirically founded realizations that every person of conscience, courage, and talent who sees life steadily and sees it whole must at some time experience: that human life wholly motivated by worldly self-interest is, metaphorically if not quite literally, hell on earth and that human life has never yet been wholly so motivated " 'but apart there grew/ . . . /Some root of knighthood and pure nobleness. . . .' "[8] The latter realization is the self-redemptive, soul-saving quality that human history tells us inheres mysteriously in the race and that the poet, with his special but by no means unique gift, must recognize, track, and assist others to develop their capacity to see too. It is an example, not of the "blind optimism" often associated with such Browning poems as *Rabbi Ben Ezra,* but of a minimally corrected pessimism: that is, an awful vision of the worst reality of the human condition saved from the hopelessness toward which it points by a vision of the "'root of knighthood and pure nobleness.'" This corrected pessimism, if one has imaginative faith and can use it, is a sufficient basis for hope at the least romantic human level.[9]

To the degree that one accepts this as the ultimate outcome of the poem's reading of the human situation, one will see a sharp contrast between it and the customary view of Browning's religious buoyancy—what Hardy called his "lucky dreamlessness"[10]—and this, too, has relevance to the generic character of the poet-speaker in Books I and XII. Either the speaker is being presented as having a world view different from Browning's, or Browning's world view had undergone considerable alteration and enlargement in the contest with his subject, both as fact and as an imaginative sense of fact, that finally brought *The Ring and the Book* into existence. The latter is my own interpretive preference in the matter, and it leads me to the further tentative conclusion that, in the contrast between his earlier and revised views of life's true reality and of the poet's role in it, Browning saw the poet in the more generic terms that Wordsworth had described in the Preface to *Lyrical Ballads,*[11] and this is the view he is developing in Books I and XII.

The presence of certain specific autobiographical facts in Book I is not being questioned, nor is the fact that the speaker plays a very specialized role. Book I is entitled "The Ring and the Book," and the speaker is a poet, author of our poem *The Ring and the Book.* Moreover, the purpose of Book I is to tell us how that particular poem came into being from the initial discovery of the Old Yellow Book to the final "spirt" of acid that made the rounded "ring" "justifiably golden" (I, 1388–1389). Indeed such facts, including the fact of the speaker's specialized role, are absolutely essential *to either way of reading Books I and XII.* However, it is also essential to remember "one fact the more." The speakers at the center of the poetic "ring"[12]—Pompilia, for example, and Caponsacchi and Guido— are no less specialized in their roles than the poet-speaker in Books I and XII is in his, and the "autobiographical facts" with which they deal far exceed any known facts incorporated into the first book. And yet, no serious reader would question the poet-speaker's assertion that he has mixed imagination quite generously with their "facts" or that the constructive poetic re- sult of such mixing is that their monologues, like the poem as a whole, "mean, beyond the facts." Why, then, should the crit- ic's mind boggle at the idea of the same sort of imaginative ge- nericizing's taking place in Books I and XII?

The really constructive critical question is one of affect. What difference does it make? How does it enlarge or refine our critical judgment of what is going on in Books I and XII and our assessment of the poem's ultimate outcome, including our willingness to admit that outcome in our way of perceiving and relating to life? Potentially, I think, in quite substantial ways, and they will be the focus of the balance of this chapter.

To see the poet-speaker in Books I and XII as an equal among equals strips his ardor of any dogmatic overtones. He becomes a representative character very much like ourselves, and though he has done something that we have not done— namely, write a long poem based on an old book we may never have seen or may see[13]—we are free to accept his account as literally or as metaphorically as we like and to submit its moral- aesthetic conclusions to our own experience and evaluative judgments. He has, he tells us, learned something very basic about writing. He has learned, he thinks, to be

> more careful whoso runs may read
> Than erst when all, it seemed, could read who ran,—
> Perchance more careless whoso reads may praise
> Than late when he who praised and read and wrote
> Was apt to find himself the self-same me. . . .
>
> (I, 1381–1385)

Even so understated a recognition of the new importance he places on the reader's *understanding* of and *assent* to what is said in Book I and elsewhere is an invitation to read freely and

critically and therefore to assess what is said as much in relation to ourselves as to the speaker.

When we apply this principle to the aesthetic theory pervasive in Book I and the aesthetic practice pervasive in the poem
as a whole, the result is a general loosening up of the speaker
and reader roles. It becomes a subject of our experience as well
as his, and we become participants rather than mere onlookers. Our understanding assumes a sympathetic rather than a
purely analytical bent, and we are readier to assent, if we reasonably can, readier to see what he is trying to say rather than
what he literally says.[14] That aesthetic, based on the general
loosening up and taking into account implicit as well as explicit meaning, can be summarized as follows. The living truth
is the highest thing the human mind can conceive of (" 'Let
God be true . . .' " [XII, 453]); it is the golden idea around
which man shapes his myths, the object of his alchemist dreams.
But of course man's alchemy doesn't work, and he never succeeds in this life in making his golden dreams come true. Perhaps the closest he ever gets to truth is what Henry James called
the "cloud of gold-dust" from the "Golden Isles" of poetry.[15]
Not only can he not create truth; it is unlikely that he can even
know the truth on this earth (" 'since truth seems reserved for
heaven not earth/[Man] Should learn to love what he may speak
one day,' " [XII, 606–607]). Still, the human mind persists in its
struggle after truth, so if man cannot know truth per se and
yet his mind persists in the struggle after it, then the best that
he can hope for in this world is some intimation of it, some
sign that it does in fact exist.

Fact itself becomes for most people such a sign: people say
"this is the fact," meaning "this is true." But fact is in itself inert; it can hide as well as embody the very sort of truth man is
capable of. So a quality not inherent in fact must be brought
to it if the intimation, the sign, that is inherent there is to be
released into our consciousness. That quality is called *imagination,* and it is man's one wholly distinctive talent. Man shares
with the rest of animal nature the laws of survival and reproduction, even of intelligence and the retention of knowledge,
but imagination seems to be a talent peculiar to man alone. Only
man is capable of an imaginative sense of fact, and all men are

capable of it to some degree. It is, therefore, the distinguishing mark of man, and by its use and development man is capable of realizing the "arch-prerogative" of his nature, namely,
"to rise, reach at, if not grasp and gain/The good beyond him"
(I, 715–716).

Imagination is what Wordsworth called the "grand and simple" reason. It is the "simple" capacity, "grand" in its results,
to see in one image of truth—a fact—another image of truth
closer to the true truth—*to see things under the aspect of eternity.*
No man is entirely lacking in this capacity, and no man has it
to perfection, but poets not only have the gift of it to a re-
markable degree, but also develop a special enthusiasm for it,
cultivate it, and spend much of their lives propagating an
awareness of its nature and its results. Thus poets become our
most experienced and, on the whole, trustworthy advocates and
guides to its usefulness and value. They are human, of course,
and not infallible; indeed, they can be egregiously wrong.
Therefore, much of the purpose and all of the dynamism of
poetry would be lost if we simply succumbed passively to its
struggles after approximations of the truth as if they were truth
itself packaged and revealed, as, at the other extreme, the high
if relative value of poetry's special kind of experience would
be lost if we were wholly out of sympathy with poetry's way of
dealing with life.

The poet-speaker's presentation of himself in Book I of *The
Ring and the Book* should, I suggest, be seen in this light. He is
an enthusiast who has undergone a prolonged and personally
conversional experience of how the poetic imagination works.
Having been converted, he is eager to convert. It is not a little
truth that he seems to have discovered, but a truth as grand
as life itself—scenic and panoramic, past and present, inner and
outer, epistemological, psychological, moral, aesthetic, and
transcendental. And it is very simple: he found an old book,
and out of it he made a new poem. The facts were all there,
but inert, dead, incomplete; through the universal human capacity, the virtue, of his imagination, they now have energy,
life, completeness. It is a grand mystery with a simple explanation and, if we will, exemplary for us all. It is not truth itself, of course; that would be impossible. But it moves fact that

has been dead for almost 200 years so far in the direction of live truth that it provides a firm platform, an empirical base, for the well-disposed spirit of man to make the inductive leap into the unknown but wholly believable with considerably reinforced confidence. In short, he can begin to " 'learn to love what he may speak one day' " (XII, 607).

Like most persons in a state of enthusiasm and excitement over a personally satisfying and widely relevant discovery, the poet-speaker follows his own special kind of logic. It is neither pure theory nor pure experience that he gives us, but a thorough kneading together of the two. Nor is the one to be understood as poets understand things (including ourselves as poets) without the other. Therefore, one must follow in close detail the process by which the one was born of the other.

The process being more than a particular instance (meaning "beyond the facts"), the processor assumes more than a particular role. As it is generalized, he is generalized too. He assumes the mantle of the artist addressing not "men" but "mankind" (XII, 854–855), and with this assumption he alters the reader's (that is, "mankind's") role in the affair. It is no longer simply to what Robert Browning thinks about his art that we are asked to be attentive; it is now a larger, darker question (I, 411–412)—how art works and why—and our attention is directed at what we think about it perhaps even more deeply and hopefully than we have ever thought about it before.

The process has representative stages that, though similar in what is thought about, are quite dissimilar in how they are thought about and to what effect. The first stage is embodied in I, 141–363, in which we get our first "bookful" (I, 364). It is a very sketchy, impressionistic account, though the speaker assures us before giving it that he has "mastered the contents, [knows] the whole truth" contained in the book (I, 117–118). The question with which the event is framed is an old one— can husbands kill unfaithful wives with impunity?—and, being a lurid question, it releases a lurid contest of contrary opinions. This quality of the story's story is given particular emphasis, but the issues that particularly magnetize the speaker are special ones: (1) the fact that the matter took the form of the written word—print or chirograph—and thus has become a primary illustration that life is language, turned into language, so to speak, on the spot as its innate way of rejecting death and giving life some measure of permanence; (2) the fact that the winnowing procedure triggered by the event forced the parties to it into melodramatic role-playing, using all the resources of language to make a clear-cut, black-and-white issue of the truth; (3) the enormous emphasis placed on " 'the precedents, the authorities!' " (I, 213 ff.), by which every judicial instance from the Greeks, Hebrews, and Romans was adduced in an avalanche of learning; (4) the appeal to the Pope on the grounds of "clericality" as the "parlous plea" (I, 269) that really opened the Pandora's box of public opinion; (5) the ironic reversal that that appeal resulted in, the Pope emerging out of the general pollution with an awesome grandeur that not only rerooted law in morality but also moved the place of execution to the turf of the privileged, the "cavalcading promenading place" of those who conceive of themselves as being above both morality and the law.

The initial stage of the process, though rhetorically dramatic, is raw and essentially superficial; its emphasis is almost entirely on external action. Seeds of significance are planted, but the account has a tabloid character of *what* with almost no attention to *who, where,* and *why.* It is a human cataclysm with almost none of its humanity revealed in the telling—little more than a circus act or a natural catastrophe. To show this, the speaker begins to reveal a sampling of the second, deeper thoughts that knit the event together into a more imaginative, profounder whole—complicating nuances, teasing questions that, while they resolve nothing, point toward the human tissue that, except at the most primitive level, is worthier of our attention (I, 383–409).

The speaker repeatedly interrupts his account of the process with which he is essentially dealing to address the "British Public" directly, the first instance being I, 410ff. On the strict autobiographical level, of course, this is an admission of Browning's awareness of a general lack of popularity with his countrymen. On the generic level, however, it is a reinforcement of the point, fundamental to his purposes, that when the laughing stops over the darkness of the question, the question and the darkness remain. We are all full of proverbial wisdom about the prevalence of truth. As John Stuart Mill had recently said in *On Liberty,* the triumph of truth over persecution has become a household word that all experience contradicts. The instance of the lost truth of this book, of this event, is further proof of truth's recurrent defeat. Not only is it unknown in London; it is unknown in Rome, where for a time it caused the greatest stir imaginable, pushing aside all thoughts of all else. Now no public records can be found to corroborate it— all burned long since by the French. All sorts of political considerations also intervene—suspicion on the part of the Roman Church, the customs of the country, a certain national and religious xenophobia. Cultivated politeness takes the place of cooperation, interest shifting from a recognition of the truth and human significance of the event to cultured small talk, curious questions reflective of sophistication rather than earnest interest and showing an attitude toward poetry as little more than a parlor game among the privileged—" 'make-believe,/And the white lies it sounds like' " (I, 455–456).

At this point the speaker recognizes that the truth lies in the book or nowhere and that some inner resource of his own is his only hope of mining it. If there were no book, he could fudge the matter easily enough; he could fabricate the matter in such a way as to accommodate whatever view of truth he might prefer, and falsehood would appear to do the work of truth (see also XII, 851). But the book does in fact exist—its truth has already been created and has begun to recreate him. So the hard task he assigns himself is to assay it, make it workable and endurable, and so shape it that others will have access to it on an ongoing basis also. There is some "make-believe," some fabrication, to the process, but the truth is enlarged not diminished by it. The make-believe—the act-as-if effort at as sincere and earnest a depth as possible—is centered entirely in the poet's or fabricator's effort to enter into the inert mass of truth, give it renewed life, and supply for it a shape or carriage that promises a greater degree of permanence than it had.

This brings us to the second stage in the process (I, 476–678), that of journeying outward in time and place and inward in imaginative consciousness. That there is make-believe in this act of generative intercourse between the self and the not-self, the present and the past ("Why, all the while, . . . /The life in me abolished the death of things,/Deep calling unto deep: as then and there/Acted itself over again once more/The tragic piece," I, 519–523)[16] is deliberately underscored by the manner in which this central stage in the process is framed by the poet-speaker. The connection he wants to make is between the word and the world ("while I read and read,/I turned, to free myself and find the world," I, 477–478), and the connecting metaphor is the stage: he "stepped out on the narrow terrace, built/Over the street and opposite the church,/And paced its lozenge-brickwork sprinkled cool" (I, 479–481). From this narrow, carefully crafted eminence, the backdrop balanced by the façade of an elegant drawing room and "Felice-church-side," the stage lighting provided by the glow of windows "fringed for festival" and a sky sporadically illuminated by remnant flashes of a setting sun on banks of clouds, the background music emanating from a cloistered choir chanting praises at once familiar and mysterious and appropriate to a midsummer night's dream, the stage properties being stately "terrace-plants" among which the fireflies wax and wane, promenaders in the street's gathering darkness contributing "A busy human sense beneath [his] feet" (I, 493), the poet-speaker embarks upon a journey to the underworld—dead time, dead place, dead persons, dead truth. Like his ancient predecessors and following their example—"Step by step, missing none and marking all," and persisting till "the ghastly goal" is reached—he accomplishes the ultimate purpose of all such journeys: "The life in [him] abolished the death of things,/Deep calling unto deep . . ." (I, 520–521).

Thus the theatricality of the process of interpenetration—its essential make-believe—is deliberately emphasized. Paradoxically, "make-believe" is the artist's way of making people believe, of breaking through their habit of inattention and, by heightening the thing seen, heightening too the consciousness of the seer. In doing so, however, the serious artist enters into an implicit contract with his audience that is so different in degree from that represented by the first, external stage of storytelling that it becomes a difference in kind. He promises that what he has to offer is the unalloyed truth; that it reaches to the red heart of tragic human experience; that he has himself made the dark journey he is solemnly inviting them to take; and that he has invested all his talent as an artist in creating the perspectives within the perspective that will enable each, according to his capacity and sympathy, not only to find the central truth of this human drama of beauty and fearfulness (I, 525), but also to purify and strengthen each in the truth-finding process itself.

Having rendered in some detail this second, interfusing stage of the creative process, the preparation of the materials with which the artist can work and in which he has a reasonable expectation of permanence, the speaker pauses to bring the reader or apprentice-artist along (I, 679–697). He is not working with raw facts nor is he imagining the facts; he is working with a fusion of the two. He did not originate the myth or action or plot; he found it. Hence illumination rather than origination (invention) is his proper focus. He could not work honestly without the myth or story; without him or his equivalent the story would suffer a second and perhaps final death. Only the combination works. But human history shows that this kneading together of the man and the myth toward an act of human salvation (I, 734) is, like everything else in life, subject to abuse. A "sceptical dilettante"[17] like Faust and his imitators will both solemnize and trivialize the sacred process, putting personal fame ahead of truth and adulterating the search for knowledge by subordinating it to some lower goal such as the search for power. The result is a grotesque rather than a tragic vision looked at from inside the "mage," though tragic to the nth degree looked at from outside him, such incomparable talent being polluted at its human source. On the other hand, there is the redeeming example of Elisha, far more ancient and wholly free of the modern ambiguity embodied in Faust. His power had, he knew, originated in a source far greater than himself, a power that he acknowledged humbly and reverenced with a simple faith that knew no mockery. His pact was with no lesser spirit, and the life-and-death reality of human existence was no farcical play-game or devil's-fun. His act was whole because his faith was whole, and the life of which he was the renewing agent was a sign of a real truth, not a brilliant sham.

With this implicit purgation of his own spirit—this rejection of discipleship to Faust, the modern "mage" with his bag of tricks and cynical motives, and identification with Elisha, ancient exemplar of awe-inspiring talents and a self-effacing conscientiousness—the poet-speaker attempts to launch the third stage of the creative process, that of crafting the art-object itself. However, the act of disengagement, the disappearing act by which the craftsman wholly effaces himself and enables the product of his craft, the poetic ring, to become complete, rounded, autonomous, sufficient to itself and to the future, is very difficult. As he has become a part of it, it has become a part of him; the life that he has breathed into its erstwhile inert stuff, its dead fact, has in turn breathed new life into him—"A spirit laughs and leaps through every limb,/And lights my eye, and lifts me be the hair . . ." (I, 776–777)—so that he hardly knows how to name this vital reciprocation, this resuscitation that evinces a strange life-giving power of its own. He tries again to tell the tale, but the life has gone out of it again, and the result (I, 780–823), though conscientious, circumspect, and balanced, is not even as "lively" as his first effort to tell it (I, 141–363). It is a singularly crucial moment in the creative process and in the way we view *The Ring and the Book*. The very idea of the objective and the subjective has become muddled. Is it *it* or is it *he*?

Then, whether under the influence of despair or of a sudden inspiration, the craftsman in him sees the secret. *He* cannot tell the tale; it must be allowed to tell itself. "Let this old woe step on the stage again!/Act itself o'er anew for men to judge . . ." (I, 824–825). Otherwise, no matter how "silverly [*his*] tongue [may] troll," the truth will look like falsehood *even to him*, and the artist will have wasted his labor (XII, 841–853). It is not his, the generic poet's, job to mediate the truth, even though at that crucial moment he may have thought he knew it better than anyone else. What gives him a unique adjudicator's power to say "how heart moves brain, and how both move hand" (I, 828) except for himself? By what authority does he presume to clean up reality, separate truth from falsehood? And even if, by no more than luck, he happened to get it right, what purpose would it serve even to those who might be said to need it most? They could not see it in so unreal a form, and their faith in poetry's worth would only be further weakened. Language is the indispensable instrument of revelation, what "we call evidence," but it must be presented as their language, not his, even if there is make-believe in the showing. The poet can best demonstrate his faith in imagination's capacity to discover, assay, and illumine truth by cutting the umbilical cord between himself and it and allowing its mysterious, redemptive power to function in others as it has functioned in himself, not smothering its precious new life in a presumption of personal indispensability. As resuscitated truth has a life of its own, the reader must be acknowledged as having a life of his own too. Thus the reader's relationship to the poem is analogous to the poet's relationship to it: truth can never become a living thing to the reader unless he too mixes something of himself with it and reenacts, in his "due degree," the regenerative process exampled in the poem.

The poet has performed a service of exceptional value. As the agent of a power far greater than himself, a power to which people give different names and which is better known than understood, he has happened upon a depository of human reality that has "spoken" to him in a quintessential or exemplary way. Being a depository of human reality that, despite the unlimited energy at its nucleus, has long since disappeared from human cognizance, it cannot be easily corroborated from sources external to it. What value it has must be found in the thing itself through a process of concentrated, uninhibited scrutiny that ultimately transforms itself into an ever-expanding, delicate though spirited, extrapolation—a species of microcosmic-macrocosmic formulation.

There is also compensation for the lack or dearth of extratextual corroborating evidence. As the exemplary depository cannot be strengthened by external "proof," so it cannot be dissipated by the tangential distractions of special interests attempting to influence the view that the empirical student of reality takes of it. It is, insofar as such a consummation is possible, "de-politicized." Indeed, the happy principle of de-politicization must be pressed into more than usual service. Being free of factitious or diplomatic external considerations, this exemplary depository must also be kept free of even subtler internal political considerations—the predilections, predispositions, prejudices of the poet. Thus, like any good empiricist, he must devise a technique for filtering out such personal impositions on the truth per se, his additions to it of the vitalizing imagination not being permitted to adulterate its essential quality of truth. Such an undertaking is clearly not for the faint of heart or cowardly, and the robustness of tone assumed by the poet-speaker is relevant to this issue. His faith in the justness and value of what he is attempting to do is whole, its obvious difficulties inducing in him not a single doubt.

Having recognized the simple secret of technique—the aesthetic necessity of *how* rather than the tempting deception of *what*—the poet is ready to proceed with his crafting, and this is what we observe him doing in the approximately 500 lines that follow (I, 839–1329). In this crucial sequence, the poet-speaker does what the overall technique he has adopted forces him to do. In a dramatic novel or stage play, he would have had alternative ways of accomplishing his goals—stage directions, collisions of personality in staged actions, exchanges of dialogue, interspersed passages of description and characterization, and so forth. But a series of technically self-enclosed monologues in which no one of the speakers addresses an audience in which another speaker is present does not allow for the use of any of these more conventional devices. On the other hand, the poet's sacrifice of these formal strategies to soundings at a profounder depth does not obviate the need for some of the creative qualities that, in the poetic tradition, they can be seen to generate.

The fact is, of course, that these traditional strategies have not been abandoned; they have been transformed on the same principle of internalization by which the whole poem is shaped. They have become implicit rather than explicit, embedded in the necessities of personality, occasion, and goal in which they originated in the first place. For so bold a technical departure on so grand a scale, the simultaneous internalization of per-

haps the most elusive and imperative of all secular subjects—
the quest for the truth of the human situation—and of the
strategies by which poetry had traditionally effected its diverse
revelations, Browning had no precedent even in the experimental canon that he had himself been vigorously evolving over
a quarter of a century. Partial or fragmentary examples could
be identified there, and there were more or less minor mirror-
ings of his manner and matter in the literature of the West
from Euripides and Aristotle to Christopher Smart and Alfred
Tennyson. But even his most practiced readers, lovers of truth
and poetry with the very widest literary experience, could have
seen nothing quite like this before. Hence, for both the poem's
sake and their own, readers needed some indication of what
was expected of them lest from old habit they perceive the poem
mistakenly and curdle its essential freshness at the source. This,
essentially, is the purpose of this final stage in the creative process that the poet-speaker has been taking himself and the
reader through in Book I.

This is the climax of the *poet's* story: it completes his account
of how, from that day in San Lorenzo Square when he found
"the Book" to the moment just before he draws the curtain and
exhibits "the Ring," he gradually worked his way into the truth
of his strange discovery and found there the need, the will, and
the secret of how to make a poem that would enable others to
make an analogous discovery and undergo an analogous process of transformation. He had told the *poem's* story three times
with quite unsatisfactory results. Only as he gradually learned
that, as he had not created the book, he could not create the
truth that the book contained, did he see that he had to get
out of the way and let truth make her own appearance. By an
accident so fortunate that it seemed to have preternatural
overtones, he had found the book, and his initial excitement
over its dramatic contents had so deepened and widened with
continuous immersion in them that, like the Ancient Mariner
in Coleridge's poem, he had begun to see human life itself
wonderfully concentrated in the book's images. Being also a
poet dedicated to the idea of lending his mind out, he was of
course determined and eager at every stage of his self-immer-
sion in this strange and wonderful tale to pass it on to others.

However, the profounder his apprehension of the implications of the book became—as he became possessed by the conviction that man's very life in this world was imaged there—he found that old ways of telling were incommensurate with his intensified and expanded sense of this story's particular needs. He had come upon one of those extraordinary conjunctions by which one's life, even at its best level of organization and refinement, is metamorphosed. The necessities of the tale, the told of, and the teller had become interfused and interdependent in such a new and important way for him that they demanded a new kind of poetry and a new kind of poet. Thus three stories emerge simultaneously in *The Ring and the Book,* the poem's story (the transformation of the myth or action), the poet's story (the transformation of the mythmaker), and the story of the poem itself (the transforming reciprocation of the myth with the mythmaker resulting in the birth of a new species of poetry or, more precisely, of poetry under a new aspect). This creative trinitarianism does not require us to make odious comparisons among its parts—to designate one as more important than the other; all three are real, and a continued awareness of all three conditions the liveliness of our response to the poem and our availability to its imaginative influences.

To perceive this long climactic sequence of Book I as guidance to the reader on how best to perceive just what is going on in the poem is to see it as an extended invitation to co-create it. That in turn raises a question that becomes more real, even more potentially troublesome, the more attractive and challenging one finds the idea of genuine co-creation: why in giving us a poem in which we are assigned the role of co-creators has the poet prejudiced the issue by making so transparent his own value judgments?

As has already been suggested, a conclusive disposition of the moral issue inherent in the poem's action or myth is not the basic object of the poet's labors. It is an important aspect of the *substance* with which the poet is working, but it is not the focus of the ultimate *significance* that he derives from that substance. Despite its apparent solidity, the moral issue is an inconstant, properly subject to each viewer's individual judgment, in a poem in which the poet is attempting to reveal a constant on which all sympathetic readers can agree and on which they can invest their faith enthusiastically. Making a moral judgment or elaborating a so-called moral case is the manifest activity of each of the sample speakers, and if that were the poet's basic goal, the reader could cooperate fully with that goal simply by choosing the judgment or the case he liked best or admired most and voting for it. Indeed, that has been the procedure customarily followed by the commentators on the poem, and it has regularly resulted in the choice of the Pope as winner of the contest, a result that has then been translated into the assertion that the Pope speaks for Browning. Such a parlor-game approach to *The Ring and the Book* is unsatisfactory critically because, however solemn or churchy or sententious the critic-players may be, it diminishes to a quite secondary poetic role the three principals at the heart of the ghastly ordeal (Pompilia, Caponsacchi, and Guido), and, worse still, it seems to imply that Browning employs all this elaborate machinery—21,000 carefully manufactured lines of poetry, history, drama, romance, epic, rhetoric, theology, philosophy, mysticism, music, painting, and a plethora of classical and Christian mythology—to say that life is a parlor game. But "here's the plague/That all this trouble comes of telling truth,/Which truth, by when it reaches him, looks"—very much like humbug.

Applied to the question under discussion, this suggests that, even if one concedes that the poet's predisposition on the moral issue is transparent, the implied fault, like the issue, is less critical than it is sometimes thought to be. But is it a fault? Is the poet's predisposal of the moral issue as real as it appears to be? Is his practice in this respect as inconsistent with the aesthetic principles of the poet-speaker as some commentators have held?

We have, in the first place, to consider his options. One option that the poet-speaker had declared off limits was what may be called the Faust option—to fake a position that would be " 'mistily seen, murmuringly heard,/Mistakenly felt . . .' " (I, 758–759). Although it might have made him interestingly elusive, it would also have introduced a trivializing tone that would have jeopardized the life-and-death seriousness of his primary

subject—human salvation. He would employ the grave grotesque as a strategy of character revelation in the case of Guido,
but his good humor was not to be allowed to topple into terrifying farce lest his whole purpose be lost. Another option,
centered in character rather than in technique, might have been
the Tertium Quid option, a calculated appearance of neutral-
ity, but the very reality of Tertium Quid made that option unacceptable. The affect of that neutered Third Something-or-
Other is fascinated disgust of the kind inspired in us by snakes,
a threatening sleekness that blends a perception of beauty with
a deep feeling of repulsion. Even had we admired a narrator's
marvelous circuitousness, we could hardly have overcome our
distrust. The only genuine option available to the poet engaged in charting the route to the underworld and instructing
his readers on how to bring saving sunlight to that "ghastly goal"
(I, 518) was the one he took, namely, a frank, full-bodied acceptance of his Apollonian role and the faith that his readers
would understand that, on the moral issue, he was not essentially different from the representative characters whose "sample-speeches" he had rendered in such detail and, despite a
comparable firmness of moral disposition, was to be scrutinized with the same care and detachment.

Before the reader allows the critics' judgment that the poet
has arbitrarily prejudiced the moral issue to take too firm a hold,
he should also acknowledge the fact that no credible make-believe would have made Guido just, Pompilia craven, and Caponsacchi simply shabby. Even if one believes that Guido finally repents and is saved, which I do not, he must admit that
Guido is dragged kicking and screaming from the depths of
corruption; even if one believes that Pompilia, as some of the
secondary sources suggest, was not as lily pure as the Pope says,
one can hardly deny that she struggled heroically with devastating odds and had a conversional impact on a variety of strong
characters, including Guido, that only a woman of enormous
stature could have had; and even if one believes that Caponsacchi succumbed too readily to the soft, sensuous regimen of
the Church and that his St. George had the longings of a Don
Juan, one must acknowledge that he braved death and disgrace to rescue Pompilia from her desperate plight and yielded

to the elemental fiery baptism that burned both the impurities and the prospects for happiness from his vulnerable human heart. So much of what some see as moral prejudice may in fact be moral fairness, and Browning's choice may simply have been not to fake his characters, good or bad, in the interests of a sophisticated evasiveness that could hardly have been both honest and poetically sound.

Finally, if Browning's poetic purpose was to chart the route to the underworld and to instruct his readers in how to bring the saving light of their imaginations to that labor—to enable "deep" to call to "deep" and "life" to abolish "the death of things" (I, 520–521)—then these ad hoc moral judgments were mere grist for his poetic mill and should not be made a critical end in themselves. Such "a full look at the Worst" restores the principals to the primary place in the poem. *Who* they are, *how* they spent their portions of life, *what transformations* they experienced will be the central metaphors in the poet's recognitions and the keys to his saving sunlight. This, in turn, will provide a different clue to the significance of the judgments made by the other speakers in the poem and an organic basis for deciding why the poet found it necessary to render Guido in two monologues, carefully spaced, instead of one. Further, it will redefine the action of the poem, putting a proper premium on change, which the poet calls the touchstone of life, and help us better to perceive that Book I is also a "sample-speech" in which we need to determine *who* the speaker is, *how* he has spent his portion of life both before and after finding the Old Yellow Book, and *what transformations* of soul he has experienced. Like *The Ring and the Book* as a whole, it too is a conversion of history to poetry, and again like the poem, its purpose is to teach us how to invest fact with metaphor and how to use our life to abolish the death of things.

The epilogic character of Book XII justifies both its length and its brevity. It is a carefully controlled tidying-up of both the myth and the meaning of the poem, and despite the apparent casualness of its method, it looks to the future with sober clarity and residual hope. The make-believe is over; the "old woe" has had its moment on stage, its poetic moment. The curtain has fallen, the Roman candle has burned itself out, the seventeenth century has vanished again into the tomb of time. What has been will be again, of course, but not exactly as it was and rarely recognized as a symbolic reenactment of the same essential pattern. Man is memory, but so strong is his inclination to forget that he seems perpetually determined to de-create himself. It is an awful paradox: what he pays for most dearly—pain—he casts away most improvidently. Even imaginative memory, the moments of racial history in which poets invest the maximum of metaphoric content, is quick to fade, its relative compensation being that, though it may fail in "grace," it yet may "succeed in guardianship" (XII, 867)—that is, even if it does not touch a particular reader into life, it yet preserves the life that is in it; it touches no one into life once and forever, but must, like King Arthur, be enabled to come again and again according to the capacity and sympathy of the individual. Otherwise, despite all we may know, we understand nothing.

The poet-speaker in Book XII is the same whose voice we heard in Book I, but he projects a very different mood. The long voyage launched in the earlier book with an expectation and enthusiasm that cut through all difficulties however imposing is now ended; he, like his co-creative reader, is both wiser and sadder. But life goes on, and lest he deceive himself as to just what has been achieved in this grand dramatic demonstration of human life at both its polar extremes and at its intricate inner levels, he must look to an end that, except metaphorically, cannot really be since "that clear, perpetual outline of face and limb, under which [he has] group[ed]" things is only "a design in a web, the actual threads of which pass out beyond it."[18] To do this, he represents four "reports" of the day Count Guido and his four henchmen died—three letters and a portion of a sermon preached the day before at San Lorenzo by Don Celestine, the "barefoot Augustinian" who had been Pompilia's deathbed confessor.

The first letter is from a Venetian visitor in Rome who has come both for Carnival and to be an observer/participant in the socially stimulating gamble of Papal succession. He is a cocktail party attitudinizer, *au courant* in a superficial, flashy, gossip-column style, who pretends to have irrefragable knowledge of the most intimate secrets of Rome's great ones. Whatever his personal lineage, he makes a great show of sympathy for all things aristocratic while at the same time maintaining the disengagement of a gambler who makes light of his losses. He knows nothing of the tragic events leading up to this climax, nor is he troubled much to know. His chief concern is with some pundit's quatrain, which we assume to be scurrilously witty, and with Guido's impeccable comportment in public prior to his execution, expressing his disappointment only in the ugliness of Guido's face when his severed head is exhibited to the crowd.

It is a grotesque vignette, both comic and horrifying, and its effect is shockingly deflationary. The world is full of such people, and if that is what it means for "Civilization and the Emperor" to replace "Christianity and [the] Pope" (X, 2028–2029), mankind faces a very chilly prospect. That is only one possibility, of course, but it is a real one, and if one would take a spiritually realistic rather than a spiritually romantic view of the influence of the most exemplary of tragic events on the way even privileged people order their priorities, such possibilities much be frankly faced.

The second letter is from Archangeli, failed defender of Guido, and the poet-speaker introduces it with a reminder that his bittersweet task is coming to an end and with the ironic information that it is to the mysterious recipient of this letter, a Florentine lawyer named Cencini, friend of the Franceschini and "brother-in-the-devil" to Archangeli, that he owes the "book" upon which his "ring" is in part based. Thus their devils'-fun has at least led to such truthful revelation as the poem contains, and though falsehood may not "have done the work of truth" (XII, 853), it has yet made truth possible, "to mouths like [the poet's], at least" (XII, 840).

This second letter is significant in yet another way. It is in two parts, one written for public consumption (XII, 239–288), the other for the eye of the addressee only (XII, 291–390); one is basically a translation from the poet's source, the other entirely his own creation. Hence, in the two parts of this one letter we have an illustration of what the poet-speaker means by his claim in Book I that the whole truth is in the "book" from which the "ring" is made. It is not all there literally, just as the two parts of the letter are not literally there, but imaginatively implicit in the first part is the second part, needing only to be enabled to emerge. As Michelangelo had freed David from the block of marble in which he was imprisoned, the poet-speaker has freed his characters from the block of fact, the historical documents, in which they were encased. Some need a more radical mode of liberation than others, but the principle is the same for all: "the heart and inner meaning" is what the poet wants to make "vividly visible," and such intensification of "the expression of things" is an imaginative transformation of more literal kinds of truth.[19]

The first (public) part of Archangeli's letter has all the inflated ceremoniousness that we have learned to expect of his florid, insincere, at once self-abasing and self-congratulatory style. It is a confession, in the grandest rhetorical manner, of a personal culpability wholly lacking in personal truth. In the second (private) part, he more than makes up for this assumed loss of public face by being venomous toward the Pope and toward his victorious adversary Bottini and by maintaining brazenly that his defense of Guido had been "superb" and that he had salvaged as much as could be saved by learning and eloquence of the Franceschini credit and fortune in the face of a Pope who had already made up his mind and who looked upon the law as a mere "leash of quibbles" to lead broken-spirited men around by the nose. There is no truth or merit in things, only excuses, face-savings, undisguised hostilities, and eagerness for the next main chance—" 'hot and hot next case!' " (XII, 326, 390).

What, then, does this letter tell us that we did not know already? Nothing, perhaps, but it serves an important imaginative purpose nonetheless. The poet-speaker, in recognizing and acknowledging the vast difference between one rhetoric and another as a costume of the same basic truth, reminds us of the deceptive power of language. The elaborately coded rotundity of the former is just as revealing as the meanness of the latter, and knowledge of that fact may, if one has the knowledge and the will to use it, protect one from being victimized by the velvet trap of mean-minded men using pontifical professional language. "Gomez" is the next poor victim waiting in the wings, and Archangeli has an insatiable appetite for sustenance like Gomez's flesh and blood. Also, the metaphoric role of Hyacinth ("Cinuccio," "Cintino," "Cinone," "Cinuzzo"), the doting Archangeli's young son and his correspondent's godson, gets stunning illumination: he is both the man-hawk's excuse for devilry and the nestling-hawk being carefully trained to use his beak and talons on victims in the future. He already prefers to see a man's head "chopped/From trunk" to seeing it saved (XII, 335–337), and it is Bottini's " 'nose' " or beak that he is sure his father could have " 'argued-off' " (XII, 355–356). Law is a suitable profession for such a well-plumed bird of prey, certainly; they fit together like hand and glove, as if made for each other. It is a sobering revelation, eliminating another large section of mankind from trustworthiness, but the poet-speaker is valiantly trying to winnow his options and to discover where to invest his faith lest the pain of those who have induced his moral meditation—Caponsacchi, the Pope, Pompilia—be wasted.

The last two reports—Bottini's letter and the extract from Don Celestine's sermon—are interleaved, and this emphasizes a different contrast from that of the two parts of Archangeli's letter to Cencini. It reminds us that, although two words cannot occupy the same space at the same time on the printed page and that therefore things must appear to have a sequential character, many of the currents are going on simultaneously, crossing and recrossing in a welter of motives and mental and moral attitudes. Now that Guido is dead, Bottini has no competitor in the sinkhole of human corruption that is one enormous dimension of life in *The Ring and the Book;* compared to him, Archangeli is noble, a kingly predator who tears only the flesh and spills only the lifeblood of his victims and who has a recognizable, naturalistic motive—the welfare, so conceived, of his nestling. Bottini, on the other hand, is insatiable for the very soul of his victims. Even the "fine gold of the Temple dim[s]" at his touch (XII, 731, 746), and he would track saints to their heavenly rest. He casts pollution over everything, converting every success to failure, finding the basest motive in every action. He would strip Noah's dove, Pompilia, Don Celestine, the world itself of the humble glory of gentleness. To adapt the barefoot Augustinian's words, Bottini skulks in safety, lurks, defies moral law, and worships only obscenity. Moreover, no motive can be discovered for his moral putrescence: he is totally isolated, even his correspondent being unnamed, and he seems to be growing old in festered solitude feeding on his own rottenness. To have the fragment of Don Celestine's sermon enfolded in Bottini's letter is itself a metaphoric gesture suggestive of some unnamed obscenity that, like the preacher's illustration, reaches back to primitive times before Paganism or Christianity became the official religions of Rome, some uncleansed pollution of the race that has lingered on through great upheavals and changes of worship and surfaces still with unaccountable frequency in men like Bottini.

Don Celestine's is the last moral-imaginative statement made by a persona in *The Ring and the Book*. Therefore, structure alone would dictate the need to weigh it carefully. But the fact that it is the exhortation of the confessor who supported Pompilia in her preparation for death and is composed under the influence of that experience suggests that it is the embodiment of how one good man of a particular disposition might interpret it for himself and for the world. It may or may not coincide with Browning's view as it may or may not coincide with our own, but those are not the conditions under which it is offered, and since we can never be certain of the former or, except on a strictly private basis, of the latter, that can hardly be considered its poetic purpose. It gives our moral-imaginative judgments something additional to work with, something to think about, something perhaps to admire and imitate; it does not relieve us of the need to judge.

" 'Let God be true, and every man/A liar' " (XII, 453–454, 600–601): it is as subtle and undogmatic a text as a man of whole but humble faith could enunciate. It goes a long way toward reconciling the simple, childlike, but terrifyingly austere position that Pompilia comes to occupy with the philosophically elaborate, quintessentially scholastic, apex-of-tradition position taken by the Pope, and the fact that it is tonally closer to that of Pompilia shows the power and organic influence which a few days spent with her have had on an Augustinian priest trained and practiced in quite a different tradition. The "grammar" of Don Celestine's "assent" is crucial. "Let God be true" is a subjunctive construction that suggests at once condition, imprecation, and command. *If* God is true; *may* God *be* true; God, *be true!* That is where faith comes in. If one's faith in God is whole, then what man does on this earth, be it ever so false, foolish, stupid, ill-tempered, and mean-minded, does not matter *insofar as our capacity to judge goes.* Heaven is for heaven, earth for earth. Only to the degree that one's faith in God is not whole does he demand that heaven's rules be given earthly application—that God prove Himself by " 'right[ing]/ Wrong on the instant' " (XII, 469–470) or by making foolish, weak, ignorant men speak truth on this earth as though they were already possessed of the wisdom, strength, and knowledge of eternity.

Though " 'Pompilia's purity prevail[ed]' " (XII, 472), that does not mean that " 'all truth triumphs' " over persecution. Indeed, for every such triumph, there are countless disasters. In the present case, nearly every imaginable impediment that circumstance and the blind, light-despising mind of man could devise was erected against the success of the young martyr's " 'convulsive' " " 'struggle' " " 'from death to life' " (XII, 568). Even her public defender, the lawyer appointed to rescue her " 'from calumny' " (XII, 579), submitted " 'for best defence, that wickedness/Was bred of [Pompilia's] flesh and innate with [Pompilia's] bone' " rather than that she was the chance-sown, cleft-nurtured seed of an hour's sexual passion (XII, 581–584). In the end, only the miracle of " 'What I call God's hand, — you, perhaps, — this chance/Of the true instinct of an old good man/Who happens to hate darkness and love light, — ' " (XII, 592–594) banished her enemies and allowed her " 'vexed star culminate in peace' " (XII, 590)—not any inherent power of human truth to triumph over human persecution and certainly not any machinery devised by man to " 'Rescue the drowning orb from calumny' " (XII, 579). This and this only " 'demand[s] assent' " to Don Celestine's text that if " 'God is true,' " as evidenced by this " 'one proof more,' " then let " 'every man [be] a liar' "!

The reader can hardly fail to be struck by the sharp difference between "voice" in Don Celestine's " 'What I call God's hand,—you, perhaps,—this chance/Of the true instinct of an old good man/Who happens to hate darkness and love light, —'." and "voice" in the Pope's "what I call God,/And fools call Nature" (X, 1072–1073), a difference that the similarities in syntax seem clearly meant to emphasize. It may be partially a difference in temperaments, of course, but it may also be a difference in experience and role. To the Pope, Pompilia has a mysterious reality like that of Mary of the Immaculate Conception, the Virgin Birth, and the Assumption. He has never seen her, never acknowledged her imperfections; his response to her has been magnificently symbolic, like an act of adoration. She has redeemed his reign as Pope and renewed his youthful dreams of heroism; she has given him the strength to defy the world and to rescind the Church's truce with the future. Don Celestine, on the other hand, has seen Pompilia up close and personally; he has counseled her, helped her through a critical stage of spiritual paralysis, enabled her to add valor to purity, nobility to goodness, heroism to patience. In consequence, he has undergone her law at the deepest, most sanctuarial level.

Like Pompilia and unlike the Pope, Don Celestine is reconciled to the realities of life on this earth; he is not furious with things as they in fact are; he invokes no apocalypse against the future. Like her and unlike the Pope, he does not see his God in grand cosmic metaphors or divide Him into the attributes of the schoolmen. Like her and unlike the Pope, he does not rate people on a moral scale or imagine life as a struggle between two mighty Manichaean opposites contending for the soul of man. Like her and unlike the Pope, he preaches no gospel of baptismal exclusivity and frankly admits that there are many dimensions of life not circumscribed by his personal choice:

"For many a dream would fain perturb my choice—
How love, in those the varied shapes, might show
As glory, or as rapture, or as grace:
How conversancy with the books that teach,
The arts that help,—how, to grow great, in fine,

Rather than simply good, and bring thereby
Goodness to breathe and live, nor, born i' the brain,
Die there,—how these and many another gift
May well be precious though abjured by me."
                                    (XII, 622–630)

Like Pompilia, Don Celestine has a comprehensive understanding of " 'the world's calumny,/Stupidity, simplicity' "; he
knows full well how disastrous are the usual results of weak,
pathetic, innocent souls' efforts to remain unspotted by a world
grown dark in corruption; he acknowledges unequivocally " 'that
who trusts/To human testimony for a fact/Gets this sole fact —
himself is proved a fool . . .' " (XII, 601–603). But like her
and unlike the Pope, he does not presume to speak for God,
to take upon himself the wreaking of God's vengeance upon
the world, and to strip God's design for mankind of all the finest achievements of non-Christian, secular culture and reduce
it to a stark penfold of moral probation. " 'God tries the heart,' "
says Don Celestine, " 'Yet [I] weigh the worth of worldly prize
foregone,/Disinterestedly judge this and that/Good ye account
good' " (XII, 613–615). That the Pope does not do.

About one thing, however, Don Celestine has no doubt—
renouncing fame. He obviously did not learn this from Pompilia, having " 'long since renounced [the] world' " (XII, 612)
and chosen to " 'glide unnoticed to the grave' " (XII, 610).
However, the short, intense experience of her in these last few
days has shown him what a counterfeit for genuine joy is this
" 'Arch-object of ambition — earthly praise' " (XII, 632), this
" 'imperishable' " hot-air bubble that perishes at a touch (XII,
640), compared to the true dilation of the spirit that transcends even mortality. Thus she has renewed in him the central current of himself and, like deep calling to deep, enabled
him to realize the paradoxical joy of the self losing the self.
The original choice was his, but only the "chance" of knowing
her has made him realize what a happy choice it was!

The poet-speaker himself makes the final aesthetic statement of the poem, and it is one of the simplest, firmest, fullest
defenses of the role of poetry in the quest for truth in our literature. It is a characterization of *all poetry*, not just of modern

poetry, as essentially a poetry of indirection. The poet speaks
to all mankind, not just to those who share his views, his culture, or even his language. Whether he uses a confessional or
a dramatic mode, whether he writes lyrics or epics or ro-
mances, it is his role to mediate the experience rather than the
thought, so *choosing his subject* as to appeal to the great primary
human emotions and so *treating his subject* as to enable the reader
to co-create it as nearly as possible as he would, *with imagination*, have found it in nature. This done, the thought will inevitably follow, but it will be a poetic, not a philosophical,
thought. It will "bring music from [the] mind" (XII, 860); not
argument, but voices in evidence, "truth with falsehood,"

> Uproar in the echo, live fact deadened down,
> Talked over, bruited abroad, whispered away,
> Yet helping us to all we seem to hear. . . .
> (I, 831, 834–836)

Its imagery will appeal to the body's eye and to the soul's also,
thus enabling us to see in particular objects—people, places,
frames, actions, designs, patterns—the endless rhythms of our
race, often at their most passionate points. In doing this, the
poet honors several principles that capable, free-spirited, conscientious persons in all ages have held to be imperative: that
the facts—the known truth—of man's life in his universe be
honestly represented; that a perpetual effort be made, especially by poets and scientists, including historians and philosophers, to discover in this infinity of factual details patterns of
coherence that will give mankind a sense of the comprehensi-
bility, meaning, purpose of his life in this universe; that poets,
including scientists, historians, and philosophers with more than
the usual gifts of poetic imagination, attempt unflinchingly to
identify in these patterns of coherence sound bases for human
reconciliation, however minimalist, with the "insistent, and often
grotesque, substance"[20] of man's life here; that poets lend their
minds out in such a way as to enable their readers to undergo
at an internal, transformational level the "substance" of the life
they represent and experience the actual birth of the reconciliation ("the best consummation possible," as Hardy calls it[21])

rather than simply comprehend it on an intellectual or philosophical or scientific plane, thus, in Plato's terms, realizing the
difference between what was or is (history) and what might have
been or may be (poetry).

This last point is comprehended in the poet-speaker's phrase
"do the thing shall breed the thought,/Nor wrong the thought,
missing the mediate word" (XII, 856–57) and is often seen as
peculiarly modern. It does, of course, have a high degree of
modern relevance, and *The Ring and the Book* is a landmark in
modern poetry because of the massive, consistent, and effective use it makes of it. But it is not peculiarly modern; indeed,
it is conspicuously ancient. When the poet-speaker says that "Art
remains the one way possible/Of speaking truth, to mouths like
mine, at least" (XII, 839–840), he is saying that, against the
background of all the fashions, experiments, adaptations, revolutions in the efforts of man to tell the truth, poetry ("Art")
"remains" the "one way possible" for poets ("mouths like mine")
to do so. One age's science, philosophy, history are not those
of another age except as they aspire to the condition of poetry, and poetry that yields its birthright to science, philosophy, history is no more than the object of intellectual curiosity
to another age. But poetry that is inspired by its special way of
supposing and stating fact—poetry that aspires to no other goal
than fulfilling the law of its own being—is independent of
fashions, experiments, adaptations, revolutions and as relevant to one age as it is to another. So while it is judicious to
see *The Ring and the Book* as a great monument in the peren-
nial search for a "modern expression of a modern outlook,"[22]
it is injudicious to assess that fact disproportionately—to see it
as having a critical significance it does not have and, in over-
stressing Browning's real but proportionate modernism, to di-
minish his greater right to be measured against the poets of
all the ages.[23]

The Ring and the Book brings us ultimately to two texts: " 'Let
God be true, and every man/A liar' " (XII, 453–454) and "Art
remains the one way possible,/Of speaking truth" (XII, 839–
840). In that juxtaposition, the poet's quest in the poem ends.
As part of this juxtaposition, "Let God be true" becomes less
ambivalent, less "subjunctive," than in the context of Don Ce-

lestine's oration. In fact, it becomes indicative: if the intimation that men in all ages have used the trope *God* to designate is a reality, a "true truth," then there is a genuine basis for man's reconciliation with all the ugly evil concentrated in this image of the world called *The Ring and the Book*. There has been a lot of "God talk" in the poem and very little evidence of a God, but if that evidence can be believed—the testimonial voices of Caponsacchi, the Pope, Don Celestine, and Pompilia—then catastrophe has not been turned into despair despite all the terror inherent in the truth. But the truth must continue to be told because it is in the whole truth that freedom from despair is to be found—the truth of love as well as of hate, of Pompilia as well as of Guido, of both the Pope and Tertium Quid, of Don Celestine as well as of Archangeli and Bottini. Moreover, it must be told in such a way as to break through the barriers, to span the distance, between the head and the heart. Only thus can one take full possession of it and answer Goethe's double question organically and in the affirmative: "Yes, it is *true;* yes, it is true *for me*."

Notes

1. Robert Langbaum, *The Poetry of Experience* (New York: Random House, 1957), pp. 115, 135.
2. Richard D. Altick and James F. Loucks II, *Browning's Roman Murder Story* (Chicago: University of Chicago Press, 1968), pp. 38–39, 74–75.
3. Mary Rose Sullivan, *Browning's Voices in "The Ring and the Book"* (Toronto: University of Toronto Press, 1969), pp. 210–213.
4. Langbaum and others put inordinate interpretive stress on the obvious and imaginatively rather trivial reversals of tone at the end of many of the monologues—e.g., II, III, IV, VIII, IX. See *The Poetry of Experience,* for example, p. 115.
5. Though the poet-speaker repeatedly uses the trope *God*, it is important, I think, to poeticize rather than theologize the name. He chooses to use that metaphor, as others speaking of the same concept or reality might not choose to use it, but there is no proof that it has for him anything more than a rich metaphoric content.
6. The relevance to the resurrection motif at the end of Pompilia's monologue is both significant and, I suggest, corrective of the way it is customarily read.

7. How Mary Rose Sullivan found "the poet" to speak in an "exultant tone in the first *and last* books" (p. 213, emphasis added) completely escapes me.

8. Arthur to Lancelot, in *The Holy Grail*, ll. 880–882.

9. The view of the poem's ultimate outcome presented here is significantly different from those reached by both J. Hillis Miller and Mary Rose Sullivan. Though limited, it is not so "momentary and evanescent" as Miller says it is, and "the impossibility of joining finite and infinite" does not have quite the negative results *for man* as Miller sees it as having (*The Disappearance of God: Five Nineteenth-Century Writers* [Cambridge: Harvard University Press, 1963], pp. 152–153). Sullivan, on the other hand, seems to me to wink away the difficulty Miller points to and simply to let her God-like poet leap the impossible distance between the finite and the infinite (*Browning's Voices*, pp. 209–214).

10. Florence Emily Hardy, *The Life of Thomas Hardy 1840–1928* (London: Macmillan, 1962), p. 383.

11. In his characterization of the Faust-type described above, the poet-speaker puts "true" words in Faust's mouth that seem to be taken almost directly from the Preface.

12. Altick and Loucks speak of Books I and XII as "ringing" the poem. While this is an understandable use of the term, it assigns a secondary and negligible meaning to what the poet-speaker intends by "this Ring" and thus introduces an unnecessary quibble.

13. *The Old Yellow Book: Source of Robert Browning's "The Ring and the Book"* was published in its entirety in 1908, edited by Charles W. Hodell, and has been reprinted. For forty years, however, most readers of the poem could not have seen it.

14. The literalist approach accounts in large part for the dissatisfaction many commentators have expressed with the speaker's use of the "ring" as a "figure" or "symbol." They have often abandoned hope of defending its intellectual integrity, claiming or conceding that it does not hold up under close scrutiny.

15. Henry James, "The Novel in *The Ring and the Book*," in *Notes on Novelists* (New York: Scribners, 1914), pp. 389, 400.

16. Sexual intercourse is, as seems inevitable, implicitly analogous to the creative act Browning is trying to illuminate, an analogy pressed to a quite bold degree even in the crucial instance of Elisha "stretch[ing] him on the flesh" to give life to a corpse (I, 760–771). The analogy holds steady: God creates, but man propagates. No attention is drawn to the Hermaphroditic resonances inherent in the transfer from biological to artistic generation, but a conceptual form of the ancient myth becomes a recurrent background presence in the poem.

17. The term is Carlyle's, especially in *Heroes, Hero-Worship and the Heroic in History*.

18. Pater, Conclusion to *The Renaissance*.

19. Thomas Hardy says that the purpose of his art "is to intensify the

expression of things . . . so that the heart and inner meaning is made vividly visible" (*The Life*, p. 177).

20. Hardy, Preface to *The Dynasts*.
21. Hardy, Apology to *Late Lyrics and Earlier*.
22. Hardy, Preface to *The Dynasts*.
23. To speak, even in support of Browning, of "the conditions for modern intellectual and moral conviction," as Robert Langbaum does, is an example of such disproportion. It is implicitly dogmatic and puts the poetic premium where Browning did not. See *The Poetry of Experience*, p. 135.

3.

Imaginative Mirrorings:
Books II, III, and IV

If, as was said in Chapter 1, *The Ring and the Book* functions in a basic sense as a course in critical-creative reading, then the three "sample-speeches" presented in Books II, III, and IV can be expected to satisfy, at an initial level, the requirements of such a purpose. *How* they are read thus becomes the primary consideration, and if Book I has an organic rather than a merely descriptive relationship to the rest of the poem, then one must look there for the most useful indications of just what kind of reading is meant. Moreover, if the principle of organicism maintains itself, one can expect Books II, III, and IV to illuminate Book I to a degree comparable to the way Book I illuminates them. Such is in fact the case.

In his description of the final stage of the creative process (I, 824–1347), the poet-speaker had spoken of "voices" ("by voices we call evidence" and "Here are the voices"), and though voices clearly imply speakers and speakers or characters are clearly "the insistent, and often grotesque, substance"[1] of the poem, characters are not *all* that is suggested by "voices." For

example, the wording with which this decisive stage is introduced is quite particular: "Let this old woe step on the stage
again!/Act itself o'er anew for men to judge . . ." (I, 824–825).
Not this old event or even this old drama, but "this old woe";[2]
and not these old characters acting it out again, but "Let this
old woe . . ./Act itself o'er anew. . . ." The issue is not one of
substance, which the characters clearly supply, but of *significance,* which exceeds character.

This, then, would be one highly refined but clear indication
of how we are to read the poem. Though *The Ring and the Book*
is one of the most empirically founded of poems, it is to be
read very imaginatively. Thus, after we have mastered the indispensable question of what Half-Rome, Other Half-Rome, and
Tertium Quid *are*—including, of course, what the poet and we
see them to be as distinct from what they see or pretend to see
themselves as being—we are then faced with the critical-creative question of what they *signify* on a level of imaginative
reality suggested by the qualitative, all-encompassing phrase
"this old woe." A Thomist might put the question as, "Those
being the accidents, what is the essence imaged there?" as a
Kantian might ask, "Those being the appearances, what is the
reality?" or a Platonist, "What is the idea?" Without pressing
the question to any one of these philosophically idealist posi-
tions—though that might be quite legitimate—the reader can
yet accept the *poetic* principle inherent in every aspect of the
aesthetic position experientially as well as theoretically defined
and enlarged in Book I that, though he must not imagine the
facts, he must view the facts as imaginatively as possible. If "do
the thing shall breed the thought" (XII, 856) means anything,
it means that the thought bred is not to be prosiac but poetic,
imaginative rather than merely analytical.

Unfortunately, no sufficient evidence of such an imaginative
or poetic level of reading exists in the standard commentaries.
For example, Langbaum's summary point about Half-Rome is
that he "reveals toward the end that he is a married man wor-
ried about his wife's fidelity, and that *his whole account,* with its
emphasis on Guido's just revenge, is by way of a warning that
he wants delivered to his rival" (emphasis added).[3] And Langbaum says of Tertium Quid that his "assumption that there is

neither right nor wrong in the case, but self-interested motives on both sides, is itself a prepossession that . . . leaves him in the end as 'wide o' the mark' as the other two."[4] Altick and Loucks also see the essence of Half-Rome summed up in his "surprise ending,"[5] and except for the sudden turn in the last lines of Other Half-Rome, they see his monologue as "an apparently judicious weighing of evidence on both sides, one which anticipates in form and technique the following speech of Tertium Quid, thus presaging the theme of the safe 'middle course' which will reappear in a number of subsequent books." He is, they say, "a creature of deep sensibilities verging on the poetic."[6] Mary Rose Sullivan sees Half-Rome as "frank, highly opinionated, self-confident, sure both of the rightness of his convictions and the accuracy of his knowledge of the case," but after an extended analysis of such matters as speaker, addressee, motive, tension, tone, mode of address, facts, and opinions, she concludes simply that, being "blinded by his pressing personal fears and drives, his reading of the Franceschini case is not to be trusted!"[7] Sullivan is also quite skeptical about the poet-speaker's characterizations of the participants in Book I and finds reasons to fault him. For example, she says that "Other Half-Rome's speech reveals that the '*swerve*' [toward the side of truth in his monologue] is due less to a '*fancy-fit*' as the poet had claimed than to a characteristic intuitive reaching after the right answer by a sensitive and imaginative nature."[8]

The fact that one could quarrel endlessly with each of these general commentaries on *The Ring and the Book* is not the important point.[9] The really troublesome issue is implicit in the following question: where in these various monuments of analysis is the evidence of a robust poetic imagination? After one has fully acknowledged their intellectual resourcefulness, the meticulousness of their research, their mastery of detail, the alertness and ingenuity with which they perceive and draw interesting connections, one is still compelled to ask what happened to the poet's own promises. Where is the truth "shall mean, beyond the facts," the music of the mind deeper "than ever the Andante dived"? What in all this analytical detective work could "save the soul beside"?

Not all souls are saved, of course, or saved alike, and perhaps a critic should not be held responsible for a poet's promises. But as Matthew Arnold said of Christianity, it really should be tried before it is abandoned.

What idea, then, does Half-Rome embody, what manifestation, aspect, metaphor of human life does he give imaginative visibility and carriage to, that qualifies him to launch in an exemplary way "this old woe"? What makes his monologue an apt opening for a vision of mankind's condition that is narrowly and obliquely redeemed by a tragedy that, while we may draw from it a reasonably firm if minimalist hope, offers us a catharsis that purges away none of the old problem and gives us only so much moral cleansing and spiritual exhilaration as imaginative understanding and inner resolution can effect? [10]

Half-Rome is both the embodiment and the exponent of a male sexism so virulent and disguised that it pollutes the world in which he himself exists and transforms life at its potentially tenderest and most re-creative center—that of "the great constringent relation between man and woman," of the "relation most worth while in life for either party" [11]—into one of the most psychologically, morally, and aesthetically imprisoning realities of the culture the poem probes, into one of its greatest sources of human cruelty, self-righteousness, and injustice. That is the ominous note, disguised as black comedy, on which "the ring" of *The Ring and the Book*—that is, its experiential and imaginative center—begins; and it is the terrifyingly ominous note on which it ends when, in Book XI, Guido projects the "nucleus" of himself—a wolfman uncompromisingly at war with what he calls "eunuchs, women, children," all the "shieldless" metaphors of his psychic culture—into eternity. It is not all of what the poet-speaker means by "this old woe," but it is a very large part of it, and it leaves no other part untouched. Thus the seed from which Book XI will grow is clearly planted in Book II, and though it would be oversimplifying and critically disproportionate to say that Half-Rome is a "little Guido" or a "Guido-in-the-making," he is much more, imaginatively, than the pro-Guido advocate that the commentators have stressed. The two characters share sympathies, thoughts, patterns of response that make them mirror-images of each other, and one of the crucial critical effects of recognizing this is to draw Guido

closer to the mainstream of life and to make him representative rather than a fairy-tale "incarnation of evil." [12]

Half-Rome is a man who vaguely sees his life besieged at what
truly is its center—his love life—but who, at the same time, has
no capacity to recognize and acknowledge that he is personally
compacted in such a way as to make it virtually impossible for
him to bring the matter to anything but a very ugly resolution.
Indeed, the farfetched procedure he pursues so relentlessly and
absurdly in his monologue—cornering a "cousin" of the "jack-
anapes" by whom he feels aggrieved and sending him a
threatening message costumed in the ghastly parable of the case
before them—is an elaborate exercise in futility that seems to
be motivated by the "not-unpleasant flutter at the breast" (I,
872) that the spectacle inside San Lorenzo church has stirred
up in him. Being the kind of man he is, he has seen that solution as admirably suited to his own problem, and in a heady
fantasy sees himself as a natural hero fulfilling with impunity
"the natural law" (II, 1477). So in defending Guido, he is really
defending his myth of himself, trying to persuade himself, in
his oblique way, that he can really do this thing and get off
scot-free. Ironically, he bullies his interlocutor with an imperious bravado likely to have a result quite opposite to the one
he projects. Though he rattles the sabres of male superiority
with near-sadistic ferocity, there is nothing heroic, or even
straightforward, in the manner in which he is issuing his challenge. If the situation he reveals is real rather than the progeny of a paranoid imagination—a wife imprisoned in the house
of a cruel keeper-husband whose plight has been discovered
by a sympathetic romantic hero—such a challenge is more likely
to lead to her rescue than to craven cowardice on the part of
the romantic "cousin"; if it is all a fantasy instead of a fact, it
accomplishes the poet's purpose—obliquely to reveal the innermost secret reality of each of his speakers—even more poig-
nantly. While the reader is not justified in spinning too elaborate a fiction around Half-Rome or any of the other characters, the fact that Half-Rome identifies his situation so fully with
that of Guido and selects the elements in his case-making so
carefully from his point of view and so suggestively from ours

rather compels the imaginative reader to construct as much as possible of what he is *not* told from the few hints he is given.

In addition to his imperviousness and incompetence as a human strategist, the dominant characteristics of Half-Rome as revealed in his monolgue are a male sexism that is both physically cruel and deep-rooted in an abstract distrust of the whole female sex and an anticlericalism that is ultimately disdainful of Christianity itself and finds its models among the primitive pagan gods. These, together with his personal myth, are the chief bases of his strong sense of identity with Guido, but the fact that he is so contemptuous of modern Roman civilization and so knowledgeable about Arezzo hints that he may even be a fellow-Aretine.

Guido can do no wrong, and Pompilia can do no right. These are the firm, broad strokes of Half-Rome's argument, the fundamental premises that rule every detail of his case as he intends it. That case has a certain primitive, animalistic ingenuity, but little subtlety, and the poet does not subject it to the many opportunities for dramatic irony that it provides. The character of the speaker is simply not worthy of the intricate levels of imaginative deflation that would be the result. The only gospel he has to impart is the gospel of his primitive self, and if he were not so totally and naively skeptical, he might see the happy accident of meeting this particular man in this particular place at this particular moment as an awesome example of the very providential collusion or predestination that he so grossly rejects.

The "great constringent relations between man and woman" express themselves in many and various ways—*quot homines, tot relationes*—but one of the most common and most devastating is male sexism. Half-Rome embodies a hardened and tyrannical form of it, so deep, unexamined, and lethal that it poisons every thought, feeling, belief, fantasy, and maneuver of his life. The Guido of Book XI is so paranoid about his maleness that he will go to any extreme to assert it, sees himself as virtually de-created by even a momentary misgiving concerning it, and can think of personal immortality only in terms of keeping it wholly intact.

Pompilia and Violante are only Half-Rome's ways of focusing his fear and hatred of all women. He speaks of honor *(Honoris causa)*, but what he is really advocating is the innate right of the male to use every strategy imaginable in a deadly warfare between "good" men and "bad" women. It is the nature of women to "play off the sex's trick" (II, 75) against the honor of man and, like Eve, to "lure" him "to his fault and fall" (II, 168–169) or, like Helen of Troy, to make of him a strutting cockerel and to lay waste all his genuine faith in and efforts toward civilization (II, 998–1009). So violent is Half-Rome in his convictions that he sees as a mark of high gallantry Guido's so disfiguring and fraying of Violante's face with a Genoese dagger that her eyes can no longer be identified with certainty. Pompilia, the "child-cheat," should have been plucked from the breasts of Violante, the "mock-mother," and crushed like a snake while Violante was simultaneously throttled (II, 61, 231–247). Womankind is a "beast-fellowship" (II, 569) compounded of trickery, connivance, seduction, and meretriciousness designed to keep men enslaved.

Half-Rome's inflation of the grand moral effects that would accrue from a judgment in Guido's favor, prophetic of Guido's own peroration in Book V—

> The better for you and me and all the world,
> Husbands of wives, especially in Rome.
> The thing is put right, in the old place,—ay,
> The rod hangs on its nail behind the door,
> Fresh from the brine. . .
>
> (II, 1538–1542)

—must strike most readers as absurd, and absurd it in truth is. But it is not an absurd view for Half-Rome to hold; it is the logical outgrowth of his virulent sexism. He is a fixated ideologue, his whole world view controlled by this one monolithic idea. It is the ghastly idea of a ghastly representative of humanity. It converts the one relationship upon which the two basic laws of man's nature depend—survival and regeneration—into a concentrated struggle of serpents and wild beasts. Mere lust becomes the only source of attraction; the rest of life is spent in hateful, suspicious efforts to outmaneuver an adversary. At the heart of Half-Rome's argument is a profoundly ironic contradiction. Though he asserts the superiority of the male, he must in truth hold the female to be superior. Otherwise, his anxiety would not be so intense, his condemnation so generalized and exaggerated, and his need for the law to shore up his side so acute. All the gentler emotions—faith, hope, love, humility—are thus wrung out of him, and he is left only with the role of the tormented tormentor.

Half-Rome's anticlericalism, his disguised contempt for Christianity's mode of explaining phenomena, and his recurrence to pagan points of reference are consistent with his sexist attitudes. He has created a myth of the female and a myth of the male, both of which are significant overlays of historical reality but neither of which approximates a poetic (that is, an imaginative, ideal) reality. Hence, his mode of argument becomes an aggression of ingenious case-making. Of course, to the degree that his myths are discordant with reality, both historical and poetic, they de-create the very objects they were meant to vivify. Hence, his Guido and Pompilia are fantasy-figures, the progeny of a sick imagination, rationalized intensely by the speaker as a bulwark against despair over his own affairs. Guido is the long-suffering, Job-like martyr-saint with whom he wholly identifies himself; Pompilia, extended and reinforced by Violante, is the seductive, treacherous, calculating, fatal "wretch," her soul "putrid" and her body writhing "viper-like" "through every ring" of her even after multiple stabbings (II, 1444–1448). Priests are the greedy, wanton allies of these women-things, casting a fairy-tale aura over the facts, treating men like imbeciles, hiding realities behind some fabrication they call God. They collude with "law" to create a eunuch-like civilization in complete contradiction to "natural law" and erase the good "old way trod when men were men!" (II, 1524).

The single incident in the overall drama by which the values of the various speakers are measured and exposed is that at the inn at Castelnuovo, where Guido overtakes Pompilia and Caponsacchi just before they begin the last short leg of their journey to Rome. Each of the three principals sees himself or herself as reaching there a crucial revelation about life and his or her capacity to cope with or even transcend its terrifying reality, and each speaker's way of perceiving and appraising this incident is a strategy the poet uses to enable the reader to get a more or less precise insight into the true character of each. It is the only incident in the poem in which Guido, Caponsacchi, and Pompilia are brought face to face in full view of the world and measured in specific relationship to each other.

Half-Rome is even more adamant than Guido in yielding no quarter to Caponsacchi and Pompilia, though he unwittingly reveals the grounds for taking a view quite contrary to his own. Half-Rome is so gratified that the runaways did not escape capture at the last moment that he is quite voluble in his use of innuendo, blanket charges, and sarcasm. He conveniently ignores the fact that Guido had chosen this moment to make his entry in the hope of discovering Pompilia and Caponsacchi *in flagrante delicto*, though he insinuates that, had he been earlier, he would have found them so—"One couch in one room, and one room for both" (II, 981). Rhetorically, he sets up the expectation that the fugitives will fall on their knees, confess their sin, and plead for a quick and easy death (the fulfillment of his own fantasy) in order to make their very different response seem heinous rather than heroic, and he compares them to such defiant, self-indulgent, bandbox lovers as Helen of Troy and Paris. Caponsacchi is "the bold abashless one" (II, 1011) whose defense, which is quite clear and cogent (II, 1012–1019), Half-Rome uses to excuse Guido, who is the opposite to bold and abashless, for calling in the Public Force "in aid and witness both" (II, 1021–1022). Pompilia, too, "sprang upright/I' the midst and stood as terrible as truth" (II, 1029–1030), but Half-Rome chooses to interpret her magnificent heroism—a besieged, child-mother making a last stand for the honor of truth against terrifying odds—as only the frothy street-invective of a guilty fishwife. Against the popular sympathy that sets toward Pompilia and Caponsacchi as a result of this dramatic triangulation, he opposes the essentially colorless "facts" that Caponsacchi is a priest in a cavalier's clothing, she a "truant" wife, and Guido a mortified husband. Though his own description of Guido shows him to be a craven coward—"trooping after, piteously,/Tail between legs" (II, 1061–1062)—and his would-be discovery of the alleged love letters a transparent deceit—"ferreting" while "their backs were turned" (II, 1068–1070)—Half-Rome insists on being blind even to his own language and on portraying Guido self-reflectively as a long-suffering saint at the climax of a tragic drama.

Stripped of its diplomacy and comic pretense of fair play, Half-Rome's portrait of himself and of human life as viewed from inside his psyche is ugly enough. But though it is shrouded in essentially transparent diplomacy and pretense and perhaps somewhat exaggerated for imaginative effect, it is not unrepresentative, and even the exaggeration is extenuated by the strong peculiarities of temperament and situation. Thus it is fair to conclude that his is a point of view on one of the central issues of life in this world that has a very large constituency in his culture and, metaphorically, in all cultures. Even if this is not the self he might exhibit under the most favorable, ego-soothing circumstances, it is the self that surfaces under even oblique provocation, and it is under such circumstances that the truth is customarily tested. It would require a complex change of scenario to make him in any literal sense an equivalent to Guido, but not a change in attitude toward the central issue of the relations of the sexes. He is a half-civilized wolf who remains restive under the softening, ameliorating, humanizing influence of civilization (religion, law, equality) and longs to reinvoke the law of the human jungle in the most imperious and yet delicate of all human relationships.

In Book I, the poet-speaker describes Half-Rome as "Honest enough, as the way is," his honesty being neutralized and his "feel for truth" faulted by a "hidden germ of failure" (I, 848–852). Attentively considered, it is a very sobering observation. It implies that Half-Rome's ghastly view is really not so extraordinary "as the way is," but that, stripped of its peculiarities of language, temperament, and plot, it is a fairly representative mirroring, imaginatively, of the way things are, and though the speaker is not an "honest" man in any deep personal sense, much of what he believes and says is an honest if frightening reflection of what his culture has taught him to say. To the degree that the reader concurs with that judgment, he will not waste his moral energy scoffing at the dogged, outrageous impercipience of Half-Rome, but will rather examine himself in an effort to discover how his own monistic, adamant, perhaps subliminal fixations cripple his own "feel for truth" and make him dishonest where he would not be so, even if his culture, on the whole, still allows it.

To move from Half-Rome's monologue to Other Half-Rome's is to move from one view of guilt and innocence in the case to an opposite view, but more importantly, it is to move to a quite different way of apprehending life, of "supposing and stating" the so-called truth. This is a far subtler point than at first appears, and it shows how ultimately literary, how basically and essentially poetic, the imaginative process controlling the development of *The Ring and the Book* really is.

Whether or not Half-Rome's hard-line male sexism represents a majority view in the culture mirrored in the poem, that of late-seventeenth-century Rome, it is impossible to say with finality. It is repeatedly asserted that Rome favors Guido; the personified enemy the Pope creates to do battle with favors him; statistically among the speakers the bias tilts his way; and the men of Arezzo support him overwhelmingly. However, the majority of Browning's readers since 1868–1869 certainly would not consciously and forthrightly adopt Half-Rome's tough sexist stand. In fact, most of them would probably tend to literalize it and wave it away as absurd, thus freeing themselves of the personal discomfort of recognizing and dealing with its pervasive, hidden, deadly presence in their own lives and culture. Browning obviously knew this, but he knew, too, that his poem must not be sacrificed to a head-on collision with sexist points of view. Art, like the Church, makes haste slowly, depending for its affect, not on argument, but on "the force of reserve, and the emphasis of understatement."[13]

Instead of argument, Browning used a form of imaginative evasion to trap the sentimental reader in a comfortable, self-massaging deception—the reader, for example, who thinks emotionally, succumbs to rhetoric, and protects himself from life's harshest truth through an escape into stereotyped fairy-tale formulae. He apparently trapped most of the commentators.

Other Half-Rome does not tell the truth; he writes a novel. His "feel/For truth" is even less authentic than Half-Rome's, and if he is successful, it is the result of accident rather than inner merit (I, 883–885). As Half-Rome looks forward to Guido, Other Half-Rome looks forward, not to the Pope, as is often said, but to Bottini. His vaunted sensitivity turns out to be little more than self-protective touchiness, and the result is a cultivated evasion of the "other half" of the truth.

Other Half-Rome, like Half-Rome and Tertium Quid, speaks a "sample-speech" (I, 865, 896, 941), and he provides a suitable point through which to examine the full implications of the poet-speaker's use of that metaphor. Most explicitly, of course, it means that they represent large constituent points of view—pro-Guido, pro-Pompilia, and (as Tertium Quid would have it) critically disengaged. In addition, they occupy different points on a time metaphor, with Half-Rome closest to the actual event ("This threefold murder of the day before," I, 846), like a near-eyewitness guessing at what he does not actually see; Other Half-Rome a further "day" removed, the event having lost its initial chill; and Tertium Quid in the evening of yet another day, the matter no longer being newsworthy in that all its "novelty" is played out. There is a suggestion of timelessness in this carefully designated time scheme, the days representing eras and the speakers embodying such different narrative modes as the rough-and-ready reporter, the romantic collector of yesteryear, and the detached, analytical historian of the distant past. Other Half-Rome, for example, is wrapped in a cluster of characterizing images: his is a "fancy-fit"; he chooses his side quite arbitrarily and under pressure, as he might choose "pink" instead of "drab" in a tournament of eggs; his is a "fountain-sport," like "Bernini's creature plated to the paps," who "Puffs up steel sleet which breaks to diamond dust,/A spray of sparkles snorted from his conch"; he is "High over the caritellas, out o' the way/O' the motley merchandizing multitude . . ." (I, 887–903 passim). The most finely turned irony runs through this cluster of images, suggesting ever so subtly that Other Half-Rome is not, like Half-Rome, "honest enough," but dishonest in the most elegant fashion.

That Other Half-Rome is impressive, most readers will acknowledge. He is tender, sympathetic, ingratiating, and he embroiders his incidents, his characters, and his characters' speeches with fascinating detail. But when one tries to find the right voice in which to read his monologue aloud, as all of the monologues require, every male voice strikes a wrong note except one of controlled ironic melodrama, and this voice not only undercuts his sense of exaggerated emotional engagement; it also begins to prepare us for the horrifying dramaturgical display of Bottini. The irony is not the speaker's, of course, but the poet's, and he uses it to puncture subtly the most impressive of all poses—that of sincerity.

> Another day that finds her living yet,
> Little Pompilia, with the patient brow
> And lamentable smile on those poor lips,
> And, under the white hospital-array,
> A flower-like body, to frighten at a bruise
> You'd think, yet now, stabbed through and through again,
> Alive i' the ruins. 'T is a miracle.
> It seems that, when her husband struck her first,
> She prayed Madonna just that she might live
> So long as to confess and be absolved;
> And whether it was that, all her sad life long,
> Never before successful in a prayer,
> This prayer rose with authority too dread,—
> Or whether, because earth was hell to her,
> By compensation, when the blackness broke
> She got one glimpse of quiet and the cool blue,
> To show her for a moment such things were,—
> Or else,—as the Augustinian Brother thinks,
> The friar who took confession from her lip,—
> When a probationary soul that moves
> From nobleness to nobleness, as she,
> Over the rough way of the world, succumbs,
> Bloodies its last thorn with unflinching foot,
> The angels love to do their work betimes,

Staunch some wounds here nor leave so much for God.
Who knows?

                                                                (III, 1–26)

It is not the action but how he feels about the action that
assumes primary importance in Other Half-Rome's monologue; even judgment is secondary to the sentimental, rhetorical orchestration of judgment, *what he says* being subordinated
to *how he says it*. He has not effaced himself like the poet-speaker
in the final creative phase of Book I, has not "disappeared";
he has exploited a chillingly tragic occasion to display self-consciously the delicacy of his sentiments and the range of his
rhetoric. Other Half-Rome's is the most self-consciously "poetic" of the monologues in *The Ring and the Book* and invites
evaluation in such severely critical terms as classical versus romantic, mimetic versus expressive. By "romanticizing" the truth,
he is de-creating it and substituting something else in its place,
the word for the fact, himself for his subject.

Since *The Ring and the Book* is, in a comprehensive sense, a
course in critical-creative reading—in how the poet takes history and transforms it into a language-art that aspires in varying degrees to the redemption of the past, reconciliation with
the present, and hope for the future—it is not surprising that
its creator was throughout keenly attuned to the subtlest nuances, capacities, and abuses of language. "The style is the man"
is an integrated assumption, not a platitude of *The Ring and the
Book*. All the speakers have a reasonable level of education and
have trafficked with the world; therefore, they share, to a large
degree, the standard language and style of their time and culture. In addition, their situations are more or less standard-
ized: each speaks an apologia of sorts, of a common subject
matter and of himself. They have, too, one common creator,
the poet of the piece, who, though he has "disappeared" from
sight, is still under the poem's splendor and wonder and must
be "instressed/stressed."[14] So 95 percent of their "style," so to
speak, is common style, and it is only within a very narrow gauge
that their rhetorical individuality can be expected to manifest
itself. Such distinguishing elements as tone of voice, motive,
point of view, sense of self, quality of thought and argument,

respect for truth and the use of evidence, imagery and other kinds of analogy, literary experience, professional alignment, literary ambition and judgment—these can, in general, be identified in the various monologues.

What is at first surprising is that Browning used so delicate and demanding a lesson in critical-creative reading so early in the poem. And yet, since it is difficult to think of any alternative available to him, the reader is best served perhaps by simply accepting three premises: that *The Ring and the Book* is one of the toughest poems in English—one of the most ambitious, integrally complex, operating simultaneously at multiple levels, offering fewer compromises and concessions; that, in making such demands on the reader, the author believed that the poem held commensurate rewards; and that a routine, literal-minded, obvious reading of the poem will produce results, however interesting the reader may find them, considerably below the results that are actually there and perhaps even different in kind from those the poet intended and hoped for.

It is important that the reader give Other Half-Rome the credits he deserves; that is an essential part of the poet's equation. First, he does come down on the right side. He sees Pompilia's more obvious virtues and Guido's more obvious vices with clarity and, in general, he renders them succinctly, cogently, and gracefully, though occasionally, in a fury of creativity, he seriously miscasts Pompilia. So even if he is successful by accident, he deserves the credit of success. Secondly, his narrative technique, his rhetoric of telling, is very often impressive. The myth of Violante and Pietro singing their duet in paradise (III, 115–228) is very well done rhetorically. The imaginary portrait of Paolo making his elegantly dishonest presentation to Violante (III, 264–376) is a small masterpiece having not even a distant parallel elsewhere in the poem; it gives us our most complete picture of the sleek, aristocratic, imperturbable, eminently plausible Roman diplomat and would-be Cardinal of the time. The sketch of Pietro the self-satisfied *petit bourgeois* and his gossip critics (III, 388–434) is very fine—economical, vivid, amusing, and shrewd:

'Oh, make your girl a lady, an you list,
But have more mercy on our wit than vaunt

Your bargain as we burgesses who brag!
Why, Goodman Dullard, if a friend must speak,
Would the Count, think you, stoop to you and yours
Were there the value of one penny-piece
To rattle 'twixt his palms—or likelier laugh,
Bid your Pompilia help you black his shoe?'

Home again, shaking oft the puzzled pate,
Went Pietro to announce a change indeed,
Yet point Violante where some solace lay
Of a rueful sort,—the taper, quenched so soon,
Had ended merely in a snuff, not stink—
Congratulate there was one hope the less
Not misery the more: and so an end.

(III, 420–434)

The cunning maneuvers of Violante in seeming to be repentant while slyly achieving her goal and putting the matter beyond recall are presented, though briefly, with perfectly scaled
dramatic power (III, 438–460), and the pathos of Pompilia's
situation as innocent victim is presented without excessive sentimentality in the extended simile of the lamb that is at once
petted, bartered, and destined for the knife:

Who all the while had borne, from first to last,
As brisk a part i' the bargain, as yon lamb,
Brought forth from basket and set out for sale,
Bears while they chaffer, wary market-man
And voluble housewife, o'er it,—each in turn
Patting the curly calm inconscious head,
With the shambles ready round the corner there,
When the talk's talked out and a bargain struck.

(III, 461–468)

The sequence on Violante's quickness "at the bye-road and the
cut-across" in taking advantage of the special provisoes of the
Holy Year to cleanse her soul while confounding her enemies,
concocted almost wholly out of the speaker's imagination, looks
many ways at once in its terse, sobering, ironically amusing
revelations of the cloak of institutional high-mindedness that

calculated duplicity often wears (III, 540–612), as is Pietro's aria of salvation at the prospect of getting his money back (III, 622–645), which is also spun entirely from the speaker's imagination. The representation of Guido's two levels of thought—the public level as dialogue, the private level as interior monologue—is well managed (III, 689–737), and so is the episode of the forged letter and the use Paolo makes of it in his machinations on Guido's behalf in Rome (III, 738–771). Though highly romanticized, the account of Pompilia's escape from the prison of Guido's palace and her and Caponsacchi's rendezvous and whirlaway toward liberty is verbally taut, emotionally intense, visually clear, and altogether captivating (III, 1064–1090).

Of course, not all of Other Half-Rome's monologue is pure gold dust from the realms of gold. He uses a number of far-fetched and inflated figures of speech that draw attention to themselves rather than to the subjects they are meant to illuminate, but more importantly, he repeatedly casts Pompilia in the poses of a queen of melodrama that are quite false to her authentic character, even as he himself generally delineates it: " 'I submit myself!' " (III, 1170) and " 'do with me what you will!' " (III, 1348), he has her saying, complete with end-stop exclamation marks. One of the passages that ends so is particularly revealing. It is an extended passage (III, 1121–1170), but the speaker tries to compress into its fifty lines Pompilia's account of her decision to flee, the flight itself, and the incident at Castelnuovo where she sprang from her bed, seized Guido's sword, and attempted to slay him on the spot. Pompilia, who is detailed and exact rather than prolix, takes more than 300 lines to cover this same material in her monologue, and it should be remembered that Other Half-Rome himself has devoted 113 lines to the fascinating but nonessential delineation of Paolo's suave seduction of Violante. Moreover, the speaker, who has shown himself to be subtle and shrewd in interpreting other aspects of the tale, seems uncomfortable and clumsy in this sequence. He omits entirely Pompilia's pregnancy epiphany as a motive for flight and compares her to a martin in the late autumn seeking sanctuary in the warm south from the "white teeth" of winter, though the flight takes place in April. He puts questionable imagery into her mouth—" 'the weak flesh fell like piled-up cards,/All the frail fabric at a finger's touch' " (III, 1142–1143)—and ignores her concern lest, by pushing farther on the journey, she injure the unborn child and thus destroy the very motive of the flight. The motive he assigns for the sudden violence with which she rebels at Castelnuovo is ambiguously romantic, lacking entirely the metaphysically based heroism with which she says she was driven— to "lay low/The neutraliser of all good and truth," on a "clear . . . impulse to serve God/Not save myself,—no—nor my child unborn!" (VII, 1595–1596, 1600–1601). And though Pompilia in that context calls Guido "the old adversary" and "the fiend" (VII, 1618, 1621), she never resorts, as Other Half-Rome makes her do, to images like a " 'scorpion' " that she would pin, " 'through [his] poison-bag,' " palpitating " 'to the wall.' " That is his myth, not hers.

Such uncharacteristic clumsiness on Other Half-Rome's part suggests, too, why in another longer passage he seems befuddled and evasive. This is the sequence (III, 788–1063) beginning

> Now begins
> The tenebrific passage of the tale:
> How hold a light, display the cavern's gorge?
> How, in this phase of the affair, show truth?

and the subject is the exact nature of the Pompilia-Caponsacchi relationship. The speaker seems throughout the passage reluctant to allow either Pompilia or Caponsacchi to be completely honest. He backs and fills, complicates and equivocates, ultimately leaving the question as moot as answering it with another question would leave it. His problem seems to be more particularly with Caponsacchi, to whom he gives the benefit of the doubt and then casts doubt upon the benefit. In this context, he also seems rather inclined to undercut Don Celestine's reputation, whose cues he has otherwise taken, calling him "that poor old bit of battered brass/Beaten out of all shape by the world's sins,/Common utensil of the lazar-house—" (III, 796– 798). On no other issue does he so hedge his bet: "Anyhow/Here be facts, charactery; what they spell/Determine, and thence pick what sense you may!" (III, 836–838).

Only one explanation seems adequate to the character and dimensions of this curious aspect of Other Half-Rome, and in it, I suggest, we have the reason for the failure even of his success. He is numb to "the great constringent relation between man and woman" as one of the indispensable realities of human life. He is intense in his apprehension of Pompilia as a saint, a martyr, a miracle, and a mystery, but he cannot encompass her as a woman. He can enshrine her in a saint's legend, but he cannot accept her as a whole human being. As a result, he makes her the center of a myth and, to a significant degree, de-creates her, as Angel Clare will do with Tess in Hardy's novel on "the great constringent relation between man and woman," *Tess of the d'Urbervilles.* This is what gives constructive metaphoric content to the poet's representation of Other Half-Rome as a bachelor; it suggests, too, why even Half-Rome's monstrous magnification of the male sexist point of view may be considered more "honest" than this ingratiatingly deceptive, essentially inhuman fairy tale. Early in his monologue, Other Half-Rome seems to contemplate one of the great moral mysteries of human experience:

> Though really it does seem as if she here,
> Pompilia, living so and dying thus,
> Has had undue experience how much crime
> A heart can hatch. Why was she made to learn
> —Not you, not I, not even Molinos' self—
> What Guido Franceschini's heart could hold?
> Thus saintship is effected probably;
> No sparing saints the process!—which the more
> Tends to the reconciling us, no saints,
> To sinnership, immunity and all.
>
> (III, 105–114)

But when one considers the severely limited perspective he has on human life, his myth depriving Pompilia of one of the two greatest passions known to mankind, the mystery loses almost all its force. Undoubtedly submitting to Guido sexually was one

of the intensest, most self-destroying agonies Pompilia had to
bear in the phantasmagoria of her marriage to a crippled, ugly,
bestial ogre but it was the fiendish hate, not the sexuality, that
she abhorred. Nowhere does she evince the disgust with human sexuality that seems to be a controlling if hidden premise
of Other Half-Rome. She declares that there was nothing erotic
in her relationship with Caponsacchi, but she does not cringe
before the idea or equivocate it in any way. That is simply not
the way it was, he being he and she being she, but in her
thoughts of paradise, after all their earthbound obligations have
been met, the idea that he and she may "Know themselves into
one" (VII, 1834) is the climactic point in her vision of transcendent fulfillment. It is only from counterfeit lovemaking in
a counterfeit marriage that Pompilia's quite human soul shrinks,
and Other Half-Rome's implicit rejection of the enormous relevance for good and ill of human sexuality to the subject before him largely disqualifies him as a useful guide to that subject. In this particular respect, his point of view looks forward
to the Pope's naiveté.

Some of the ways in which Other Half-Rome ignores or
sidesteps this subject are indicative. His nervous discomfort on
the one subject on which the plot will not let him be silent—
the Pompilia-Caponsacchi relationship—is one. He also de-
taches himself from the realistic facts of Pompilia's conception
and birth by making them a part of Violante's interior monologue in moralistic self-exculpation. He compresses the three-
year mental and physical subjection of Pompilia to the brutal-
ities of Guido into an eleven-line analogy of a ferret in a chicken
coop:

> Accordingly did Guido set himself
> To worry up and down, across, around,
> The woman, hemmed in by her household-bars,—
> Chased her about the coop of daily life,
> Having first stopped each outlet thence save one
> Which, like bird with a ferret in her haunt,
> She needs must seize as sole way of escape
> Though there was tied and twittering a decoy
> To seem as if it tempted,—just the plume

O' the popinjay, and not a respite there
From tooth and claw of something in the dark. . . .
                                              (III, 776–786)

The pregnancy epiphany, which reverses Pompilia's suicidal
despair and gives her an individual affirmative role to play as
a blessed life-force who takes charge of circumstances, is diminished to the tender but comparatively trivial instinct to nest,
as if she had literalized the incident of the "blessed building-
sparrow" (VII, 1223–1259):

> So when the she-dove breeds, strange yearnings come
> For the unknown shelter by undreamed-of shores,
> And there is born a blood-pulse in her heart
> To fight if needs be, though with flap of wing,
> For the wool-flock or the fur-tuft, though a hawk
> Contest the prize,—wherefore, she knows not yet.
>   (III, 1533–1538)

Finally, two passages, the one from early in the monologue,
the other its final turning, reveal the disproportions of judgment to which Other Half-Rome's blindness, whether willful
or unconscious, leads him.

The early passage is the first part of the rhetorically graceful myth of Violante and Pietro singing their duet in paradise:

> For see now: Pietro and Violante's life
> Till seventeen years ago, all Rome might note
> And quote for happy—see the signs distinct
> Of happiness as we yon Triton's trump.
> What could they be but happy?—balanced so,
> Nor low i' the social scale nor yet too high,
> Nor poor nor richer than comports with ease,
> Nor bright and envied, nor obscure and scorned,
> Nor so young that their pleasures fell too thick,
> Nor old past catching pleasure when it fell,
> Nothing above, below the just degree,
> All at the mean where joy's components mix.
> So again, in the couple's very souls

You saw the adequate half with half to match,
Each having and each lacking somewhat, both
Making a whole that had all and lacked nought;
The round and sound, in whose composure just
The acquiescent and recipient side
Was Pietro's, and the stirring striving one
Violante's: both in union gave the due
Quietude, enterprise, craving and content,
Which go to bodily health and peace of mind.
But, as 't is said a body, rightly mixed,
Each element in equipoise, would last
Too long and live for ever. . . .

(III, 115–139)

This passage contains Other Half-Rome's vision of prelapsarian perfection, his idea of Eden before the fall, of eternity spared the "fatal germ." It is the bourgeois ideal, both Victorian and universal, of domestic bliss, and it is, especially in moments of personal or national distress and moral fatigue, broadly attractive. It fulfills the longing for a past that never was and a future that will never be; it is behind the failure of memory that lets old age say "to be young were very heaven" and the failure of prescience that allows youth to dream only of "bluebirds over the white cliffs of Dover"—of "love and laughter and peace ever after." And though it is not true, it explains many bourgeois values, sacrifices, and taboos, including the domestic sterilization of the classical ideal of the golden mean and the domestic sanctification through silence of human sexuality. Other Half-Rome positively idealizes such falsehood.

The final passage reworks the issue in quite a different way, and the poet structures it so as both to suggest and to disguise its import:

One's honour forsooth? Does that take hurt alone
From the extreme outrage? I who have no wife,
Being yet sensitive in my degree
As Guido,—must discover hurt elsewhere
Which, half compounded-for in days gone by,
May profitably break out now afresh,

Need cure from my own expeditious hands.
The lie that was, as it were, imputed me
When you objected to my contract's clause,—
The theft as good as, one may say, alleged,
When you, co-heir in a will, excepted, Sir,
To my administration of effects,
—Aha, do you think law disposed of these?
My honour's touched and shall deal death around!
Count, that were too commodious, I repeat!
If any law be imperative on us all,
Of all are you the enemy: out with you
From the common light and air and life of man!

(III, 1677–1694)

The disguise is in the last three lines, where the speaker trumpets our popular judgment of the scoundrel Guido in clarion tones and assures us once again that his judgment of the case is "sound." In the preceding lines, however, the speaker draws an extended analogy that suddenly casts doubt on his disinterest as a judge in the matter. It has never been made clear as to just whom he is addressing in his monologue and that it is not in fact a soliloquy. The syntax of the final verse paragraph seems to equate the "Sir" of line 1687 with Guido himself, and the last three lines are clearly addressed to Guido. If he is in fact apostrophizing Guido, then his monologue becomes a cunning but petty act of revenge over a slight that he has never had the nerve to confront his "enemy" with before, and all of the poetic purring that has preceded it has been an elaborate exercise in insincerity. But even if that is not the point of the poet's sleight of hand, the analogy itself is ridiculous. For a presumably sophisticated man of the world, sensitive, epigrammatic, astute, poetic, knowing, to compare seriously an admittedly inferred slight to his honesty in a civil matter—a slight that may or may not have been intended—with a multipronged, calculated, widely advertised onslaught on a nobleman's name, fame, peace, and worldly happiness—which is the way Guido presents the offense to his "honour"—demonstrates at the very least that he has no understanding of "the great constringent relation between man and woman." In the face of that, even the highly speculative issues of self-interest and petty revenge shrink into matters of little importance.

That Other Half-Rome has severe limitations as a critical participant in life is not a moral judgment on him, of course; he suffers from one of the largest, most representative wounds of humanity, a refusal to acknowledge the robustness of reality and a self-deceiving inclination to wink it away, and it is up to the individual reader to extend him the honed empathy of critical-creative understanding. On the other hand, the fact that he arrives at what most readers would accept as the right judgment of the shocking case before him is a relatively minor consideration in light of the human reality he sacrifices to it. His maneuvers are subtle, but their results are devastating. As in the case of Half-Rome, one may wish to consider his failure in human capacity as specialized and thereby resist identification with him. That, in its turn, would be a fault very much like his fault. The poet is suggesting not only that, well considered, the particular fault suffered by Other Half-Rome has a center in a far larger and more representative number of persons than is generally recognized and admitted; he is also suggesting that it has a degree of uncentered presence in us all.

It should be clear, then, that the poet-speaker is not exaggerating when he declares that "our human speech is naught,/Our human testimony false, our fame/And human estimation words and wind" (XII, 834–836). Nothing in *The Ring and the Book* can be taken to say what it literally appears to say, to mean what it literally appears to mean. Everything is in a perpetual process of transformation, altering light, changing perspective. Even honesty is being eroded by a "germ of failure" obscure but relentlessly working, and dishonesty of even the shrewdest sort, fail-safe dishonesty, crumbles even as it is being put into place. To be perfectly true (or perfectly good or perfectly beautiful) is as much of a delusion and a dream as to be perfectly false. Such phrases are just a few of our ragged uses of language, and to believe them about ourselves or to expect them in others simply adulterates such possibilities of goodness, beauty, and truth as the world does offer. We may love them as ideals, but we cannot hope to know them as realities on this earth. Truth for its own sake, truth as a beautiful idea, is available to us in some sense and degree, but we have to work at it, pay the highest price for it, and be content with such slight portion of it as we receive, not supposing that our portion is the whole vision or that it is necessarily better—that is, truer— than another's. Mostly, we see what we like to see or what we are in the habit of seeing, and therefore we need to work more on our habits of seeing than on the objects seen. That is the object of the poem, its dynamic way of providing us with a "noble exercise of our imagination."[15]

The manifest markings of Tertium Quid's monologue are a cynical self-conceit, a manner of address so punctilious and self-conscious as to have a vulgar edge, a contempt for "the mob" so encompassing and emotionally violent that not even its wit can save it from our antagonism, and a network of illustrative images that is curiously discordant with the self-image the speaker is at such pains to project. Such characterizations of Tertium Quid, being interpretive, go far beyond what the poet-speaker in Book I tells us, but they are consistent with his characterization. In setting up this "elaborated product," this *"third something"* (I, 915–942), the speaker's irony becomes far more cutting than it has been before. Tertium Quid's is distinctly the Roman view, the "finer sense o' the city," urban, sophisticated, rational, authoritative:

> Here, after ignorance, instruction speaks;
> Here, clarity of candour, history's soul,
> The critical mind, in short; no gossip-guess.
> What the superior social section thinks. . . .

This is the voice of the "new tribunal" of the "educated man" to whom the Pope will give the back of his hand—the voice of "Civilization and the Emperor" at the apex (X, 1975–1976, 2028), the "spirit of culture['s]" voice (X, 2016).

Thus we have two problems fused—a representative point of view ("a sample-speech") so ironically rough-handled by the poet-speaker in Book I and a character who is given the role of spokesman for that point of view; and since "One and one breed the inevitable three" (I, 914), there is the additional problem of determining if there is an organic rather than a perfunctory connection between the two and how deep the connection runs. It is a delicate critical challenge, certainly, but perhaps not an impossible one.

Audience plays a much more pervasive role in Tertium Quid's monologue than in the two previous ones, as the poet-speaker in Book I, by drawing unusual attention to the audience's presence, promises:

> Eminence This and All-Illustrious That
> Who take snuff softly, range in well-bred ring,
> Card-table-quitters for observance' sake,
> Around the argument, the rational word—
>   (I, 937–940)

The heavy irony has been purged from these lines. They are presented elegantly but sympathetically, and since the speaker loses his audience in the end, we can conclude that, in the main, he does not speak for them. Moreover, since they are bona fide members of the uppermost class even as witnessed by Tertium Quid's elaborate efforts to advance himself with them, their alienation after repeated indications of dissent suggests that his view is in important respects different from their view. Therefore, Tertium Quid's assumptions and arguments are presumably idiosyncratic rather than representative or are representative of a narrower subclass than that of the class as a whole. The Pope will later concentrate his ire on a particularly personified "brisk junior," the "younger" representative who, "should the old authority be mute,/Or doubtful, or in speaking clash with new,/ . . . takes permission to decide" (X, 1995, 1988–1990), and this would encourage one to consider the possibility that Tertium Quid is a spokesman, not for "old authority," but for a new branch of the upper class, a counterpart to or equivalent of the *nouveau riche*, namely, a new intelligentsia.

This, I suggest, is the truth of the matter. Browning is not doing something so dubious as masking/unmasking the true aristocracy of civilization and culture. He has created an aristocrat *manqué* representative of a new breed, common in the Renaissance and after but identifiable in all ages, of culture-climbers—ambitious, haughty, insecure, intemperate, often virulent, sometimes parasitic—who are filling the vacuum left by an older, truer aristocracy that has either abandoned leadership in a new, rapidly changing, idea-crackling age or, from a paucity of numbers and a tendency to massage traditional values that have themselves fallen into disrepute, has lost the capacity to monitor adequately a burgeoning present and future. These new "brisk juniors" ape the rituals of the older, truer aristocrats, but there is an identifiable strain of vulgarity in their cynicism, self-conceit, punctiliousness of manner, and haughtiness toward the putative lower classes, including the "burgess-life" (IV, 65), from which they may themselves be sprung.

Tertium Quid, as was said at the beginning of this discussion, has these manifest markings. In addition, the storehouse of imagery upon which he draws to illustrate his points provides firmly rooted evidence of the likelihood that his origins were in the very "mob" toward which he shows such violent contempt. No one of these images, taken alone, would prove much, but cumulatively they mirror a mind deeply dyed with the experiences of a product of the lower orders of society. Even a cursory listing tells a critical subterranean story.

(1) "last bale to boat/Crammed to the edge with cargo—or passengers? (IV, 29–30)
(2) "barking for the wife:—bow—wow!" (IV, 48)
(3) "the wick shall moulder out some day,/Failing fresh twist of tow to use up dregs. . . ." (IV, 79–80)
(4) "As watchman's cresset, he pokes here and there,/Going his rounds to probe the ruts i' the road/Or fish the luck o' the puddle." (IV, 87–89)
(5) "How long now, would the roughest market-man,/Handling the creatures huddled to the knife,/Harass a mutton ere she made a mouth/Or menaced biting?" (IV, 127–130)
(6) "like a stone you kick up with your foot/I' the middle of a field/ . . ./ . . . made alive/By worm, and fly, and foot of the free bird?" (IV, 230–231, 236–237)

(7) Creeps out a serving-man on Saturdays
To cater for the week,—turns up anon
I' the market, chaffering for the lamb's least leg,
Or the quarter-fowl, less entrails, claws and comb:
Then back again with prize,—a liver begged
Into the bargain, gizzard overlooked,—
He's mincing these to give the beans a taste,
When, at your knock, he leaves the simmering
soup. . . .

(IV, 360–367)

(8) "Clung to the higher perch and crowed in hope" (IV, 399)

(9) "the grey mare,/The better horse,—how wise the people's word!" (IV, 472–473)

(10) As when a cook . . . will Excellency forgive?
Strips away those long loose superfluous legs
From either side the crayfish, leaving folk
A meal all meat henceforth, no garnishry. . . .

(IV, 542–545)

(11) "from inside your own house and home,/Gnats which yourself have closed the curtain round,/Noise goes too near the brain and makes you mad./The gnats. . . ." (IV, 560–563)

(12) " 'This thrust I have to parry by a guard/Which leaves me open to a counter-thrust/On the other side,—no way but there's a pass/Clean through me.' " (IV, 615–618, the putative words of Guido)

(13) "A pet lamb they have left in reach outside,/Whose first bleat, when he plucks the wool away,/Will strike the grinners grave. . . ." (IV, 665–667)

(14) "Out of the bower into the butchery" (677)

(15) "If haply they might wriggle themselves free./They baited their own hook to catch a fish/With this poor worm. . . . (IV, 707–709)

(16) 'T were hard to serve up a congenial dish
Out of these ill-agreeing morsels, Duke,
By the best exercise of the cook's craft,
Best interspersion of spice, salt and sweet!
But let two ghastly scullions concoct mess
With brimstone, pitch, vitriol, and devil's-dung—
Throw in abuse o' the man, his body and soul,
Kith, kin, and generation, shake all slab
At Rome, Arezzo, for the world to nose,

Then end by publishing, for fiend's arch-prank,
That, over and above sauce to the meat's self,
Why, even the meat, bedevilled thus in dish,
Was never a pheasant but a carrion-crow—
Prince, what will then the natural loathing be?
                                        (IV, 726–739)

(17) "While blotting out, as by a belch of hell . . ." (IV, 754)

(18) You do n't expect he'll catch up stone and fling,
Or try cross-buttock, or whirl quarter-staff?
Instead of the honest drubbing clowns bestow,
When out of temper at the dinner spoilt,
On meddling mother-in-law and tiresome wife. . . .
                                        (IV, 761–765)

(19) " 'may live like flies in honey-pot' " (IV, 784, the putative
words of the Comparini)

(20) "Do you fright your hare that you may catch your hare?"
(IV, 919)

(21) " 'whether goat or sheep/I' the main, has wool to show and
hair to hide' " (IV, 1222–1223, the putative words of the
Court)

(22) " 'to scream and scratch/And scour the fields' " (IV, 1227–
1228, *idem.*)

(23) Bull-like,—the indiscriminate slaughter, rude
And reckless aggravation of revenge,
Were all i' the way o' the brute who never once
Ceases, amid all provocation more,
To bear in mind the first tormentor, first
Giver o' the wound that goaded him to fight:
And, though a dozen follow and reinforce
The aggressor, wound in front and wound in flank,
Continues undisturbedly pursuit,
And only after prostrating his prize
Turns on the pettier, makes a general prey.
So Guido rushed against Violante, first
Author of all his wrongs, *fons et origo*
Malorum—increasingly drunk,—which justice done,
He finished with the rest. Do you blame a bull?
                                        (IV, 1565–1579)

The subterranean story implicit in this network of images, I
suggest, is the life experience of a child reared among the
harshest, seamiest forces of a situation dominated by violence

and want. There is a persistent, perhaps obsessive, pattern of food imagery, especially as it is associated with penury, the slaughterhouse, belching, vomiting, and domestic violence, as if the speaker—to borrow from his "bull-similitude"—remembers bodily hunger as his "first tormentor," "First/Author of all his wrongs, *fons et origo/Malorum*," the very thought of which makes him "increasingly drunk" (IV, 1569, 1576–1579). To the degree that one finds this persuasive, the more plausible if not more attractive one may find Tertium Quid's rage against the middle class with its petty physical comforts and faith in social machinery, his sympathy with Guido's struggles to improve his situation, including a lenient view of his use of craft and violence, and his ill-disguised hostility toward Pompilia, with whom he may share common origins. He has an unusually vivid familiarity with the sights and sounds of the brothel (IV, 148–191), and behind his critique of that stock-in-trade of the street corner, Punch and Judy, may perhaps be the vestiges of the street-wise youth (IV, 1282–1299), as may be, also, his intimate knowledge of the pimpish marriage broker who ostensibly deals in "perukes" (IV, 437–451).[16]

If much of the distasteful arrogance underpinning Tertium Quid's vulgarly punctilious manner can thus be explained as originating ultimately in his formative background and his flight from it, that aspect of his "sample-speech" cannot be taken as representative of the true aristocracy, but must be seen as a peculiarity of his individual character. What, then, of his arguments? Do they have a merit that is quite independent of our *ad hominem* reactions? His claim that they do—"The long and short is, truth is what I show" (IV, 1618)—demands separate examination.

Fortunately, the poet has safeguarded his reader from an endless series of quibbles on this issue by building a system of demurrers into the poem's own process. The monologue is punctuated with points of dramatic interaction between the speaker and his well-accredited audience. Though His Excellency and His Highness do not speak and the speaker is too cunning to confront them directly, it is clear which of his argumentative efforts misfire, and these must also be discounted as representative of the true aristocracy.

There are seven instances of this kind: (1) his attempt to launder Violante's guilt, thrice compounded, over pawning Pompilia off as her own natural child (IV, 211–317); (2) his attempt to erase the qualitative distinction between the Comparini's gross foolishness and Guido's gross knavery (IV, 505–635); his effort to reduce the conflicting claims respecting the authenticity/forgery of the love letters between Caponsacchi and Pompilia to simply a question of one party's word against the other (IV, 1011–1117); (4) his too-commodious attempt to pass swiftly over the issue of Guido's cowardice at the inn at Castelnuovo (IV, 1118–1212); (5) his effort to justify Guido's triple murder as the inevitable result of a final, intolerable outrage against him (IV, 1300–1391); (6) his attempt to construe Pompilia's deathbed testimony as evidence, not of her probity, but of her relentless effort to get revenge (IV, 1424–1520); and (7) his attempt to justify Guido's defiance of the very law he had invoked unsuccessfully and then taking the law into his own hands as the only choice society itself had left him (IV, 1521–1617).

It is a crucial list, certainly, but not a surprising one, and most readers will be gratified to find that it is their list exactly. Is it to be dismissed, then, as too obvious and the monologue's legitimacy as a "sample-speech" discredited? Not at all, unless one insists upon being incorrigibly literal-minded. Browning is not harpooning traditional blue-bloodedness any more than Matthew Arnold, in calling aristocrats "Barbarians" in *Culture and Anarchy,* was returning them to slingshots and arrowheads. The princes of the past had lost their hold upon the future and their default had created a vacuum of leadership which a new breed was rushing in to fill. Being immune to new ideas in an age of new ideas, the old aristocracy could hardly be the future's brokers. Both Browning and Arnold saw the new breed of "aliens" as essentially classless and far more numerous than was generally recognized. But in their works, Browning and Arnold invested these "aliens" with very different metaphoric contents, and in those different metaphors they lodged quite different expectations, not of their importance, but of their salutariness.[17]

Tertium Quid is a *soi-disant* aristocrat, self-styled "superior," "curious," "historical," "critical," "authoritative."[18] He is "something bred of both" Half-Romes, a hybrid offspring, not of the traditional aristocracy, but of the two faulted "halves" of the society as a whole. To use a metaphor out of animal husbandry with no indelicate intentions, he was sired by a hard-line male sexist out of a romantic feminine mythicist. In the evolutionary process, his genetic inheritance is transformed into a hermaphroditic impotence, not in the idealized, self-contained, delicately aesthetic classical sense, but in an aggressively valueless, self-imprisoned, disturbingly distasteful modern sense. Tertium Quid's "sample-speech" according to this reading of his monologue is one scenario of a world always in the making that puts natural law above such imperfect but civilizing influences as religion (e.g., Christianity) and the societal values that religion's institutions sustain in an admittedly disheartening, sometimes positively grotesque, fashion and prefers the fragile spinnings of its own wits to any altruistic promises—social or metaphysical, moral or religious—that might dim the flare of its own self. Imaginatively translated from its locus in historical time and in the particular fiction of the poem, the character of Tertium Quid embodies those self-manufactured, *soi-disant* uppercrust but essentially classless persons who are neither brutally forthright like Half-Rome nor fragile to a fatal fault like Other Half-Rome (the abrupt hard-liner and the bleeding deacon, so to speak). They see themselves as above life's fray and, having no center of their own, they draw a bit from here and a mite from there and thus fabricate a hybrid self that ultimately stands nowhere for nothing. Being neither naturalists nor mythicists but rationalistic fast-steppers whose agility derives from the fact that they bear no burden of belief in either God or man, they seem to be in the ascendancy especially in an age that

> hangs between; in doubt to act or rest;
> In doubt to deem [itself] a god or beast;
> In doubt [its] mind or body to prefer;
> Born but to die, and reasoning but to err.[19]

They may tread the world's drawing rooms and cater to the confidence of the great, but they are, in mirror-image, street people dependent for survival on the sharpness of their wits. Life is for them at best a gamble, and the airy structures they build frequently tumble like a house of cards. On the issue of sexuality and the relations between man and woman, they are little more than eunuch-like equivocators. Their humor tends toward superciliousness, centrifugal bitchiness, and camp, and they are likely to misjudge and lose the very audience they would most like to identify with.

The portrait is extreme enough to offer us the option of dismissing it, but it is not the worst case, as Books IX and XI will prove. Despite its specialization, objective, conscientious, imaginative readers will perhaps see enough particles of themselves refracted in it to be grateful for an insight, however faint and fleeting, that without it they might never have achieved.

At the beginning of this chapter, the issue of the organic relationship of Book I to the rest of the poem was raised. An effort was made there to show how the poet-speaker's remarks in I, 824–1347 point the reader's study of the characters and their handling of the fiction ("facts") of the poem toward the highest imaginative level—the level that, in idealist philosophies, might variously be called the *essence, reality,* or *idea.* It was also suggested that if the principle of organicism truly holds, then the balance of the poem should feed back in a constructive way into Book I.

On the basis of the analyses given in these pages of Book II, III, and IV, one can, I think, say that the organic principle does in fact hold true, and the test is very simple and empirical. It is only through a careful study of the successive monologues that the real significance of Book I begins to emerge. Critics have sometimes faulted Book I as an intrusion on the reader's independent experience of the poem's central "ring,"[20] or they have found one or another of the poet-speaker's explanations to be wrong.[21] Such criticisms evaporate in light of a different view of what the poet in Book I is really doing— namely, bringing critical conceptualization to the very point at which it transforms itself into an act of creation. According to this view, Book I assumes the character of a vision on the threshold of realization, of actually becoming. It is not really a question either of intrusion or of some misdirection of detail. The poet-speaker says that he now sees how to "do the thing shall breed the thought"—how to create an idea of character that contributes significantly to an idea of life—how, specifically, to reach beyond moral judgment in this case to the larger human reality in which moral judgment itself subsists. This does not preempt our role as ultimate judges, but it does subject it to the same principle of indirection to which the poet has subjected himself. Analytical criticism of the poet's idea of character in the context of life is not quite enough; we are asked to create a competing idea of our own and to measure its legitimacy and usefulness against the one he offers. That, after all, is the imaginative spirit of the poem, and ideally it should be the spirit of the criticism too.

Notes

1. Thomas Hardy, Preface to *The Dynasts.*
2. The comparison with Tennyson's characterization of *Idylls of the King* is irresistible—"accept this old imperfect tale,/New-old" ("To the Queen")—as is his use of the metaphor "voice": "The voice of days of old and days to be" (*The Passing of Arthur*, 135).
3. Robert Langbaum, *The Poetry of Experience* (New York: Random House, 1957), p. 115.
4. Langbaum, pp. 117–118.
5. Richard D. Altick and James F. Loucks II, *Browning's Roman Murder Story* (Chicago: University of Chicago Press, 1968), p. 41.
6. Altick and Loucks, pp. 42–43.
7. Mary Rose Sullivan, *Browning's Voices in "The Ring and the Book"* (Toronto: University of Toronto Press, 1969), pp. 21–40.
8. Sullivan, p. 56.
9. Sullivan and Altick and Loucks have written big books, and they say many other things, of course, but these citations are, I believe, indicative of their critical methods and results.
10. This does not distinguish the poem's tragedy from that of its classical predecessors, where the problem is also both internal and external, the bases of redemption as much in ourselves as in the poetic action, and the cathartic effect stoic rather than romantic.

11. Henry James, "The Novel in *The Ring and the Book*," in *Notes on Novelists* (New York: Scribners, 1914), p. 409.
12. Langbaum, p. 110.
13. Florence Emily Hardy, *The Life of Thomas Hardy 1840–1928* (London: Macmillan, 1962), p. 363.
14. Gerard Manley Hopkins, *The Wreck of the Deutschland*, 11. 38–39.
15. James, p. 410.
16. I am grateful to Diane Yvonne Clunan, who as a student in a doctoral seminar at New York University sharpened my interest in the role of imagery in this monologue and in the poem generally.
17. For an analysis of Arnold's mythic intent in the class labels he used, see my essay "Facing the Enemy Within: An Examination of the Moralist Mythos in *Culture and Anarchy*," in *Matthew Arnold's Prose: Three Essays in Literary Enlargement* (New York: AMS Press, 1983), pp. 67–111. *Culture and Anarchy* and *The Ring and the Book* were appearing simultaneously, and there are many fascinating comparisons to be drawn between them.
18. The poet-speaker in Book I uses these epithets to characterize ironically Tertium Quid's sense of himself.
19. Alexander Pope, *An Essay on Man*, II, 7–10.
20. Langbaum, p. 135.
21. Sullivan, p. 56.

4.

"The lost are like this . . . but worse":[1] Book V. *Count Guido Franceschini*

A rush to moral judgment has characterized reader response, including professional reader response, to Guido. Langbaum's judgment that he is "an incarnation of evil"[2] has received resounding confirmation from Altick and Loucks, who have "no doubt that he is the devil incarnate."[3] Such a response seems to be conclusively authorized by the Pope's relentless, resolute, unyielding condemnation of him, and this proves that it is a fundamental strategy of the poet in *The Ring and the Book*. That condemnation was a large and basic fact of the history found in the Old Yellow Book, and therefore it demanded a large presence in the transformation of history to poetry that is the poem's all-enveloping process. The poet seems to have recognized the historical fact as such a telling potential metaphor of the way the game of life is played customarily that he invested a great deal of concentrated imagination on the process of inducing the metaphor out of it.

Our natural temptation to have at Guido is persistently reinforced by the poet's maneuvers. That he did the ghastly deed
is never in doubt; his motives are so base and transparent and
his logistics, of both action and defense of action, so essentially
incompetent that he disgusts us while we despise him. Those
who speak for and against him in generic roles—the two halves
of Rome and the two lawyers—fuel both our eagerness to see
him condemned and our anxiety lest, in this crazy, mixed-up
world, he may somehow go free. Tertium Quid is a particular
source of agony because his disengagement is so fraudulent and
his blurring of distinctions so maddening, and a large part of
our blind affection for the Pope is generated by our relief that
the matter is finally settled in a satisfactory and seemingly authoritative way.

But of course a poet's maneuvering of our habitual inclina-
tions is only the beginning, only the manifest index to a latent
reality that, while imaginatively consistent with the outward sign,
is much profounder and more evasive than any metaphoric
structure that the poet can devise as a way of pointing toward
it. Such structures require imaginative insight on our part to
make them work, and in that sense the poet's role is analogous
to our role. Still, they are clearly his devices, his structures, and
he is in charge of them. However, the deeper we get into the
"novel country" to which they have guided us, the more genuinely coequal poet and reader become, the less authority and
responsibility the poet can assume for the way we comport
ourselves. He becomes an explorer, not a schematist, and the
infinity of topographical details that he, as an honest pioneer,
is still obligated to note and, to a relative degree, organize cannot have and should not be expected to have interpretive completeness. Like us, he is consciously at work, but he is unconsciously at work too, and much of what we find interesting may
arise from the latter source and depend on our own interpretation, our own metaphoric investiture, for completion. Nothing so manifest as Guido's guilt and, put mildly, the reader's
sturdy disinclination to absolve him of it can qualify as the latent reality that the poet and the reader must explore. They
are signs, not significances.

Our expectation of imaginative coherence in the work of a

serious poet seriously offered—a critical premise that must be honorably held until destroyed by a preponderance of carefully sifted critical evidence—compels us to study these manifest indices or signs for clues to their significance. What general characteristics of the human psyche—a psyche that perpetually supposes and states, observes and concludes—is mirrored in the rush to judgment carefully aided and abetted by the poet through the example of Guido? What do we learn about ourselves by being led to recognize the eagerness we feel—an eagerness also exampled by Guido—to have our judgment unequivocally confirmed?

Guido is, prima facie, an extreme instance, of course—a particularly disgusting and despicable villain—and we, like the Pope, may condemn him, send him to Mannaia, and go "sup" with "a clear conscience," made wholly secure in our actions by the very extremity of the case. But having admitted the possibility that this is a strategy on the part of the poet, we may begin to see how this strategy leads inward toward a subject that admits of no such security through the recognition that the answers to the preceding questions must encompass Guido both as an object of judgment and as a judge since our tendencies in judging him have an elaborate correspondence in his tendencies in judging others. If, in pursuing the implications of this correspondence, we discover that the poet has strategically disguised the fact that Guido is both a distorted mirror-image of ourselves and, intratextually, a mirror-image of the character who has traditionally been endowed with the authority to speak for Browning and, through him, for us—namely, the Pope—then we are faced with a different, more complex, more disquieting problem than simply finding a thousand patent reasons to heap abuse on a disgusting and despicable villain. We may still see him as the "midmost blotch of black," but our moral ingenuity will have to work from different premises toward different ends in accommodating our greater need to be inquisitive rather than categorical, judicious rather than judicial, empathetic rather than coldly noncomplicit, imaginative rather than literal.

By the test of what actually happens in Guido's first monologue, the poet-speaker of Book I characterizes his manner quite masterfully. One may, of course, read backwards and visit upon this introductory characterization whatever severe moral judgments he may have formed in reading Book V, but that would be clearly prejudicial.

> Soft-cushioned sits he; yet shifts seat, shirks touch,
> As, with a twitchy brow and wincing lip
> And cheek that changes to all kinds of white,
> He proffers his defence, in tones subdued
> Near to mock-mildness now, so mournful seems
> The obtuser sense truth fails to satisfy;
> Now, moved, from pathos at the wrong endured,
> To passion; for the natural man is roused
> At fools who first do wrong, then pour the blame
> Of their wrong-doing, Satan-like, on Job.
> Also his tongue at times is hard to curb;
> Incisive, nigh satiric bites the phrase,
> Rough-raw, yet somehow claiming privilege
> —It is so hard for shrewdness to admit
> Folly means no harm when she calls black white!
> —Eruption momentary at the most,
> Modified forthwith by a fall o' the fire,
> Sage acquiescence; for the world's the world,
> And, what it errs in, Judges rectify:
> He feels he has a fist, then folds his arms
> Crosswise and makes his mind up to be meek.
> And never once does he detach his eye
> From those ranged there to slay him or to save,
> But does his best man's-service for himself,
> Despite,—what twitches brow and makes lip wince,—
> His limbs' late taste of what was called the Cord,
> Or Vigil-torture more facetiously.
>
> (I, 954–980)

The Guido of this passage, the product of the poet-speaker's own process of aesthetic experiment and maturation as discussed in Chapter 1 above, is relatively free of direct moral judgments. He is a playactor on a silent screen, and what we are given are the highly refined observations and inferences of a practiced critic of mime. The essential drama of his situation is enabled to emerge relatively free of the distortions of moral judgment—a middle-aged man who has killed the young wife of a late marriage, along with the putative parents who harbored her against him, has just been tortured to elicit the confession of a truth that was never really denied, and is now being tried by the Court for his own life. That under these circumstances, objectively considered, he holds together and performs with a high degree of physical control and mental coherence is impressive, even heroic in its way, and however we may eventually appraise the source of his strength, we cannot reasonably deny the reality of it.

To try to normalize Guido is one of the most difficult obligations readers of *The Ring and the Book* face. It runs against all our cultural prejudices, all the stock responses that a black-and-white, Manichaean mentality automatically triggers. We feel that we are betraying our moral heritage, becoming at best morally flabby and at worst actually complicit in evil. Unless a monster is a monster, the very idea of moral order, of the basic distinction between good and evil, threatens to collapse. One may play games at the other end of the spectrum with some impunity—question Pompilia's heroism, impugn Caponsacchi's motives somewhat cavalierly, quibble to a degree with the Pope's way of reaching his judgment—and still maintain a sufficient sense of moral order and integrity. But to try even to be objective about evil seems too much like colloquizing with the devil or toying dilettantishly with chaos. All our superstitions warn us of its consequences.

But, though difficult, it is obligatory for any reader who recognizes in *The Ring and the Book* an imaginative achievement different in both degree and kind from the popular fairy-tale rescue of the beautiful young princess from the dungeon-castle of the ogre by the handsome young prince, or the Biblical exemplum of a St. Michael or a St. George saving a female embodiment of virginity and virtue from the filthy horrors of a fire-breathing dragon, or the classical myth of Perseus slaying the monstrous dragon about to devour Andromeda, chained to a rock in Ethiopia as the sacrificial victim of her mother's sinful words. Fairy tale, exemplum, and classical myth are all patterned in the poem, but the simple, severe lines of their morality-play genre do not take its measure. The modern tragedy of circumstance has invaded the classical tragedy of character, and the stark medieval doctrine of individual guilt has been placed in dramatic tension with the modern theory of conditioned behavioral response. Neither the compounded tragedy nor the compounded morality can work well—poetically, imaginatively, dynamically—if Guido, despite the complex turmoil he engenders in the poem's action, is perceived as simply monstrous—a dragon, an ogre, a devil, or any unequivocal incarnation of evil. He must be normalized to the degree that the poetic text permits it, and if the text refuses to admit it sufficiently for it to work well, then possibly the poet has failed, not the reader.

Each reader will have to find the techniques of normalization that work best for him, but three techniques that have both general relevance to any reading process and special relevance to the particular problem posed by Guido in *The Ring and the Book* may be useful. One is consciously to set aside while reading Book V the influences external to it—reports, rumors, speculations, judgments of other speakers—and to try to see with uninhibited clarity what Guido says for himself. Another is to make a conscious effort to identify with the incidents and motivations that Guido relates, not to compare the way he looks at things with the way we look at them, but to understand, to empathize, with his way of supposing and stating how he thought and felt about them. This does not prevent our concluding, on the basis of a cumulative impression or of individual incidents, that Guido is a fraud of whatever magnitude we choose, but it does help to obviate our pretending to read his monologue when we are in fact merely subjecting it to a prepackaged editorial attitude. The third is to make appropriate allowance for individual differences of manner and language—the same allowances we would expect an audience to make for ourselves—and to consider that Guido, having had thirty years' experience of the types composing his tribunal, behaves and speaks to some degree in the light of that experience. There are conventions to observe, normal expectations to be fulfilled, and every observance of convention or respect

for formal expectation is not a sure sign of duplicity. The reader
should be relatively slow to take his moral cues from manner-
isms or failed efforts at formal propriety or other more personal peculiarities. They may ultimately be seen as metaphors
of a character's cravenness, but idiosyncrasy, however much it
may displease us, does not have an a priori moral content, despite our often unnoticed habit of acting as though it does.

The long introductory verse paragraph in which Guido presents himself to the Court is extremely ceremonious:

> Thanks, Sir, but, should it please the reverend Court,
> I feel I can stand somehow, half sit down
> Without help, make shift to even speak, you see,
> Fortified by the sip of . . . why, 't is wine,
> Velletri,—and not vinegar and gall,
> So changed and good the times grow! Thanks, kind Sir!
> Oh, but one sip's enough! I want my head
> To save my neck, there's work awaits me still.
> How cautious and considerate . . . aie, aie, aie,
> Not your fault, sweet Sir! Come, you take to heart
> An ordinary matter. Law is law.
> Noblemen were exempt, the vulgar thought,
> From racking, but, since law thinks otherwise,
> I have been put to the rack: all's over now,
> And neither wrist—what men style, out of joint:
> If any harm be, 't is the shoulder-blade,
> The left one, that seems wrong i' the socket,—Sirs,
> Much could not happen, I was quick to faint,
> Being past my prime of life, and out of health.
> In short I thank you,—yes, and mean the word.
>   (V, 1–20)

Guido has never been a star before, and this has been a large
part of his problem with life. His ancient lineage had burned
itself out by the time it got to him, and he had been left with
a nobility in ashes. Even the thirty years he has spent seeking
patronage in Rome had been, from its very inception, a grotesque mistake (an alien Tuscan trying to adapt to mysterious
Roman ways, a centuries-old patron trying to get himself pa-

tronized), and for that conspicuous failure he has had to pay
an enormous price, sacrificing to it not only the best years of
his life from the imperious demands of sexual longing at fifteen or sixteen to almost the seventh climacteric and the onset
of old age, but also an identity or healthy ego strength that
could not survive the diminishment and humiliation of an Aretine Count playing, decade after decade, the part of a Roman
lacquey. So even if his star is blighted and crossed, this is the
first star role he has ever had a chance to play, and he tries to
play it with lavish ceremony.

   He is not very good at it; in fact, he is conspicuously bad.
He is self-conscious; his efforts at wit grossly misfire; his emotional appeals are mirrors of a colossal species of bad taste; his
pretensions to rhetorical sophistication are as painful to watch
as those of a raw provincial schoolboy come to a great center
of humanistic learning to impress the sophists with his scholastic skills; the flagrant ways in which he tries to be ingratiating to the judges are enough to make one wish he were momentarily both deaf and dumb. Guido is still an Aretine lost in
Rome, a fourth-rate product of provincial melodrama bastar-
dizing classical tragedy before the most practiced critics of the
age. If he were there of his own free will, we would simply
laugh him out of town; but he is caught in a trap and is playing the part he has been ordered to play, however rightly ordered, however wrongly played. So while our theatrical sensibilities may be outraged, our sense of pathos is stirred too. Bulls
should not be in china closets, but when by chance or design
they are, they make an awful havoc in both the closet and the
heart. It would be sentimental to expect anything to improve.
The lines of character are too clear and apparently indelible.
Guido is one of civilization's incompetents trying to play civilization's game. In that he is representative rather than unique.
Most fair-minded readers can identify with that, and to call it
simply monstrous would be to call themselves monsters.

   Guido's keen sense of belatedness, the subject of his second
verse paragraph, is representative too.

>   I am representative of a great line,
>   One of the first of the old families

In Arezzo, ancientest of Tuscan towns.
When my worst foe is fain to challenge this,
His worst exception runs—not first in rank
But second, noble in the next degree
Only; not malice 'self maligns me more.
So, my lord opposite has composed, we know,
A marvel of a book, sustains the point
That Francis boasts the primacy 'mid saints;
Yet not inaptly hath his argument
Obtained response from yon my other lord
In thesis published with the world's applause
—Rather 't is Dominic such post befits:
Why, at the worst, Francis stays Francis still,
Second in rank to Dominic it may be,
Still, very saintly, very like our Lord;
And I at least descend from a Guido once
Homager to the Empire, nought below—
Of which account as proof that, none o' the line
Having a single gift beyond brave blood,
Or able to do aught but give, give, give
In blood and brain, in house and land and cash,
Not get and garner as the vulgar may,
We become poor as Francis or our Lord.
                              (V, 140–164)

Behind the painful analogy with St. Francis, which is so misconceived as to make one grin and groan at the same time, and
behind the insolent, mean-minded indictment of all those who
have worked their way up through the ranks of Church and
State (V, 184–208), there is a genuine recognition of being
alien in time, outfitted for a life that no longer exists. Like many
other people, Guido feels that he has been left "high and dry/I'
the wave's retreat":

My stranded self, born fish with gill and fin
Fit for the deep sea, now left flap bare-backed
In slush and sand, a show to crawlers vile
Reared of the low-tide and aright therein.
                              (V, 172–175)

His contempt for the peers of his condition does not negate the truth of it, and the unconscious self-mockery in his characterization of his noble predecessors as not "Having a single gift beyond brave blood" (V, 160) does not blunt the incisiveness of his characterization of himself as possessed of, perhaps largely shaped by, "A heartful of desire, man's natural load,/A brainful of belief, the noble's lot" (V, 178–179). He is a man without a medium (a fish out of water) in any way suited to his need for survival. His only talent is for aristocratic privilege, and the cultural tide has washed that away and left him a mere barbarian. Like his even more dubious brothers, he has only the options available to an impecunious nobleman: the Army, the Church, and marriage to a wealthy wife. He is easily dissuaded from the first, by himself or by others, apparently leaves the third for a last resort, and opts for the second as the most plausible, though only an extravagant self-delusion could have blinded him to the fact that it was the option for which a barbarian like himself was least qualified. Still, both the belatedness and the self-delusion find echoes in us all.

In his third verse paragraph, Guido continues unconsciously to expose characteristics that are thoroughly unattractive to us and offensive to his particular audience: crude efforts at ingratiation, a soggy wit, inept choice of rhetorical figure, self-laudation through self-depreciation at the most transparent and dismissible level, a great show of managerial acumen and stoical perseverance incredible in an incompetent lad of fifteen and contradictory of the very point it is meant to support. But out of this mélange yet another personal trait emerges that is broadly representative and contributes to the troubled failures of his life and our own. Guido is a "splitter," a divided self who neither knows who he is nor knows that he does not know. He has somehow got hold of a tawdry script about how to be a successful toady, and he has no idea that it is all wrong and bound to end miserably. He who has compared himself to St. Francis thinks that minor orders are sleights of hand to guarantee him his share of the loaves and fishes while, at the same time, he indulges in the worst clichés of courtiership—hunting, partying, and gambling. And his claim to a ready wit and exceptional skill at repartee is so ludicrous that it suggests

that his auditors have been so attentive in their incredulity that
he thinks his rhetorical style is succeeding magnificently. It is
true that he is absurd in a patently despicable way, a provincial
naif caught under a high-powered critical microscope acting
out the most pretentious delusions of grandeur as reported by
this same naif, now grown old in failure and suspect at the most
ominous level, to essentially the same critics who saw through
him then, reported, moreover, as if it had been brilliantly
planned and impeccably executed. So while it is certainly absurd, it is also genuinely pathetic. He did not have a chance
from the beginning, and since thirty-five years of failure in
dealing with life through the available options have taught him
nothing—have made him no more self-aware, no more acute
as a student of reality, no less tasteless and mean-minded—we
must entertain the thought that Guido is petrified in incompetence, has no capacity for the mythmaking process by which
our low lives are gradually redeemed, and, being deprived of
all social, moral, and imaginative talents at anything more than
a shrewd and barbarous level, cannot be judged, conscientiously, by standards wholly alien to his endowments: "So he
was made; he nowise made himself" (VII, 1731; X, 357–359;
XI, 934–941, 2098–2099). We may rail against the thought that
Guido is more to be pitied than censured, may, like the Pope,
meet it with the counterthought that it is only conclusive proof
that falsehood is so systemic in man's language that he calls a
thing truth knowing it to be falsehood; but ordinary conscientiousness both in critical analysis and in critical self-regard demands that we undergo its influence even if, in the end, we
refuse to yield to its law.

   The poet having thus implanted an ambiguity *in the critical
reader's response to Guido* that is very different from the ambiguity that the Pope finds *in Guido himself,* the central action of
the myth can begin, and it is introduced at the end of the fourth
verse paragraph. As one would expect, it is introduced with
elaborate care. The would-be sleek boy of sixteen is now the
drab man of forty-six, thirty years having been spent failing
where, according to the rule, everyone succeeds (V, 296–297).
Having transformed a young Count into a young lacquey, he
has succeeded only in becoming lacquey to a "lacquey's son"

and received as a token of recognition and esteem earned by three decades of, he says, fidelity to fasts, feasts, and functions, the "unburnt end o' the very candle" the lacquey's son had carried in a ceremony of state (V, 315–322). At the heart of this verse paragraph is a rapidly darkening irony. Prompted by a sudden awareness that change-of-life is upon him, Guido describes his decision to change his life in a network of metaphors that prove only that no change is possible; he may alter the geography and transform the fiction, but he cannot change himself. He is neither flesh nor fowl, but an aging fish out of water whose only change will be a metamorphosis of stench. The "denizen[s] o' the dung," (V, 293), as he tags all those who, without the glory of his name, have managed to achieve fame and fortune through heroic service, professional expertise, or humanistic learning, feel a natural, an unexplained, antipathy toward him which, we know, he will unconsciously avenge on a strange, sad, exquisite flower of the dung-heap, Pompilia.

Against the ceremony of language in which Guido attempts to invest his decision to cut bait in Rome with a classically noble stoicism is set the elaborate epic simile, complete with gloss, of the gaming Casino (V, 370–97). As the ritual of acquiescence in defeat is working its way through, the "watchers of his ways" covering their compunction with cheery banter while they attempt to avert a damaging scandal by seeking a consolation prize, a far more ominous voice suddenly intrudes, that of Abate Paolo, brother, priest, pimp, marriage broker, master-fixer. With all the suavity of the most cynical politician, he offers flesh as the way to wealth, both solace and a consolation prize in a wife with a dowry.

What gives this development the terrifying ring of the inevitable ill omen is already clear in seed and will immediately be made clear in flower. Though he has no capacity whatever to recognize or acknowledge it, Guido is one dwarfed, shrunken, bitter organism of hate: hate is "the truth of him" (VII, 1727). He cannot know it because such knowledge would be a modification of it, and we can never learn enough about him to explain quite why it is so. Though seemingly rare in our own experience, he is by no means unique, and even the appearance of rarity is deceiving. Like Guido, such people put a plausible front on their actions, and, like him, they have no access to the truth of their state. Those who, like Pompilia, are caged by them and perpetually wounded often live lives of quiet desperation and take their awful secrets to the grave. Moreover, partial hatred, whether vertical or horizontal in time, is by no means rare; only the rarely favored escape it. Thus we need not be quintessentially Guido-like to recognize, if we can and will, the ways in which we are tied to his representation. But the ill omen is both inevitable and terrifying because we know that Guido has only one option left, marriage, and we know, too, that in marriage his hate will have but one object, the vulnerable flesh and soul of an individual woman. Institutions like the Army and the Church (and "the Court," which Paul throws in at the last moment) are relatively immune to people like Guido; they are large, entrenched, protected by codes and traditions, and they eventually reject such alien implants. But individuals, especially the kinds of individuals a Guido would naturally select, are isolated, uprooted, and unprotected by rules of the hearth and the society that have been shaped by males for centuries to accommodate males and to make living chattel of females, including the rule that makes rejection of it by the female the darkest of crimes.

Guido's monologue undergoes an abrupt change in tone as soon as he begins to defend the marriage contract he entered into with the Comparini. Here he, not the judges, is the authority; he is master now, with no more need for deference, ingratiation, cajolery. He transforms the catechetical method of the schools into the flashy cunning of the fencing academy, thrusting and parrying with the relish of one who, after an anxious struggle in a strange arena with adversaries whose weapons and rules he did not understand, has at last found firm footing on his own turf and is playing his very own game according to his very own rules.

Though Guido repeatedly presents himself as an expert duelist, that being part of the baggage of the nobleman he carries around so ostentatiously, there is no evidence that he is in fact one, and the crudeness with which he sizes up, measures the anatomy of, his present situation is a mockery of the idea implicit in his technique. He wounds himself with every feint, and when, at last, he drives his rapier home, it is into a heart that has already been fatally wounded—his own. However, the crude, vigorous, self-indicting flourish that Guido manifests with such eye-opening confidence, while it seems to dissolve all possible doubt about his motives for actions that have always been perfectly clear, does not resolve any of the latent critical issues with which the reader must deal. In fact, it further complicates and subtilizes them.

Guido is a grotesquely brutal perversion of the concept of noblesse oblige, inverting the linguistic structure of the phrase and arrogantly investing society with the obligation to honor his demands for privilege. His blatant appeal to a profit-and-loss calculus may also be interpreted as having an analogy in feudalism's worst excesses, its tendency to exploit misfortune and drive the weak to the wall. But the very relentlessness and thoroughgoingness with which Guido maintains such a philosophy of life, with its ghastly male chauvinism, its diminishment of morality to the most venal species of self-interest, and its dismissal of idealism as merely the "gabble o' the goose" (V, 447), enforces further the possibility that such a philosophy is so deeply rooted in him, so systemic, that only an advocate of ethical monism could fairly fault him. Thus the real issue—personal responsibility for motives and actions—becomes even more tightly woven.

Also, the splitter or divided-self motif is not resolved by Guido's abrupt assumption of the masterful posture of the hard-hitting occupier of a clearly defined ideological space. Which is the real Guido—the ingratiating sycophant? the self-confident ideologue? some ambiguous compound thrice confounded by our ambiguous identification with certain aspects of the metaphor he embodies? An even more complex possibility is that even his peculiar manifestation of noblesse oblige is fraudulent, that behind the mask of a haughty impecunious nobleman walks an authentic "cit." Of course, Guido himself would rage against such an idea, and no suggestion is being made that he is conscious of so "libelous" an allegation or that he could succeed at the one role any better than at the other. But the fact is that the crucial action of his myth, the error that finally brings him down, is a full-dress manifestation of

the burgess-spirit about which he is uncompromisingly contemptuous. The profit-and-loss morality by which he justifies
his "honour" in making and maintaining the marriage contract converts the medieval man of noble lineage into the
modern aristocrat of the countinghouse, his failure at both being
germane to quite different considerations. Thus Guido's lack
of an identity, of any true sense of who he is, also becomes
further complicated and subtilized by the seemingly solid new
space he occupies with such self-destructive bravado.

Finally, Guido's representativeness, his function as a refractor of ourselves, is progressively woven into the fabric of his
defense. It is a deeply ironic stratagem on the poet's part:
whether this main phase of Guido's dramatic role-playing is
masked or unmasked, whether he is an expert fencer, as he
claims, or a pretentious poseur as ignorant of the anatomy of
man's body as of his soul, he is given the poetic function of
"strip[ping] a vizard from a face,/A body from its padding, and
a soul/From froth and ignorance it styles itself" (V, 561–563);
the poet makes him the unlikeliest heir to "Plautus, Terence,
Boccaccio's Book,/ . . . [and] frank Ser Franco's merry Tales"
(V, 559–560). The face, body, and soul are our own, of course,
and the wit of the poetic conceit is so startling and challenging
that it transforms the whole character of Guido's monologue
as a "noble exercise of our imagination." Instead of an exercise in moralistic supererogation, a chilling but tediously reiterative and somewhat obvious portrait of an extremely dangerous loser whose very incompetence releases mayhem into
the world, *Count Guido Franceschini* becomes an experiment in
the surreal, a representative that is representative, not in the
dominant image that it draws with such massive care and imaginative fidelity, but in the half-hidden, seemingly discon-
nected, odd-shaped fragments that reflect images of the viewing eye while it is intent upon looking at something so different
that it seems to have little relation to itself. Like Guido hearing
himself described as a closet cit, we may be outraged at the notion of having so disgusting a creature as a fatigued, duplicitous, child-abusing, wife-beating, soul-pimping, sadistic murderer as our guide to moral self-awareness; but self-knowledge
has traditionally demanded a terrifying price, and we quickly

realize that much of the aesthetic delight, like most edification, inheres in the very outrageousness of the literary idea.

The marketing of honor, the selling of one's "name,/Style and condition," is the first example and, roughly speaking, a paradigm of the way the poetic stratagem works.

> Softly, Sirs!
> Will the Court of its charity teach poor me
> Anxious to learn, of any way i' the world,
> Allowed by custom and convenience, save
> This same which, taught from my youth up, I trod?
> Take me along with you; where was the wrong step?
> If what I gave in barter, style and state
> And all that hangs to Franceschinihood,
> Were worthless,—why, society goes to ground,
> Its rules are idiot's-rambling. Honour of birth,—
> If that thing has no value, cannot buy
> Something with value of another sort,
> You've no reward nor punishment to give
> I' the giving or the taking honour; straight
> Your social fabric, pinnacle to base,
> Comes down a-clatter like a house of cards.
> Get honour, and keep honour free from flaw,
> Aim at still higher honour,—gabble o' the goose!
> Go bid a second blockhead like myself
> Spend fifty years in guarding bubbles of breath,
> Soapsuds with air i' the belly, gilded brave,
> Guarded and guided, all to break at touch
> O' the first young girl's hand and first old fool's purse!
> All my privation and endurance, all
> Love, loyalty and labour dared and did,
> Fiddle-de-dee!—why, doer and darer both,—
> Count Guido Franceschini had hit the mark
> Far better, spent his life with more effect,
> As a dancer or a prizer, trades that pay!
> On the other hand, bid this buffoonery cease,
> Admit that honour is a privilege,
> The question follows, privilege worth what?
> Why, worth the market-price,—now up, now down,

Just so with this as with all other ware:
Therefore essay the market, sell your name,
Style and condition to who buys them best!
                                          (V, 430–465)

Following the catechetical method, Guido is responding to a
typical question put to him by some generalized person after
things had begun to fall apart: " 'Are flesh and blood a
ware?/Are heart and soul a chattel?' " The worth of an honorable name, he says, has been the foundation-stone of his in-
struction from childhood upward, and he views it as the key-
stone that keeps society from collapsing. "Honour of birth" is
the touchstone of honor, and adding to/subtracting from a
person's honor is the basic formula by which society's system
of rewards and punishments works. This "honour," which a
man spends his whole life guarding, is not froth, a soap bubble that bursts with the first touch of passion or purse, but
sterling, minted and marketable. It will not swing an unequal
bargain in the marketplace, but fairly matched—for example,
a title against a fortune—it works. There may be extras as one
or the other bargainer may see it, and each is likely to exag-
gerate the distinction of his commodity somewhat, but both
know what "the back-bone . . . /I' the writhings of the bargain" is (V, 510–511). Of course, many people misperceive what
they think they want, and when it proves not to be the thing
they thought it was, certain types want their money back, crying
foul and making a terrible fuss over quite imaginary offenses.
In this as in everything else, breeding shows. The prince or
genuine man of the world sees these matters with clear-eyed
fortitude and makes the best of his misfortunes, whereas the
burgess or inexperienced provincial howls, indicts, exagger-
ates, and spends all his energy externalizing blame when in fact
his is a quotidian case of "purblind greed that dog-like still drops
bone,/Grasps shadow, and then howls the case is hard!" (V, 565–
566).
    Summarized in this impersonal, objective, skeletally compre-
hensive way, there is nothing very shocking about Guido's argument. It is not a romantic point of view, and one could
quibble with some of the particularities of its phrasing and with

its generalized use of class distinctions; but only the hopelessly romantic would reject it as a reasonably accurate analysis of the way of the world. The difficulties arise when two elements are added: real persons and ideal principles. We reject the social model when it begins to bear on individuals we know and love, and we reject it when we are conscious of its contention with our fondest ideals—truth for its own sake, for example, or honor just to be honorable, or love without ulterior motive. In such cases, our human affections save us from the lure of abstract social models by rooting us in a different kind of organizing principle—the day-to-day experience of living with people we admire and love. This humanization is both legitimate and essential; even though we may not be able to give it the intellectual finish of the social model, it supplies ballast to our lives and saves us from being tossed about on the crosscurrents of social and moral theory. Unfortunately, however, much of our commerce is with strangers, and only in rare instances do we make conscious connections between our ideals and our practical negotiations. Therefore, in vast areas of our lives, this humanizing influence does not take place, and though we are not, like Guido, boldly dismissive of higher ideals and brutally cynical in pinpointing "the back-bone . . . /I' the writhings of the bargain," we do regularly trade what we have, including "name,/Style and condition," for what we want, including "name,/Style and condition."

The second example, a refinement on the first, is a response to the friendly but censorious question, " 'From the bride's soul what is it you expect?' " (V, 577–578). Complete compliance, says Guido; I want everything the law allows—"all wifeliness," body and soul freely rendered. That is what the law provides, and that is what will be demanded until the law is changed, not such "troll[ing] . . . lies o'er lip" as poets inflate marriage-hymns with. The thoughts a young or old man's fancy turns to in the spring are not "of white womanhood,/The chaste and pure," but of the lust and sexual gratification written on public walls by hot young bucks. Let's be honest, says Guido. Moreover, it is "nobler" in a woman, better for her "soul," to yield her body gracefully than to be taken by force by her husband (V, 593–602).

So far, though rough, so good: most of us are complicit both in the law and in the lie, and we have let the law stand for so long because, draped in the lie, we like it. In his final image, however, Guido seems to overstep all reality and all propriety: "As when I buy, timber and twig, a tree—/I buy the song o' the nightingale inside" (V, 605–606). The nightingale sings only when it is free, and buying and selling the soul is the devil's business! That is both true and a dramatic clarification of the limitation of the mercantile metaphor and the mercantile mind. But is it so true and clear in actual practice? Is it not rather more honest to say that the blatant contradiction is only a slight impediment to the persistent expectation—that the difference between what we call lust and love is inextricably bound up with the soul's serenade and that the bargain loses its savor when the nightingale, which had been taken entirely for granted, suddenly flies away? So while we may volubly express our shock at the absurdity of the idea of "buy[ing] the song o' the night-ingale" when buying the tree, we often act as though we have done just that, the duet of the bodies being unaccompanied by a duet of the souls, the woman being unconsciously expected to stay in voice and sing alone.

In the third example (V, 607–753), the very extravagance of Guido's attitudes and images—the gross charges he throws around with an imprecision that defies credulity, the prurient and revolting current of sadomasochism that he propels with obvious if fraudulent relish—moves him into a cave of such specialized physical cruelty and strange spiritual pollution that his representativeness of anything but a sewer-culture seems eclipsed. His is an almost "unimaginable story" to healthy minds with typical social attitudes, and the idea of identifying with him appears, even on the face of it, to be impossible. Pompilia as character-assassin, scandalmonger, cockatrice, imperious nymph, and falcon-hawk are metaphors we dismiss out of hand with fitting contempt for their creator and propagator. We can believe (indeed we hope) that the marriage went unconsum-mated for months, not because Pompilia refused Guido, which she would eventually try to do, but because her childlike char-acter and total freedom from coquetry worked against his sex-ual arousal, which required the sort of ritualistic violence that stimulated now his sadistic, now his masochistic instincts (V, 678–697). Guido wants a hawk to master for his psychosexual pleasure, including the pleasures of domination or even execution and the long-drawn-out pleasure of plucking the pinfeathers (equivalent to undeveloped pubic hairs just emerging from the skin) one by one. For him to compare such unnatural motives and practices, literally unthinkable even in the category of the bestial, with the discipline sanctioned by the Church for members trying to subdue in themselves the temptations of the flesh used in reinforcement of the vows of poverty, chastity, and obedience overleaps the understanding as ordinarily defined and explodes all possibility of sympathy.

But these horrifying extremes of character, which create a chasm of disgust between us and Guido, leave his representativeness intact at one important level, namely, the set of attitudes toward the male-female relationship that he brings to the marriage state, the assumptions about the respective roles of the male and the female united in marriage, quite independent of the particular content he invests them with. He had argued initially for parity of contract, title for wealth, but the idea of other parities—parity of person, parity of family, parity of authority, parity of love—had never even occurred to him. Mutuality in marriage was to him a foreign and wholly subversive idea into which he could not enter, having long since been incapacitated for it by his ancient lineage and the culture that had evolved along with that lineage. His will was marriage's way; he would be master, she dutiful slave. If she proved less than perfectly docile, he would discipline her into submission; if she "prove[d] a haggard," he would "twist her neck!" Stripped of its fiercer metaphors, this had been the official male attitude toward and program in marriage for centuries, and the myth of *The Ring and the Book* shows to what conclusions it eventually leads.

From this point forward, the monologue moves steadily toward those conclusions, and the "plot" is given sharper focus. Marriage is still the issue, but now attention shifts from the fairness of the marriage contract or the manner of comportment in the married state to the irrefragability of the marriage vows. The Comparini, having done all they could in Arezzo to strip Guido of his "good name," flee to Rome and attempt to strip Pompilia of hers. They could not take her from her husband's house without the direst legal consequences, so they publish the story of her anonymous origins in an effort to make her inheritance, now Guido's, null and void. Guido's problem then becomes how to get rid of Pompilia without losing his claim to Pompilia's purse. It is a particular metaphor for one of the most fundamental dilemmas of man—how to free oneself from a wholly untenable situation without paying an untenable price—and the whole world, faced with some version of the same dilemma, watches with suspenseful attention for the solution, though by the very nature of the case it cannot be considered acceptable whatever it is. Guido's resolution is classic: he gets rid of the whole bundle and pays the ultimate price. In the process, he divides the whole world into two opposing camps until, by analogy with the Roman Emperors at the gladiatorial games, the Pope is given the decision of thumbs up or thumbs down. That, despite his obvious guilt, a majority of those watching seem to favor acquittal is to be expected: Guido is their surrogate in resolving a universally typed dilemma, and people not surprisingly rank justice somewhat lower than self-interest.

Looking at the remainder of Guido's monologue from this perspective, the critic has his own dilemma, and he can expect an analogous but different reaction from the watchers of his decision. He must study Guido as a universal surrogate, separating in the manner already established the particular metaphors of often horrid content, which are peculiar to individual character, and the modular metaphors of situation and response that, stripped of the special content with which Guido invests them, have a representative relevance. He must put a higher premium on judging us than judging Guido, on stripping the "vizard" from our face, the "padding" from our body, and the "froth and ignorance" from our soul rather than from Guido's. This, being harder and less immediately gratifying, is likely to cost him the sympathy of the many readers who would rather judge than be judged even at such a distance. Faced with their own dilemma—either to identify with Guido and be damned or to identify with the modular metaphors and be damned—they might choose to throw the whole matter over and, like Gigadibs at the end of *Bishop Blougram's Apology*, either give up reading altogether or return to such honest, straightforward folk as "Plautus, Terence, Boccaccio's Book,/ . . . [and] frank Ser Franco's merry Tales." As the Pope says, quoting Ecclesiastes, "of the making books there is no end" (X, 9).

Guido's need for some adroit fast-stepping and the steps he maladroitly takes form the substance of the next extended example (V, 754–931). Surprised by the revelation of Pompilia's wholly untraceable lineage, he can abruptly cast her out as waste for the dung-heap, or he can stand aloofly above the patently contemptible charge, "maintain" his wife's " 'cause/By making it his own (what other way?),' " and by saving Pompilia's wealth for her, save it for himself. This is the strategy of the outlandish letter he forges for her to sign, a strategy so transparently false in style and substance that he quickly confesses it, though he tries to save face by claiming fear of more "Vigiltorture" and the perfect propriety of the letter's sentiments in a dutiful wife. This is Guido's first essay in the fabrication of style, and his defense is a lamely conventional "defense of poetry": its falseness as history is redeemed by its impeccability as sentiment. Despite the pride he feels in his skill as a rhetorician, his soul is a parody of the poet's. Having "saved appearances," however—having taken Pompilia to his bosom and lessoned her in the basic elements of high marital propriety—he must set to work at once to alter appearances, getting in and out of his humor as quickly as a Jonsonian or Apuleian ass. The daughter of a whore must be shown to be a whore despite all his exampling and instructing her in "marital rectitude" as a way of preparing the path to Caponsacchi while dusting over the "harsh, uncouth, and ludicrous" behavior by which he impelled her along the path.

The three epithets the poet has chosen to characterize how "ungracefully" Guido "battled" in this phase of working through his dilemma—"harsh, uncouth, and ludicrous"—are quite precisely pointed, and they supply a suitable transition from the particular to the general metaphor. Like most people engaged in a sharply drawn battle of the sexes, he has absolutely no talent or skill for it. He is angry, threatened, determined to succeed while at the same time anxious about success, having found that his wife's allies have unexpected tricks of their own; in these respects he is typical. Though he is hateful, vindictive, and cruel to a quite individual degree, hatefulness, vindictiveness, and cruelty are not unusual characteristics of the protagonists in such ugly dramas, including ourselves. A typical harshness is a typical development; one does not have to be as barbaric as Guido to be genuinely clumsy or even boorish ("uncouth") is so unfamiliar a set of circumstances; and even if "hate" is not the "truth" of us, as it is of Guido, we are likely to play this unfamiliar and contradictory game of face-saving and anti-mythmaking so self-consciously and self-deceptively as to be an objective observer laughably absurd or ludicrous. In its basic lineaments, Guido's situation is our situation; like him, we must save enough face not to appear to have been fools long since, but we must at the same time not save so much face as to appear to exonerate the party at whom we are aggrieved. So we play contradictory roles that, in our fury of self-justification, seem impeccable to us and ludicrous to everyone looking on.

As Guido moves closer to the epic center of the myth—flight, capture, and trial—he is aware, as are his judges both *intra librum* and *extra libro,* that the crucial charge against him, the issue upon which his very survival may depend, is cowardice. Unless that can be erased, or at least made inert through ambiguity, his whole line of defense—in short, he—collapses. This awareness, to the limited degree that he is capable of entertaining it, monitors his next strategy (V, 931–1036). The charge he sets up to counter is this: you were not mild and exemplary in exhortation but " 'Breathed threatenings, rage and slaughter!' " However, the charge bears so much the mark of his own rhetorical style that probably its substance too has been manufactured for the purpose to which he puts it. Would that I had! he says; perhaps "my broken gods" would not then be strewn about "my deserted hearth" nor devils frolic on my "tesselated floor." No, he played the role of Christian God, not the avenger of the Old Testament or of the heroic age of Greece. He boxed ears instead of cutting ears off, brandished a corked rapier instead of abruptly severing the first joint of the ring finger. In short, he was a fool, ignoring in his benign

blindness the most blatant maneuvers of Pompilia and Caponsacchi, a pair of besotted lovebirds hiding behind the masks of
wife and priest, that, as the whole town knew, had cuckolded
him months before. So long drugged by gentleness, he had
awakened to the sad, sad truth only after a literal drugging,
looting, and absconding. This is typical Guido, so enamored of
his own rhetoric and of his self-congratulatory conviction of
astuteness that he is almost comically obtuse to the fact that his
rhetoric and his false show of astuteness are inevitably doing
him in. Not only is he rhetorically inept, conveying to this particularly sophisticated audience the exact opposite of what he
intends, but in addition, the self-admiring unction with which
he delivers it converts the despicable into the disgusting. His
implicit assumption of the character of a doomed and gentle
god, the vague duplicity with which he seeks to cast himself in
the role of a cuckolded old fool out of the fabliau tradition,
the cool, matter-of-fact detail in which he describes both physical and psychological cruelty while claiming for himself inex-
haustible gentleness and long-suffering, the minutiae with which
he inventories the escape while asserting that he knew nothing
of it until awakened by a crowd of neighbors at noon—all of
this adds up, not to an ingenue or even to genuine ingenuity,
but to what one might call the pathetic grotesque, the pitiful
miscalculations, grimly humorous, of a cruel, incompetent cal-
culator.

The modular metaphor that emerges out of the particularly
duplicitous content of Guido's gesturing here, a duplicity of
motive, action, and explanation that is at once comic, terrifying, and pitiful, is that of the grim final phase of a marriage
gone bad. It is told entirely from a male point of view, and
hence it has only a male representativeness. What it reflects is
the emotional chaos that results from the collapse of a marriage organized on the principle of male domination. The presumption of authority implies an assumption of responsibility,
and unless, like Guido, he does not believe in marriage, has no
capacity to make it work, and sees every untoward event as adequate grounds for its destruction, the male partner must feel
the collapse acutely in his exposed male ego. Under the pressure of pain and confusion, that ego will spasm wildly in sev-

eral emotional directions at the same time—rage, jealousy, remorse, inordinate self-righteousness, acute self-depreciation—
and will create fantasies to give seeming validity to each emotion. Those with a capacity for honest creativity will identify
the error, take responsibility for it, and accept the consequences as the heavy but just price of self-blindness left too
long unrecognized and uncorrected.

At the center of the monologue, supplying its structural, in-
tuitional or interpretive, and rhetorical fulcrum, is Guido's account of the incident at the inn at Castelnuovo when the three
principals are brought face to face and measured (V, 1037–
1162). As was said in Chapter 1, everything preceding flows to
it, and everything following flows from it. In a monologue of
2058 lines, it bridges the center numerically; it is the dramatic
turning point, the episode from which the total action takes its
direction toward an inevitable conclusion; intuitionally or in-
terpretively, it overleaps even the impressive traditional distinctions between paganism and Christianity, the natural man
and the supernaturalist, and finds the difference between human good and human evil in the integrity of a man's belief
and his courage to act it out without regard to self-interested
loss or gain; and all the poet's dependence on rhetoric as the
most distinctive, subtle, and trustworthy measure of a man's
moral-imaginative condition—*the style is the man, revelation is* "the
Word"—is put to a crucial test.

The poetic result is masterful—controlled, structurally balanced, consistent with all we know, reiterative of the single
crucial question, so intensely dramatic that we actually watch
the mind moving as if it were a physical thing, a rational animal, through the language.

At first, Guido plays on the Court's sympathy in the same
manner with which he began his monologue (V, 1037–1048),
though here he identifies by allusion with Lucifer instead of
with Christ, as earlier. Then he tries in the naivest fashion to
shock the court by casting aspersions on Caponsacchi as a cavalier and Pompilia as a paramour still disheveled from her late
lovemaking, not realizing that his images create around Caponsacchi the aura of a Roman hero of Imperial days, impatient with lacqueys, wishing that the horses were eagles to "Whirl

him along the league . . . / . . .[to] Rome and liberty" (V, 1049–
1062). With that, he abruptly calls his "case complete," ironically asking the Court to see the matter through his eyes (V,
1064–1066).

Though the remnant Guido is there, he is not in his usual
expansive state of mind and rhetoric. He knows that he is
walking in a minefield, and he freezes. Then comes the question that above all else he would like to avoid:

> 'Why, that then was the time,' you interpose,
> 'Or then or never, while the fact was fresh,
> To take the natural vengeance: there and thus
> They and you,—somebody had stuck a sword
> Beside you while he pushed you on your horse,—
> 'T was requisite to slay the couple, Count!'
>
> (V, 1068–1073)

There is sarcasm behind the declaration, incredulity behind the
manifesto, and Guido squirms. He tries to set it up as though
this were *his* dilemma—natural vengeance or legal redress—and
to argue that he tried the latter first and took the former at a
later time. Even he knows that is ridiculous, and any remaining doubt turns to certainty: " 'Why, 't is clear . . ./You shrank
from gallant readiness and risk,/Were coward: the thing's
inexplicable else' " (V, 1089–1091). The charge is unequivocal
and incontrovertible, and Guido flaps around hopelessly in his
own filth. He becomes so craven that even those for whom he
had expressed such haughty contempt and at whom he now
grasps frantically for companionship—lambs, eunuchs, women,
children, and all shieldless, timid things—seem to withdraw from
the leprosy of his touch. It is a foreshadowing of the litany with
which his second monologue will end, as his frenzied "Cowardice were misfortune and no crime!" is a prophetic mockery
of the Pope's " 'Call ignorance my sorrow not my sin!' "

But as Guido slips deeper into self-pollution—"I am fallen
so low/I scarce dare brush the fly that blows my face,/And thank
the man who simply spits not there" (V, 1102–1104), he suddenly thinks that he has found a stone to stand on. The Court
may be "generous" enough to see mirrored in this craven wretch

merely a man immobilized by misery who waited upon his judicial "masters" to make a decision which he was not capable
of making. It is the last straw of the drowning man, but Guido
grasps at it as if it were a divine inspiration:

> There's the riddle solved:
> This is just why I slew nor her nor him,
> But called in law, law's delegate in the place,
> And bade arrest the guilty couple, Sirs!
> (V, 1114–1117)

It seems too absurd, but then Guido's absurdity has been fully
established, and this so far turns things around in his own mind
that he quickly readjusts his mask and proceeds as if no one
had seen the crisis but himself. He accuses Caponsacchi and
Pompilia of the seedy motives that would have moved him in
language that is a mirror of himself, reducing her heroic resistance and the intuitive recognition of it by the onlookers to
a "playhouse scene" from a cheap melodrama. As his climactic
effort at diversion from the truth, he falls back mechanically
on the forged love letters, which are his own compositions, and
reels off their false filth in stereotyped clichés like a gramo-
phone.

Despite the thorough deflation of all Guido's pretensions to
honor effected in this scene, the grimness of its revelation is
suspended in an atmosphere of comic absurdity. We know what
the consequences will be. Guido will be executed, but the wife
he maligns so callously is at this same instant dying of the
wounds he inflicted on her, though he had defended these same
actions to the same Court without particular injury to himself
and without saving her and her foster parents from his dagger. The poet, we know, had all this in mind, because that is
the plot he is using to interpret reality and to suggest a unifying perspective on it. We recognize the aesthetic category in
which the poet is working: he is establishing a precarious equipoise between the tragic and the comedic views of life by making the difference between the tragic grotesque and the comic
grotesque essentially moot. But while such labeling is a useful
result of literary observation and analysis, we have to carry

judgment beyond a precise description of what is happening literarily to why it is happening. What imaginative intuition shapes or is shaped by these literary events? What is the all-enveloping perception that justifies suspending such awful grimness in an imaginative medium of comic absurdity?

The part that Pompilia plays both in this particular scene and in *The Ring and the Book* as a whole clearly shows that the twentieth-century artistic use of the absurd—human life has no comprehensible meaning, we are all spinning around like particles of dust in a whirlwind—is not that enveloping perception, though the viewpoint itself is vividly suggested as a real-case possibility from which the poem ultimately turns away. On the other hand, the reassuring sentiments expressed by Pompilia in her state of transcendent exhilaration at the climax of her monologue—which may be seen as the proposition to which complete absurdity is the anti-proposition—cannot be taken as that enveloping perception either, though to see it or the Pope's mediation of it in that way has been the overwhelming tendency of the commentators. Like complete absurdity, it is a viewpoint that cannot be ignored, but all the poem's pluralism of persons and perceptions contradicts the notion of adopting one person and one person's perception as the poetic solution offered by Browning. This is simply too monistic and mechanical—both too Guido-like *and* too Papal—to be imagination's way. Moreover, this particular episode at Castelnuovo is such a touchstone scene throughout the poem and places such a high premium on process that poetic coherence would seem to demand that process itself be an inherent dimension of any enveloping perception the poem might be said to offer.

The second half of Guido's monologue (V, 1163–2058) is quite different from the first half and does not require the same unit-by-unit explicatory scrutiny. There is the same voice, the same duplicity of intent, ineptness of figure, incompetence of strategy; and his final arrogant analogy with God-the-Father has its counterpart in the equally arrogant analogy with God-the-Son with which he began. However, the level of Guido's rhetoric undergoes a subtle change. He tries to cover up the awful revelation at the center of his monologue, but his rhetoric never again rises to the level of absurdly inflated artificiality with which he tries frantically to gain control after the terrible self-abasement of that revelation has shaped itself in language:

> Are eunuchs, women, children, shieldless quite
> Against attack their own timidity tempts?
> Cowardice were misfortune and no crime!
> —Take it that way, since I am fallen so low
> I scarce dare brush the fly that blows my face,
> And thank the man who simply spits not there. . . .
>
> (V, 1099–1104)

It takes nothing away from what was said above about this passage—that Guido is spasming desperately for a footing in the mud and grasps the least straw as though it were a divine inspiration—to say too that through the horror of being found irredeemably foul by the world there comes, faint but sure, the even greater horror of self-discovery, of perceiving if only vaguely that that is indeed the awful truth of himself. Guido does not have a Marlow as Mr. Kurtz does in Conrad's *Heart of Darkness,* and he is not prepared to say " 'The horror, the horror' " outright, but there is a suggestion in the imagery and tone he uses in this passage and in the reaction he goes through immediately afterwards that something very like it momentarily takes place.

It was a very delicate thing for the poet to attempt, and it has far-reaching implications for *The Ring and the Book* as a whole. Browning had to avoid at all costs allowing the character of Guido, archrepresentative of the most pernicious human forces, to collapse into the sentimentality of an easy metamorphosis that would contradict the meticulous care with which he had developed him and the massive presence he had assumed. The poet is neither a Manichaean like the Pope nor a vacuous sentimentalist like Other Half-Rome. In Guido, he had created a man, not a monster, as in Pompilia he had created a woman, not a cherub or an angel or a fanciful clone of the Virgin. The validity of the poem's fulfillment of its fundamental promise as an honest portrait of men and women struggling with real forces in the real world demanded it. In

Guido and Pompilia, those forces get their quintessential concentration, and the poem's honesty is lost to the degree that they are only symbols of irreconcilable Good and Evil, not real men and women.

Everything about them does not need to be textbook clear to be real (mystery is as much a part of life as is knowledge), but they have to interconnect at an organic level. The fact that they interconnect brutally at the physical level is a chief significance of Pompilia's pregnancy. We believe that the intercourse was for her a horrid experience, but it was also the key to her redemption and ultimate magnification; without the promise of motherhood, we are told, she would have despaired and committed suicide. While the moral or psychological interconnection need not come to term in Guido in the way Pompilia's pregnancy comes to term, evidence was needed that he had undergone her influence at the core of his being, and that evidence is what surfaces faintly but unmistakably in this central passage of his monologue. His very phrasing, "an alacrity to put to proof/At my own throat my own sword, teach me so/To try conclusions better the next time—" (V, 1123–1125), is a recognition of the "proof" that he has been operating all along on false "conclusions," that Pompilia has risen to a moral mastery of life while he has "fallen so low" as finally to be able to see, at least vaguely, what she truly is. Obviously, Guido is going to fight such a recognition tooth and claw since he does not have the moral or psychological strength to live with it; coming at this moment in his fabricated life, it points toward a grim conclusion for which he also lacks the strength, namely, to kill himself. He will die, of course, but miserably, not nobly by the sword of the pagan he will claim to be. But this is the beginning of a new question for Guido and thus the beginning of a new narrative curve, both of which lead inevitably to his second monologue and neither of which will be concluded until, having had his last word, he loses the head he has been trying so incompetently to save. That question is this: having had a glimpse of the "true truth" of Pompilia and of himself—that is, having seen two interconnected but vastly different ways of apprehending and conducting life and what they have respectively come to—how does he deal with that recognition? Like

Caponsacchi and the Pope, Guido has undergone the influence of Pompilia in spite of himself and to his total surprise; like them, he must come to terms with that revelation in his own individual way.

Guido returns to his narrative from a state of disconcerted abstraction: "Ah, the Court! yes, I come to the Court's self" (V, 1163), and it takes him a few seconds to recollect himself while he merely mouths phrases already used, concluding with a pitifully brave show of spirit and wit. But Guido never recovers the old individuality, as disgusting and despicable as it was. The motif that runs through his defense is that of stoical resignation to a situation deteriorating on every front. Of course, we are scarcely inclined to credit him with sincerity in this latest posture of the humble man beaten to his knees by a relentlessly inimical "fate." It is too clearly the pose of a practiced poseur and too clearly the outcome of the failure of his own dishonest machinations, including his failure to measure his opponents correctly or to believe even in the remnant workings of the machinery of justice. Still, it is clear that his defense has reached a Parnassian level—morally, psychologically, and idiomatically characteristic but no longer enlivened with his distinctive originality and verve, no longer "inspired."

The sequence in which Guido attempts to rekindle his old competitive spirit is barometric (V, 1483–1549). His claim that he "rose up like fire, and fire-like roared" upon hearing of Pompilia's delivery of a child has a characteristic touch, as does his presumption of a voice from his Nature-God calling him to a higher morality: *"Quis est pro Domino?"* But the inner debate by which he moves between these two points has a new undertone of pathos far more fascinating than the bravado that frames it. He is caught between two sets of strenuously conflicting ideas. One is the wholly familiar and attractive idea of having fathered an heir, on the one hand, and, on the other, the compelling strategic need to write the child off as "the priest's bastard and none of mine!" The other is another version of his strong sense of belatedness: the child that he had "died to see though in a dream" is born at a time to inherit, not a noble name, but the mark of Cain on his forehead. Both ideas have about them, besides the usual duplicity, a touch of the might-have-been, of natural regret and pathos, and this new note gets into the language and gives it resonances quite Shakespearean.

> What, all is only beginning not ending now?
> The worm which wormed its way from skin through flesh
> To the bone and there lay biting, did its best,
> What, it goes on to scrape at the bone's self,
> Will wind to inmost marrow and madden me?
> There's to be yet my representative,
> Another of the name shall keep displayed
> The flag with the ordure on it, brandish still
> The broken sword has served to stir a jakes?
> Who will he be, how will you call the man?
> A Franceschini,—when who cut my purse,
> Filched my name, hemmed me round, hustled me hard
> As rogues at a fair some fool they strip i' the midst,
> When these count gains, vaunt pillage presently:—
> But a Caponsacchi, oh, be very sure!
>
> (V, 1484–1498)

It is a poetic alteration of some consequence, and it can be traced to the lingering influence of that earlier moment of revelation.

This low-grade tension continues to affect Guido's account of gathering his accomplices, going to Rome, spending nine days in his brother's deserted house, making the final decision, obtaining entry, committing the triple murder, and being overtaken on the road back to Tuscany. His habits of willfulness are too ingrained, his propulsion toward self-destruction too far developed, to be any longer subject to personal choice or for the faint undercurrent of conscience to deflect him from the inevitable action. But the current is there nonetheless:

> I have no memory of our way,
> Only that, when at intervals the cloud
> Of horror about me opened to let in life,
> I listened to some song in the ear, some snatch
> Of a legend, relic of religion, stray

> Fragment of record very strong and old
> Of the first conscience, the anterior right,
> The God's-gift to mankind, impulse to quench
> The antagonistic spark of hell and tread
> Satan and all his malice into dust,
> Declare to the world the one law, right is right.
> Then the cloud re-encompassed me. . . .
>
> (V, 1568–1579)

> day by day, joy waned and withered off:
> The Babe's face, premature with peak and pine,
> Sank into wrinkled ruinous old age,
> Suffering and death, then mist-like disappeared,
> And showed only the Cross at end of all,
> Left nothing more to interpose, 'twixt me
> And the dread duty. . . .
>
> (V, 1602–1608)

> There was the end!
> Then was I rapt away by the impulse, one
> Immeasurable everlasting wave of a need
> To abolish that detested life. 'T was done:
> You know the rest and how the folds o' the thing,
> Twisting for help, involved the other two
> More or less serpent-like: how I was mad,
> Blind, stamped on all, the earth-worms with the asp,
> And ended so.
>
> (V, 1661–1669)

This is not a reformed Guido by any means. He is like an alcoholic who, despite the recognition that alcohol is destroying him, has from long abuse lost the choice to drink and suffers from a compulsion from which he no longer derives any pleasure. As Hopkins says in the poem quoted in the title of this chapter, the damned are like that—only worse, and Guido has begun to feel less remorse than the haunting, inchoate fear, the vague polluting pain, of the would-be master who is half-aware that he has become the helpless slave of his own mastery. This is not to excuse him in any sense; he did it to himself. Moreover, one can argue that he has earned society's ultimate reprisal a thousand times over. Still, it does put the question of responsibility for the triple murder into a different context and thereby reasserts the larger question of responsibility that pervades the whole poem. If Guido, even as the result of disgusting and despicable actions, has finally lost control of his actions, is he to be held responsible for a particular act though it be the most disgusting and despicable act of all? The fact that one may see the question as outrageous even on the face of it does not mean that the question is illegitimate unless one is willing to move the idea of "just deserts" back several centuries, like the Pope, to the "Vigil-torture" and the readier justice of the Middle Ages. More shocking to some readers' sensibilities will be the doubly ironic recognition that, had Guido not undergone the influence of Pompilia, neither *his* temporary distress of spirit nor *our* distress over the issue of responsibility would have taken on this distressing aspect.

Having got through his apologia, his defense with its confessional subtext, Guido shifts tone again. "But now," he says, "Health is returned, and *sanity of soul*/Nowise indifferent to the body's harm" (V, 1739–1741, emphasis added). It is as clear a confirmation of the truth of what has been said above as any poet can be expected to give. The animal instinct of survival now takes over, an instinct that has been severely threatened by the "conscience [that] doth make cowards of us all" in a way quite different from the cowardice of the "poltroon," and Guido becomes his old incorrigible self. His ego reinflates, his clumsy wit revives, he tries to out-adjudicate his judges, he dismisses what "the world calls cowardice" as a "prodigy of patience," and, with the vulgar mentality of a sea-lawyer, he transforms his role as triple murderer into that of "law's mere executant" who needs no defense except that which law gives to its own defenders (V, 1745–2025). In an unctuous peroration, he equates his acquittal with the beginning of social utopia, the restoration of male domination with the panacea for all social diseases and dislocations, and draws an analogy between the return of his son to him and the return of God-the-Son to his seat at the "right hand" of God-the-Father.

Again one is reminded of the classic pattern of the alcoholic: once the crisis is passed, the old pattern of self-destructive arrogance reasserts itself with progressive virulence. The terror of recognition changes, as if by magic, to a fantasy of triumph.

Notes

1. Gerard Manley Hopkins, *I Wake and Feel the Fell of Dark*, ll. 13–14.
2. Robert Langbaum, *The Poetry of Experience* (New York: Random House, 1957), p. 110.
3. Richard D. Altick and James F. Loucks II, *Browning's Roman Murder Story* (Chicago: University of Chicago Press, 1968), p. 52.

5.

Near-Havoc in the Heart: Book VI. *Giuseppe Caponsacchi*

It would surely be critically disturbing to think that a poet of the seriousness and stature Browning has assumed by the time we reach the end of Book V of *The Ring and the Book* would, in a poem of epic dimensions, suddenly leap from "an incarnation of evil" to "the highest in manliness and courage"[1] with no facilitating gradations in-between. That would diffuse good and evil so completely as to call into question both the seriousness and the stature of the poet and would leave even the sympathetic reader confused and incredulous. Langbaum, who makes such a leap, concedes that it "is certainly a valid criticism of *The Ring and the Book* that good and evil are not sufficiently interfused."[2] Fortunately, however, the poet rather than the critic is in charge of his subject, and Browning's passage from a human failure that is precariously close to complete in Guido to a human success that is exhilaratingly close to complete in Pompilia is through a character who is not only well advanced in self-pollution but who clings to the self-redemption that is offered him in a deeply divided way. So far is Caponsacchi from being "the highest in manliness and courage" that even at the end he is not quite reconciled to the price he has had to pay for moral maturity and faces life as a joyless prospect that only the austerest stoicism can make endurable. It is critically disproportionate to say that Caponsacchi's "action . . . is the pivot of the whole drama"[3] since in that he is subordinate to Pompilia, but in himself he embodies a large and sufficient interfusion of good and evil, and in the poem's architecture his monologue supplies the appropriate elevation, both moral and structural, away from a potential if distant Guido toward a potential if distant Pompilia.

The righteous anger with which Caponsacchi begins his monologue, though much celebrated, deserves a great deal more critical consideration than as a contrast to the obsequiousness with which Guido has conducted himself in the previous monologue. That anger has complex roots and is a major signal to the reader of one of the chief ingredients in Caponsacchi's sense of himself. Emotion is a controlling current of the self that, with a mixture of success and failure, he is attempting to image forth, both to himself and to others. We know that Caponsacchi has been rusticated for six months after playing the part of a romantic hero (priest turned cavalier turned St. George), and during that time his resentment toward these "judges" who were so blind to his stunning performance has had time to fester. Though he has not actually broken his vows, perhaps, it is clear that he has entertained private fantasies of wife, hearth, and child—has *imagined* himself married to Pompilia—and since these fantasies have been brutally foreshortened by her murder, he can convert guilt to wrath with a vengeance—and impunity. There is also some portion of whistling in the dark. Though he has learned a great lesson, he has also suffered a ghastly disappointment for which he cannot wholly blame external forces—Guido, for example, or the judges or the system. So, as we gradually learn, he is not nearly so sure as he seems to assert and is compensating for fear with a measure of bravado. Anger is very close to lust, often surfaces as a form of lust or as a strategy leading to lustful gratification, but in a priest it is much more respectable than lust. In fact, it is well precedented in the Old Testament, which gave up pagan lust

but retained pagan vengeance until that, too, was modified by
the New Testament. And if one can call his anger righteous,
then one can exercise it publicly with impunity and with some
expectation of applause. Also, as we finally learn, Caponsacchi
faces a future without joy, and that dreary prospect is enough
to make him rage against his fate, even though *fate* is not the
direct metaphor he chooses to employ. He is raging against the
light as much as he is carrying the torch of passionate truth,
cursing the price he knows he has to pay and, in the end, will
pay.

It is not to "his priestly vows and the true meaning of Christianity" that Caponsacchi is "recalled."[4] In fact, he isn't simply
"recalled" to anything. He is drawn into a voyage of moral and
metaphysical discovery, of imaginative illumination, that makes
him tragically sober but minimally reconciled to an unroman-
tic, dutiful humanity of which the priesthood and Christianity
are temperamental, familial, cultural "accidents." Caponsacchi
undergoes, under Pompilia's tutelage, a profound metamorphosis of the human spirit for which the "filthy rags of speech,"
even to a man of education, seriousness, and social privilege,
are grossly inadequate. He can rise to admirable rhetorical
firmness, as when his anger fuels the sarcasm of contempt, but
in the face of the insight borne by Pompilia he is a rhetorical
stammerer. Then he falls back on phrases and analogies that
only half reveal what he is feeling and inevitably muddle the
reader's mind with ambivalent conclusions about him. He has
no language to designate precisely feelings of a quality quite
new to his experience. Of the language of Mariolatry and of
the language of Meg and Moll he has some mastery, but of the
language of the lady with "the beautiful sad strange smile" he
knows almost nothing. His monologue is a living laboratory for
the creation of such a language, and even at the end he is hardly
accomplished at it. He is like a monk who has reentered the
world and has to create a whole new vocabulary to meet his
present needs.

Giuseppe Maria Caponsacchi—even the name is ambiguous,
as ambiguous as the role Caponsacchi, in compensation for the
ambiguity of his past, is required to play. He is to be the ambiguous husband-consort of "the glory, . . . beauty, . . . and

splendour" of life (VI, 120–121), the ambiguous nonfather at the ambiguous virgin birth. He must forever touch with his soul, never fondle with his body; Pompilia is to be ever "in [his] eyes and ears and brain and heart" (192), but never in his bed. That is the ambiguous mastery of self that he must achieve, a love that reaches a "celibate state" without ever passing through a corporeal union. He must be reborn a virgin of her soul-virginity, be immaculately reconceived.

Caponsacchi had spent "three or four years" at his priestly playacting before the onset of Pompilia. These are the same years she had spent learning the ghastliness of evil while he was learning the light frivolity of religion. They had also listened to very different kinds of rhetoric, his of the sort exemplified by the Bishop who had overcome his scruples about ordination (VI, 273–335) and the episcopal patron who had advised him on the best way to get preferment (VI, 353–392). Caponsacchi and Pompilia are alike in that they had discovered in very different ways, the one harsh and relentless, the other velvety and relentless, how counterfeit are the careers their cultures have held out to them, the Church and marriage. And they share a common bond of disillusionment with the vows they have made to falsehood. His first sight of Pompilia, reinforced by the tale Conti frames her in, works like yeast in his spirit, giving his customary religious responses the excitement of high Renaissance art. Raphael uncased becomes a metaphor for the sudden vision of Pompilia; he stops the silly faddist pretense that "Marino" is a better poet than Dante; he is drawn again to the Duomo by the joy of watching " 'the day's last gleam outside/Turn, as into a skirt of God's own robe,/Those lancet-windows' jewelled miracle . . .' " (VI, 460–462). For the first time, too, he finds an authentic tongue. He rebukes his patron, speaks honestly of his soul's deprivation, and declares his intention to " 'go to Rome' " to embark on a journey of authentic self-discovery.

The *Summa* of Thomas Aquinas symbolizes the codified, disengaged orthodoxy that has been Caponsacchi's religious reference point during his priestly career; now, however, he begins to feel the private stirrings of "liberation theology," Romanticism's conversion of faith to service.

One evening I was sitting in a muse
Over the opened 'Summa', darkened round
By the mid-March twilight, thinking how my life
Had shaken under me,—broke short indeed
And showed the gap 'twixt what is, what should be,—
And into what abysm the soul may slip,
Leave aspiration here, achievement there,
Lacking omnipotence to connect extremes—
Thinking moreover . . . oh, thinking, if you like,
How utterly dissociated was I
A priest and celibate, from the sad strange wife
Of Guido,—just as an instance to the point,
Nought more,—how I had a whole store of strengths
Eating into my heart, which craved employ,
And she, perhaps, need of a finger's help,—
And yet there was no way in the wide world
To stretch out mine and so relieve myself—
How when the page o' the Summa preached its best,
Her smile kept glowing out of it, as to mock
The silence we could break by no one word. . . .
                                        (VI, 483–502)

What is acceptable in this passage—what is *made* acceptable by the language in which it is said—is the spiritual recognition it describes. It is, we feel, a fair representation of the romantic sadness of that young man who had had religious scruples about taking priestly vows and who had allowed himself to be guided by ecclesiastical authority into both taking and mocking the vows he took. We feel, too, the authenticity of the connection he draws between his situation and the situation of all failed idealists—"Leave aspiration here, achievement there,/Lacking omnipotence to connect extremes." Knowledge of the world and of our own histories makes the recognition thus worded luminously valid, as luminous, for example, as Caponsacchi's and Pompilia's instantaneous recognition of the truth of each other and as valid as their elective affinity or soul-mating. And since no serious critic ever reads a poem, but is engaged in a perpetual process of rereading it, we recognize the coherence between this, Caponsacchi's first crucial insight, and his last, "O great, just, good God! Miserable me!" (VI, 2105). Impotence to some degree in all things is the universal condition of man, and we identify with Caponsacchi's weakness. Since it is under Pompilia's influence that he accepts the fact of his life's precarious misdirection, we can believe that, unless he loses his way among the misty feelings that are so strong a current of himself, Caponsacchi will find in Pompilia a way to a vulnerable redemption. Thus his is the exemplary dramatic role of a man of genuine aspiration crippled by the thoroughly human tendency to confuse two quite different manifestations of romantic feeling and to grasp at the lower form because of the very austerity of the higher. Like Guinevere in Tennyson's *Idylls of the King,* Caponsacchi's weakness is his inclination to accept a self-myth inferior to the one of which he is capable, and only Pompilia can teach him what only Arthur could teach Guinevere, namely, that "the highest" is "the most human too."

It is given to Caponsacchi to dramatize and explicate the "forged" love letters, thus further emphasizing his role as a language man. Being a trained scholastic who has for the past several years daily practiced the art of trafficking in the language of insincerity, he is adept at its detection. Of course, the love letters' authenticity is crucial to our view of the exact nature of the relationship between Pompilia and Caponsacchi and therefore integral to the poem's plot or physical story line. But it is also integral to the poet's pursuit of his characters' spiritual patterns, the unconscious but identifiable structures by which people attempt to create or resolve relationships with the world. This invests plot with a different content and shows how the body and the soul of the poem are themselves integrated.

In his presentation of the letter sequence to the Court, Caponsacchi's method is to give in order examples of the letter received, the letter returned, and the strategy he intended in replying in just the way he did. There is much ambiguity in the way he words his replies, and his explanation to the Court is that the letters he received were transparently false and the replies he sent were careful calculations to tease the conspirators, whom he spotted as false but dull, into a frenzy of confusion, each successive reply seeming to reflect a higher degree both of resistance and seduction and each subsequent epistolary overture becoming more unguardedly vulgar in its sentiments and more patently false in its style. Thus Caponsacchi's own method has its double aspect—maybe true, maybe false—and this had originally prompted one of the judges to ask with a benign sneer, " 'What if she wrote the letters?' " We do not know what Caponsacchi's original reply to this question was, but now he hits home with an analogy that is itself luridly dramatic and patently vulgar. If a "low-browed verger" showed him a scorpion transfixed on a point and said that it had issued from the mouth of Raphael's Madonna, he would reply that the verger's soul had left his body by way of his buttocks.

Such a climax to the love-letter sequence certainly shows the fervor with which Caponsacchi holds to Pompilia's heavenly purity, but it also reveals a good deal more about him than he intends or is even conscious of. Both his ego strength and his self-image have considerably improved since his first appearance before this same Court. In his ruminations at Civita, he has apparently processed both the events and his first formal account of the events. In that reprocessing, he has touched up his script in a manner at least faintly suggestive of Archangeli's monologue and has added stage directions and histrionics not altogether alien to Bottini's. In fact, judged by this analogy of the Madonna and the verger, he has become more dramaturgical than sensitive, careless alike of the feelings of the judge who had asked a reasonable if ironic question and of the implications for Pompilia of having such an advocate as himself.

Such analogies with Archangeli and Bottini, though subtle and distant, are important. Without in any sense demeaning Caponsacchi to their level, they teach us to see him as he in fact is. Though the "gap 'twixt what is, what should be" is not so wide in his case as in theirs, it is the same gap, and they provide implicit glosses on the end to which it can lead. We do not have in Caponsacchi a romantic hero to be easily and romantically fulfilled, but a human being with as much potentiality for ugliness and evil as they show. His life is at a precarious point, and his habits of compromise and self-pollution are real. There is a genuine portion of honesty and truth in his commentary on the letters received and sent, but there may be a significant portion of dishonesty and self-deception in it too, and the "spot of commonness" in Caponsacchi's makeup revealed by this lurid illustration of the Madonna and the verger shows to what ludicrous extremes his sensibility, puffed up and undirected, can lead.

Ironically, Caponsacchi's second appearance before the Court, though he takes a great deal of angry advantage of it, pouring into the occasion much exaggerated self-righteousness of the I-told-you-so kind, is in a sense the crux of such personal salvation as he achieves. Obviously, chewing his cud at Civita had redeemed nothing but his self-inflation. The climactic catastrophe had not taken place, and his deflation by the Court had merely made him feel abused, like a grossly devalued St. George. The brutality of the triple murder has brought about a change of kind that he has chosen to see as a difference of degree only, a mere confirmation, so to speak, of what he had told the Court six months ago, when in fact he had told the Court no such thing. He had, at that time, "cut the conscious figure of a fool,/Changed countenance, dropped bashful gaze to ground,/While hesitating for an answer" (I, 1064–1066). He does not fake the passion, but his manifest anger at and contempt for the judges is latent anger and contempt for himself; his self-righteousness is the hurt ego's mask for self-depreciation and self-pity. It is Caponsacchi's bulwark against despair; and it works, giving his severely soiled idealism a chance to work through the rubble of himself and discover a sufficient if awful truth. Thus by designating him an amicus curiae, the Court enables him to save his soul—to resist and overcome a self-strangulating pathos and reach, to a minimum but sufficient degree, the self-strengthening truth of Pompilia, of himself, and of the world in which he must now "Do out the duty" (VII, 1843). Though Pompilia is his tragic catalyst and avenue of grace, the Court provides the indispensable occasion. They give him a formal opportunity *to speak,* and that is the process of clarification he needs. They mirror back to him his own gross weakness, and through a network of responses that run the gamut of contrition, humiliation, rejection, condemnation, and empathy, they help him toward a degree of conscientiousness and wisdom that, though they cannot relieve his burden of sadness, enable him to become adequately reconciled to it. Caponsacchi's speech corrects the past, and while it does not guarantee the future, it gives him a degree of faith in it; the actual saying of it, its conversion into language, is the metaphoric evidence he needs to reinvigorate his own and reality's authenticity.

It is perhaps impossible to say just how much whistling in the dark there is in Caponsacchi's first approach to Pompilia's abode; that there is a good deal is suggested by the blatant braggadocio with which his language is laden (VI, 683–690, 691–700, 710–720). That mild form of self-deception is reinforced by Caponsacchi's rationalization of why he went to the house in the first place. He not only gives his high-minded intention in a low-minded figure—to serve Madonna by "making clowns/Remove their dung-heap from the sacristy" (VI, 681–682); he also makes no concession to the part infatuation plays in it, and this makes us suspicious. Since we cannot quite believe him, we have to think that either he is self-deceived or is attempting to deceive the Court. Thus we are inevitably reminded of Guido's earlier monologue, and the advantage accruing to Caponsacchi's new voice begins to weaken. He is not, we discover, quite the breath of fresh air we thought he was.

Another, more startling discrepancy is that between Caponsacchi's account of Pompilia's first words to him (VI, 725–880) and her account of the same event (VII, 1418–1442). The two accounts vary dramatically in both length and content. Pompilia makes no claim to reporting her words precisely ("whatever the phrase") and gives the gist, in reconstructed dialogue, as asserting her *faith* in him as God's instrument to exercise his priestly *caring* in helping her escape from the imminent danger of being "put to death" in the *hope* of saving her unborn child. Caponsacchi, on the other hand, makes no concessions to inexactness of fact or phrase, though in his fabricated version, he imposes on Pompilia a mini-autobiography, a potpourri of everything he knows or has surmised about her, a torrent of impassioned, semihysterical feelings, facts, rationalizations, and interpretations that, if actually poured out so unreservedly in their first encounter, might well make one doubt her emotional stability if not her sanity. It has the character of a script composed in solitude and nervously delivered in public for the first time. Nothing in Pompilia's own monologue is rhetorically anything like it; it corresponds in no way to the lucidity of her vision or the clarity of her phrase. It huddles into one undisciplined gush of words all the main lineaments of her own history, along with her explicatory commentary, and a full exposure of his personal reasons for self-guilt and self-exoneration. In short, it tells the Court, not what Pompilia actually said, but how he feels about what she said and would also like for them to feel. There is even a blatant contradiction at its center: in the very act of telling Caponsacchi that she will never tell about the shameful actions of "the young idle priest," she in fact tells him.

Once again, the language is made a crucial criterion of the truth of Caponsacchi, and another marker is established by which his progress can be specifically measured. He does not yet know her, and only as he begins to understand the privileged revelation that she embodies will he be able to undergo her influence and receive her law at a level of redemptive significance. Moreover, it seems fair to take this imaginary account of Pompilia's first speech to him as an oblique caution to the reader. As she is not to be judged adequately by such a voluble if generally right-minded fuzz of words, what the poet is doing being much more austerely honed linguistically and much more processively staged dramatically, so we in turn may miss more than we gain by dressing the significance of Caponsacchi in a loose garment of well-intentioned language that not only leaves him individually ill-defined but also dissipates all the poet's imaginative meticulousness in a vague array of language that, even if it happens to be right in its general drift, grossly devalues the care and precision with which poetry at its best, like science at its best, does its finest work and upon which it depends for its transformational impact.

Though Caponsacchi does not yet understand the revelation of Pompilia (did not understand it in the face of the event itself, had not penetrated it on the occasion of his first appearance before the Court, has yet to learn it even at this point in his monologue), her influence is being felt. It is reflected in the new note of sobriety his language begins to assume—in his revision of the Madonna-scorpion simile (VI, 909–917) and in such delicate, lucid, and economical tropes as the following:

> Pompilia spoke, and I at once received,
> Accepted my own fact, my miracle
> Self-authorised and self-explained. . . .
> (VI, 918–920)

> "As I
> Recognised her, at potency of truth,
> So she, by the crystalline soul, knew me,
> Never mistook the signs."
> (VI, 931–934)

But this moment of "crystalline" illumination does not last and is never again recovered with the preternatural clarity that Caponsacchi assigns to it. He does not become an instant saint, and the old ambiguities again assert themselves. They make their reapproach in the most ingratiating guise, of course, and the passage in which Caponsacchi recreates his metamorphosis-ecstasy is one of the most lyrically impassioned and sensuously captivating in the whole poem.

> I put forth no thought,—powerless, all that night
> I paced the city: it was the first Spring.
> By the invasion I lay passive to,
> In rushed new things, the old were rapt away;
> Alike abolished—the imprisonment
> Of the outside air, the inside weight o' the world
> That pulled me down. Death meant, to spurn the ground,
> Soar to the sky,—die well and you do that.
> The very immolation made the bliss;
> Death was the heart of life, and all the harm
> My folly had crouched to avoid, now proved a veil
> Hiding all gain my wisdom strove to grasp:
> As if the intense centre of the flame
> Should turn a heaven to that devoted fly
> Which hitherto, sophist alike and sage,

Saint Thomas with his sober grey goose-quill,
And sinner Plato by Cephisian reed,
Would fain, pretending just the insect's good,
Whisk off, drive back, consign to shade again.
Into another state, under new rule
I knew myself was passing swift and sure;
Whereof the initiatory pang approached,
Felicitous annoy, as bitter-sweet
As when the virgin-band, the victors chaste,
Feel at the end the earthly garments drop,
And rise with something of a rosy shame
Into immortal nakedness: so I
Lay, and let come the proper throe would thrill
Into the ecstacy and outthrob pain.

(VI, 945–973)

It is more than a renascence; it is "the first spring" of which all later springs are mere approximations and copies, mere repetitions of renewals that can never equal the wholly new order that the initial spring established. It outstrips the most delicate promises of the most inspired idealists—the pagan Plato and the Christian Thomas alike—admitting the very metaphors ("that devoted fly," for example) that their imaginations rejected. It abolishes old things and furnishes the world entirely anew; all former fears become veiled opportunities and death the gateway to life. It is a glorious vision of a glorious state, but it is not quite as beatific as it seems.

It is an intense rendition, a description gracefully veiled, of the ecstasy of lost virginity, a verbal enactment of the "initiatory pang," the torn hymen, the passivity to invasion, the suspended moment, and the "little death" of the virginal experience of sexual union and fulfillment in which Caponsacchi is cast in the female role: "so I/Lay, and let come the proper throe would thrill/Into the ecstacy and outthrob pain."

The unmistakable sexual analogue is not, in any sense, a devaluation of the experience he intends to celebrate. Religion, especially the Christian religion, habitually uses sexual analogies to clarify its most sacred rituals, and it is refreshing to witness frankness rather than coyness on Caponsacchi's part. It might even be considered prurient to notice that the authority of detail with which he celebrates the sex act is surprising in a vowed celibate who has insisted that his social playfulness has been kept within proper priestly bounds. There are, however, three disquieting elements in the performance that are not entirely disguised by its admitted magnificence. First, Caponsacchi's casting of himself in the female role is distantly suggestive of the hint Guido gives that his sexual appetite is stimulated by an aggressive woman assuming the dominant role. Second, Caponsacchi's magnification of his personal ecstasy, though generously intended, is nevertheless self-inflationary, and its unmistakable sexual overtones may seem unserviceable to his efforts to prove that his relationship with Pompilia was entirely asexual. Finally, the next phase of his presumably spiritual history has so clear an analogy in postcoital depression that his analysis of it as purely a conflict of two appearances of conscientiousness becomes suspect against this strong sexual backdrop. While there is nothing conclusive about any one or even all of these elements, they are disturbing and keep our judgment of Caponsacchi in solution while strengthening our determination to keep watching him with great care.

That next phase—"I' the grey dawn"—though brief and lower-pitched, is a little masterpiece of quietly deflationary irony in which the technique the poet uses on his self-romanticizing "hero" is well illustrated. The technique is the establishment of an implicit distance between the persona's point of view and the poet's. It is a common species of dramatic irony, but though common, it is uncommonly well done, creating around Caponsacchi an atmosphere of genial wryness. Even if we credit him with full sincerity in his view of the matter, accepting without quibble that he sees it just as he says he does, we are still struck with the measurable degree of his blindness and begin to question, not his honesty or sincerity per se, but the quality of his honesty and thus of his competence to be sincere. This in turn suggests another subtle analogy with Guido, one of the most incompetent villains in literature, and raises a slight but haunting question about the real differences between them.

Caponsacchi traces a high-minded pattern in this two-day period of emotional recoil in rather highfalutin language. The

Church that had seemed so permissive and with which he had established so comfortable a relationship suddenly changes tone, now pleading with the connubial voice of " 'the Bride, the mystic love/O' the Lamb' " (VI, 977–978), now warning with the ominous voice of the grave, " 'Leave that live passion, come be dead with me!' " (VI, 1001). Having sated himself with "hips and haws," he finally discovers the apple of "perfect gold" only to discover too "the seven-fold dragon's watch" (VI, 1002–1009). Since "the lady" has taught him the "first authoritative word," then he must have the higher courage to obey, not the lady, but God (VI, 1010–1021). The very pull of the lady's call proves it to be temptation, pride arrogating to itself the presumption of being God's singular instrument (VI, 1028–1033). If the risk of sin were only mine, I'd do it; but I must not expose *her* to sin (VI, 1036–1039). It would be too horrible, though, if she thought me paralyzed by fear! No, she couldn't believe that; God wouldn't let her (VI, 1040–1048). So far I have been dutiful; that is wise (VI, 1049–1054). Still, it is a priest's duty to " 'counsel, comfort' "; so I'll go " 'counsel, comfort' " (VI, 1055–1062).

Caponsacchi, like Guido, resembles an alcoholic fighting a drink he knows, after a short period of self-harrowing, he is going to take. Therefore, he isolates himself, seeking no outside help. Also, he complicates the matter superficially rather than profoundly, putting a respectable number of obstacles in his way, but none that he cannot brush aside at will, having one large magic wand in reserve—his will. He does not want to be cured, only exercised. He refuses to acknowledge and deal with the erotic component in his response; he mythicizes the Church because it is so easy to reconfigurate his own myth; he defines fear in external images (the Archbishop, Count Guido) that stimulate feelings of defiance or courage; he rationalizes defeat into victory, victory into defeat. The issue here is not the desirability of the overall outcome; that is a larger, more encompassing irony. The issue is personal honesty, the level of genuine sincerity with which one confronts his dilemmas regardless of their fortunate or unfortunate result.

The gulf that separates Pompilia's and Caponsacchi's perceptions of reality is again pointed up in their respective accounts of her response to his failure to keep their engagement. According to her, there was "No pause i' the leading and the light!" When he failed to come the first night, she prayed, having left " 'God the way' " knowing she had " 'the will' " (VII, 1455, 1458–1461). In his account, she spent the two days " 'Breaking [her] heart' " and, upon his appearance at last, massages his resolution by making her very salvation wholly dependent on him: " 'shall I be saved or no?' " (VI, 1065–1073). That is the role he likes—to be both *the will* and *the way*—as he says to her, " 'Now follow me as I were fate!' " (VI, 1076). It is a role that, despite its need for cleansing, he plays well. It is the beginning of Caponsacchi's active phase, and he takes charge of his tongue as well as of logistics with a new directness and vigor. Even his exchange of Thomases—Aquinas for the converted Apostle—has a ready clarity and flair that are convincing.

Caponsacchi's redirection—his gradual movement from romantic self-deception and pathos toward a true tragic vision—is signaled by a change of tone and a pointing of the stages or structure through which he will pass on the way. Both occur simultaneously:

> So it began, our flight thro' dusk to clear,
> Through day and night and day again to night
> Once more, and to last dreadful dawn of all.
>   (VI, 1152–1154)

There is a new note of seriousness in Caponsacchi's voice, his metaphors assuming a character at once more solemn and more potentially sublime. Though the poet does not so mechanize his spiritual progress as to tie it literally to the rhythms of two days interspersed with two nights, he yet has alternating periods of darkness and illumination, and that "last . . . dawn of all" is made "dreadful" by Caponsacchi's first truly tragic recognition—that the marriage of good and evil, the twilight union of dark and day, is the terrifying truth of human reality in this, our earthly dispensation.

Caponsacchi prefaces his narrative of the journey that climaxes at Castelnuovo with a few remarks about his desperate need to speak. After alluding to the worldwide myth that souls whose reputations are treated unjustly cannot find peace even in the grave (VI, 1155–1162), he says, "Men,/You must know that a man gets drunk with truth/Stagnant inside him!" (VI, 1162–1164). It is a rich, even profound, remark mirroring the sagacity Caponsacchi has begun to distill from his experience. Although it is directed at the portion of his narrative he is about to relate, it inevitably glances back over what he has already told and, without altering it, reconciles us somewhat to its faults. It is his recognition that the perspective built up in his own mind during those months alone at Civita was a distempered fairy tale that has dissolved in the light of the catastrophe that has now taken place and that his narrative now has a wholly different character from his first deposition before the Court.[5]

The parable with which Caponsacchi describes his thoughts and feelings on the first dark leg of the journey (VI, 1183–1192) continues to reflect, in a subdued or remnant fashion, the view of a romantic adventurer. The conclusion he wishes to sustain—"You know this is not love, Sirs,—it is faith" (VI, 1193)—is not so luminously self-evident as he says it is. The parable, accepted as proof to himself that, as he says, " 'I have caught it, I conceive/The mind o' the mystery,' " is of two martyrs who, having been blessed in dying together, awake in the tomb and fearlessly wait " 'through the whole course of the world' " for the signal to arise, he being entirely content " 'because she lies too by my side.' " To die for love and to be content with entombment together until the end of time is Caponsacchi's romantic dream, not Pompilia's, who wishes to live until her life-giving mission is accomplished and then to join God. It is his way of sublimating the fear that he refuses to acknowledge and is to that degree a self-deception. Pompilia, on the other hand, knows how terrifying true suffering is, and she controls as best she can a mortal fear that she frankly acknowledges—even the fear that a sudden cessation of pain may be a proof of hopelessness rather than of hope (VI, 1216–1227).

Throughout the first day of the journey, Caponsacchi watches eagerly for some sign of affection returned by Pompilia and is acutely disappointed when she acknowledges only his official role as "kind" rescuer and "priestly" intercessor (VI, 1234, 1274). Pompilia, for her part, scrutinizes his every change of expression to find there the least sign for hope or fear. She takes note of his apparent strength and her own weakness, wondering aloud if, in the emotional economy, strength has its "drawback" as weakness has its. She has accepted Caponsacchi at his own self-estimate and is not judgmental when, in explaining his smile at the "great gate" of an ancient bishop's villa, he puffs himself as being on the cutting-edge of things, not an anachronism seeking patronage from an "obsolete" past (VI, 1249–1265), a faint but instructive analogy with the Pope's characterization of him as "the first experimentalist" (X, 1909).

Having pleaded with Caponsacchi to keep traveling through the second night, her countenance reflecting a profound anxiety—" 'Unless 't is you who fear,—which cannot be!' " (VI, 1290)—Pompilia comes very close to physical and emotional exhaustion. As a result, she begins the second day with a waking nightmare of Guido demanding her sexual favors. Then Caponsacchi does something profoundly ironic. This modern priest on the cutting-edge of religious time, this "first experimentalist," becomes a medieval exorcist casting out demons: " 'Let God arise and all his enemies/Be scattered!' " (VI, 1299–1303). It is a stunning contradiction, and it shows how fundamentally need dictates response in a desperate situation and how relative to the mental attitude of the user are such terms as *obsolete* and *anachronistic,* the common rituals so designated being born of need, not time.

When, later in the day, Pompilia awakens from a sleep of exhaustion, she seems startlingly indifferent to her arrival at the very destination toward which she has drawn herself so compulsively as to endanger her physical and mental health and the health of her unborn child:

> 'if it might but last!
> Always, my life-long, thus to journey still!
> It is the interruption that I dread,—
> With no dread, ever to be here and thus!
> Never to see a face nor hear a voice!
> Yours is no voice; you speak when you are dumb;
> Nor face, I see it in the dark. I want
> No face nor voice that change and grow unkind.'
>   (VI, 1311–1318)

It is a subtle, complex moment in the "journey" of them both, physically, mentally or emotionally, and spiritually. Pompilia is our first concern. She has reached a point of numbness in which only changelessness seems equivalent to peace. Stasis rather than buoyancy or exhilaration appears to be the charmed state of body, mind, and soul, the idea of change having coalesced with the idea of catastrophe. Subliminally, it has prophetic overtones: the journey's end, like the past, promises disillusion with promises, counterfeit joys, more tests of the spirit than the spirit feels it can endure. The waking nightmare is the predictive metaphor: "No worst, there is none"[6] and since the worst is yet to be, how sweet it were to cling forever to what by comparison is so fair, the voiceless, faceless, seemingly benign present.[7] This illusion has, of course, a dark underbelly, the anxiety it is meant to mask being the reality it foreshadows. But we know that is only a temporary condition: as Pompilia has not exploited pathos in the past, she will rise to reality's even more tragic demands in the future. In the meantime, it is proof of her genuine humanness, and this we are reminded not to forget when her heroism elevates her to heights we may be tempted to assay as abstractly idealized.

Caponsacchi's gloss on this speech and the truth it embodies—"That I liked, that was the best thing she said" (VI, 1319)— is also barometric. The intimacy with and trust in him that it reveals is naturally gratifying, and its similarity to his own parable of the entombed martyrs seems to validate that parable's aptness. But Caponsacchi is an alert and observant man, and he would be just as aware as we are of the temporary depletion of body, mind, and soul that Pompilia's speech reflects and could not conceive of it as containing "The mind o' the mystery." Further, her disembodying of him—voiceless, faceless— strips his parable of the physical metaphor of lying side by side and emphasizes a purely spiritual intimacy. Thus his pleasure in hearing her words shows that he is getting a fuller understanding of her and is becoming more satisfied with an angelic rather than an erotic myth. The verbal event thus represents a measurable movement in Caponsacchi's development.

The next and final stage in the journey consolidates that movement and carries it forward by several distinct measures.

Following a brief rest stop, they travel on, but after a period of seeming calm, Pompilia becomes so distraught that her mind begins to turn. Despite Caponsacchi's inclination to flee like the wind to Rome, it is Pompilia who insists that to push farther would kill her, and she is carried "motionless and breathless" into the inn at Castelnuovo. That is the last stage of their physical journey together, but within its frame, Caponsacchi gains spiritual stature that is synchronous with his shedding of the last remnants of erotic attachment.

In soliciting the aid of a woman at the rest stop, Caponsacchi says three things of significance: he refers to Pompilia as " 'my sister' "; he diagnoses her problem as " 'her head is hurt' "; and he speaks of the " 'Comfort' " that " 'you women understand!' " (VI, 1323–1326). The precision of his speech and the aptness of its content have a simplicity that is admirable in a new degree. Human brotherhood is becoming his motive, sympathetic objectivity his method, and a deeper understanding of the peculiar strength of womanhood his reward. He shows a new capacity to listen, less need to talk, making himself useful in the humble ways of an attendant rather than a master. Pompilia is tender, observant and inquisitive,[8] resolute, profoundly self-searching without any sign of self-dramatization, and even in the face of a foreboding greater than her consciousness can bear, she is determined to stay, not flee, because " 'I have more life to save than mine!' " (VI, 1407). Caponsacchi quietly internalizes all these metaphors of a limitless, finely tuned human faith and a self-immolating conscientiousness and undergoes their transforming influence. Even his total absorption by the thought ("Taken up wholly by the thought," [VI, 1381]) that she had spoken of him as " 'my friend' " rather than as " 'a priest' " (VI, 1383) has now no touch of the former romantic gratification; it is rather a species of awe that so sacred a being as she has proved herself to be should call him friend. He, too, sees the fierceness of the sunset, and he carries her into the inn "motionless and breathless pure and pale" (VI, 1411) with the reverence with which he has handled the host (cf. VI, 1617–1620). Throughout the night, he keeps watch as if guarding a softly lighted sanctuary, and his terrified sense of "impending woe" is "Lest hell reach her!" (VI, 1418–1426).

That is the state of Caponsacchi's body, mind, and soul when he suddenly comes face to face with Count Guido. It is the beginning of the end for all three of them—Guido, Caponsacchi, and Pompilia; from the events of this fateful morning, destiny merely has to work out its appointed course. This is the crucial reference point in all their lives. It releases Pompilia from goodness to grandeur, from domesticity to epic heroism, enabling her to pass beyond admirable action to awesome transcendence. It is the missing link in Guido's elaborate network of rationalizations, the unmaskable evidence of a cowardice at the core of his being that all the histrionic bravado of his second monologue, which is rooted in it, cannot hide. It is the touchstone of Caponsacchi's degree of success in life, the exemplary event by which he will ever after recognize the difference between what he is and what he is not, the metaphor in which the reader can see concentrated *The Ring and the Book's* most representative man.

Language itself is the chief refractor of the scene. Guido speaks first in a superb demonstration of how poetry moves life to the distance of form and idea. It is not the speech that an outraged husband, or even a husband pretending to be outraged, would make on a literal, realistic, reporter's level to the man who has presumably filched his honor but who has had the unaccountable good luck or uncanny shrewdness not to be caught, as one might have expected, *in flagrante delicto.* Such a speech would have been possible, of course, and it might have had its challenges for the writer and its uses for the reader. But they would have been the challenges and uses of prose, not poetry, the decorum or proprieties of prose imposing severe restrictions on their style. The poet, on the other hand, has to accomplish too much of a nonrepresentational kind in too relatively short a space to be able to function under such restrictions. Language is both a mask for Guido and a revelation, and the poet wishes to reveal how inherent in the mask itself is the character of the man who wears it. Guido hovers somewhere between the comic absurd and the horrifying, and hence the very grotesqueness of his manner of speaking in these circumstances is the awful truth of him. The hiss of the serpent is heard in the sibilants, the half-strangulated howl of the hyena, both cowardly and hungry for blood, in the aspirants and gutturals. For such a sidewinding, hit-and-run creature to don the costume of High Renaissance culture—Latinate, mythological, pirouetting on stylized turns of phrase, burying every semblance of truth under a network of textbook conventions—is at once comic and horrible, a witty parody in which the morality of the Italian Renaissance itself is massively implicated. To the "Civil Force" he may wish to appear the cultivated courtier who maintains a modish demeanor even in this most distasteful of situations, but he cannot pretend even to himself that he is fooling Caponsacchi. Thus his performance becomes a blatant example of something between arrogant defiance and arrogant incompetence, and since he will be exposed as a craven coward almost within the instant, his stylistic artifice must be seen as a cunning poltroon's way of guarding himself against the physical violence he so richly deserves.

The insight forced upon us by this pairing of Caponsacchi with Guido is a sobering one, and it is Caponsacchi himself who articulates it. He is paralyzed into speechlessness and inaction by "the speech" (VI, 1482), the myth of the romantic hero suddenly and conclusively collapsing into the austere truth:

> During this speech of that man,—well, I stood
> Away, as he managed,—still, I stood as near
> The throat of him,—with these two hands, my own,—
> As now I stand near yours, Sir,—one quick spring,
> One great good satisfying gripe, and lo!
> There had he lain abolished with his lie,
> Creation purged o' the miscreate, man redeemed,
> A spittle wiped off from the face of God!
> I, in some measure, seek a poor excuse
> For what I left undone, in just this fact
> That my first feeling at the speech I quote
> Was—not of what a blasphemy was dared,
> Not what a bag of venomed purulence
> Was split and noisome,—but how splendidly
> Mirthful, what ludicrous a lie was launched!
> Would Molière's self wish more than hear such man
> Call, claim such woman for his own, his wife,
> Even though, in due amazement at the boast,

He had stammered, she moreover was divine?
She to be his,—were hardly less absurd
Than that he took her name into his mouth,
Licked, and then let it go again, the beast,
Signed with his slaver. Oh, she poisoned him,
Plundered him, and the rest! Well, what I wished
Was, that he would but go on, say once more
So to the world, and get his meed of men,
The fist's reply to the filth. And while I mused,
The minute, oh the misery, was gone!
On either idle hand of me there stood
Really an officer, nor laughed i' the least.
They rendered justice to his reason, laid
Logic to heart, as 't were submitted them
'Twice two makes four.'

                                    (VI, 1472–1504)

These are the remarks, not of the "warrior-priest" of the Pope's myth—the "hero," "athlete," primitive Christian gladiator who sprang into "the mid-cirque, free fighting-place" at "that un-caging of the beasts" (X, 1127–1168 *passim*)—but of the poor, but recently disciplined, and as yet unpracticed apprentice convert who for the first time sees the truth of something he has been taught and has even preached for years—namely, the grotesque marriage of good and evil that is the true human condition. It is a moral victory of sorts, but not such a one as instantly prepares a man to lead the imaginary Crusades of the Pope's fond dream. Nor are we easily persuaded that the event had the impromptu clarity that Caponsacchi gives it here. There is no indication that it was a part of his earlier deposition, and it is reasonable to believe that "the misery" he speaks of—the guilt, the self-doubt—is something he has tried to work through during the months of isolation at Civita and that it has been brought to a head only by the catastrophe itself. We can hardly doubt that it will occupy a central place in his moral conscious-ness for the rest of his life, but we must give it balanced weight in reaching a critical understanding of Caponsacchi both as a dramatic character and as a poetic instrument of our own self-measure.

Caponsacchi's speechless paralysis is then paired with Pompilia's systemic heroism. It is a scene whose character as melodrama is transformed to authentic tragedy by the exhilaration we experience at the magnificence with which this nameless young woman springs from a swoon brought on by physical and mental torture greater than her consciousness could bear and does as if instinctively what these two socially privileged males either have no notion of doing or no power of bringing to reality:

> She started up, stood erect, face to face
> With the husband: back he fell, was buttressed there
> By the window all a-flame with morning-red,
> He the black figure, the opprobrious blur
> Against all peace and joy and light and life.
> 'Away from between me and hell!'—she cried:
> 'Hell for me, no embracing any more!
> I am God's, I love God, God—whose knees I clasp,
> Whose utterly most just award I take,
> But bear no more love-making devils: hence!'
> (VI, 1523–1532)

As there is no flab in Pompilia's language, there is no hesitancy in her movement. Spontaneity validates her truth, which has the leanness and incontrovertibility of an axiom, and gives sharp perspective to Guido's circuitous falseness and Caponsacchi's sadly ineffectual hindsight. Moreover, the luminosity of her metaphysics has its social corollary:

>   'Ha!—and him
> Also you outrage? Him, too, my sole friend,
> Guardian and saviour? That I baulk you of,
> Since—see how God can help at last and worst!'
> She sprung at the sword that hung beside him, seized,
> Drew, brandished it, the sunrise burned for joy
> O' the blade, 'Die,' cried she, 'devil, in God's name!'
> (VI, 1540–1546)

As Pompilia's monologue moves from this dramatic turning point to an ever-mounting, ever-expanding lyric apostrophe, an aria of transcendent affirmation, Caponsacchi's moves irregularly, with alternating phases of firmness and collapse, toward an elegiac lament. It renders *in parvo* a forecast of the life he will have to live from this day until he too "rises" through death to the life that, through "the revelation of Pompilia" (VI, 1866), he now ardently believes in but dimly sees. That the revelation is real he proves by the verbal portrait he paints of her goddess-like grandeur in contrast to his own fallen littleness:

> That erect form, flashing brow, fulgurant eye,
> That voice immortal (oh, that voice of hers!)
> That vision in the blood-red day-break—that
> Leap to life of the pale electric sword
> Angels go armed with. . . .
>
> (VI, 1600–1604)

He has also passed beyond his awe at being called her " 'friend' "; she had called him " 'Guardian, and saviour' " too (VI, 1541–1542, 1610–1611). But so far from being a "warrior-saint" as a result of such praise from such a revelation, he is to the end, despite his grief, arrogant, self-righteous, abusively angry (esp. VI, 1783–1859), guilt-ridden in the name of humility (VI, 1888–1897), ferociously judgmental (VI, 1908–1954), self-pitying (VI, 2069-2070), reconciled to his relegation from life but not quite reconciled to the collapse of his earthly dream (VI, 2081–2104). These are all representative human weaknesses that, despite the revelation of Pompilia, Caponsacchi has not, like her, succeeded in divesting himself of. Hence he is by no means a saint, and the Pope's myth of him is not only fallible but deeply faulted. What Caponsacchi did for Pompilia was to rescue her from the despair that, despite her pregnancy epiphany, would have been the inevitable outcome of her failure to find freedom. What she did for him was to rescue him from the self-destruction upon which he had embarked and to lead him so far from the erosive ambiguity of an erotic priest vowed to celibacy as to give him a decent, representatively faulted man's chance to do his duty and save his soul.

Caponsacchi's solemn pronouncement of anathema on Guido is perhaps the most celebrated passage in his monologue:

> How you will deal with Guido: oh, not death!
> Death, if it let her life be: otherwise
> Not death,—your lights will teach you clearer! I
> Certainly have an instinct of my own
> I' the matter: bear with me and weigh its worth!
> Let us go away—leave Guido all alone
> Back on the world again that knows him now!
> I think he will be found (indulge so far!)
> Not to die so much as slide out of life,
> Pushed by the general horror and common hate
> Low, lower,—left o' the very ledge of things,
> I seem to see him catch convulsively
> One by one at all honest forms of life,
> At reason, order, decency and use—
> To cramp him and get foothold by at least;
> And still they disengage them from his clutch.
> 'What, you are he, then, had Pompilia once
> And so forwent her? Take not up with us!'
> And thus I see him slowly and surely edged
> Off all the table-land whence life upsprings
> Aspiring to be immortality,
> As the snake, hatched on hill-top by mischance,
> Despite his wriggling, slips, slides, slidders down
> Hill-side, lies low and prostrate on the smooth
> Level of the outer place, lapsed in the vale:
> So I lose Guido in the loneliness,
> Silence and dusk, till at the doleful end,
> At the horizontal line, creation's verge,
> From what just is to absolute nothingness—
> Lo, what is this he meets, strains onward still?
> What other man deep further in the fate,
> Who, turning at the prize of a footfall
> To flatter him and promise fellowship,
> Discovers in the act a frightful face—
> Judas, made monstrous by much solitude!
> The two are at one now! Let them love their love

That bites and claws like hate, or hate their hate
That mops and mows and makes as it were love!
There, let them each tear each in devil's-fun,
Or fondle this the other while malice aches—
Both teach, both learn detestability!
Kiss him the kiss, Iscariot! Pay that back,
That snatch o' the slaver blistering on your lip—
By the better trick, the insult he spared Christ—
Lure him the lure o' the letters, Aretine!
Lick him o'er slimy-smooth with jelly-filth
O' the verse-and-prose pollution in love's guise!
The cockatrice is with the basilisk!
There let them grapple, denizens o' the dark,
Foes or friends, but indissolubly bound,
In their one spot out of the ken of God
Or care of man, for ever and ever more!

                                        (VI, 1903–1954)

Herein Caponsacchi gives full rein to his cumulative disgust with Guido, and it is a sobering and fascinating revelation. On the one hand, it comes very close to the aesthetic category called "the sublime"; on the other, it is horrifying rather than terrifying, and hence we must see it as a faulted apprehension, tantalizing but not wholly apt, as the true sublime would require it to be. It is obviously Caponsacchi's effort, through language, to purge his body, mind, and soul of the horrible worldly admixture of divine insight and devilish manipulation and malfeasance symbolized in the contrast between Rome and Arezzo, a contrast particularly embodied in the barefoot Augustinian, Pompilia's confessor, and Vicenzo Marzi-Medici, Governor of Tuscany. But the distressing irony of the passage is that, while we may get a grim satisfaction or even exhilaration from the relentless verbal energy with which Caponsacchi pushes Guido, coupled with Judas, "out of the ken of God/Or care of man" (VI, 1953–1954), we cannot be blind to the effect of such a satisfaction on ourselves or to the demands it imposes on our final judgment of Caponsacchi. It assumes, of course, the character of a Final Judgment, and since that is reserved to God, it cannot be allowed Caponsacchi, however indulgent toward him our sense of his distress may make us. It may even, in the eternal economy, be a correct judgment, but that does not give him the right to make it, and since it is a faulted imaginative creation, its creator is faulted too. Moreover, though we may acknowledge the power of the central parable that sustains the judgment and makes it function rhetorically—two lonely men, "at the doleful end,/At the horizontal line, creation's verge," kissing and licking and biting and clawing and mopping and mowing in a frenzied, hate-filled lovemaking—we cannot with justice condone its rigid, generic, morally exclusionary implications. It is a symbolically apt response of a threatened, male-dominated, chauvinistic, systemically Judeo-Christian culture, but it is just as clearly a stock response and hence, despite its power, essentially uninspired. It reveals what an abstract level Caponsacchi's own sexually deprived loneliness—his anger, bitterness, self-righteousness, and self-pity—has reached, but its power must be resisted as well as felt if the finer, truer, more saving view of the human condition that Pompilia embodies is to prevail. In short, this impressive judgmental fantasy, coming very near the end of his monologue, greatly enlarges our sense of Caponsacchi's pain, but it shows, too, how precariously close he comes, even under the redemptive influence of Pompilia, to the condition of the tragic overreacher and deflates any last inclination we may have had to see him as a romantic hero rather than as a heavily laden, deeply faulted, profoundly sympathetic representative of our race.

Notes

1. Robert Langbaum, *The Poetry of Experience* (New York: Random House, 1957), pp. 110, 112.
2. Langbaum, p. 135.
3. Richard D. Altick and James F. Loucks II, *Browning's Roman Murder Story* (Chicago: University of Chicago Press, 1968), p. 56.
4. Langbaum, pp. 111–112.
5. Once more an analogy with Guido is implied, but in this case it is an analogy that favors Caponsacchi. Although only Guido has two explicit mon-

ologues, Caponsacchi has two also, the implicit one delivered in such an ambiguous manner on such an ambiguous subject with such ambiguous results six months ago, and the present one, in which the stark horror of the event can be saved from a soul-crushing waste only if it is at least partially redeemed by his own spiritual transformation and by a meting out of justice so simple and severe that it proves, in this symbolic instance at any rate, that evil does not rule the world. Guido's monologues, on the other hand, turn upon a different fulcrum. Being the murderer of human objects of his monstrous hate, he can hardly be expected to see any tragic lineaments in their catastrophe. Only his own death warrant presents an equivalent catastrophe to his consciousness, and though this altered circumstance may not absolutely have demanded from him a second monologue, it certainly justifies it. It would appear, therefore, that Guido's second monologue (Book XI) rather than his first (Book V) invites comparison with Caponsacchi's explicit (second) monologue (Book VI), the first being analogous rather to Caponsacchi's implicit (first) monologue. In neither of their first presentations did they make much progress toward the truth, and in that fact they are alike. This seems to imply that there may be patterns of response in Caponsacchi's explicit (second) monologue that teach us how to read Guido's second monologue and that the influence of Pompilia is to be measured chiefly by the imperfect transformation of Caponsacchi and the moral flounderings of Guido rather than by the Pope's ecstatic reactions to her.

6. This is the title and opening statement of a "terrible sonnet" by Hopkins.
7. The condition described is comparable to that which Odysseus' sea-tossed mariners feel when they arrive at lotos-land in Tennyson's *The Lotos-Eaters*. It is also like the "death peace" that Guido experiences near the end of his second monologue.
8. As she is about to reenter the carriage, Pompilia asks, " 'How do you call that tree with the thick top/That holds in all its leafy green and gold/The sun now like an immense egg of fire?' " (VI, 1336–1338). Caponsacchi does not interpret the question, with its surreal wording, except to report it and identify the tree as "a million-leaved mimosa." But besides the obvious reference to the fertilized egg within her and to the mimosa's popular reputation as a vegetal mimic of animal life, there seems to be an allusion to mad Cassandra's quarrel with Apollo and her visions of the worldwide conflagration symbolized by the Trojan War. It is the beginning of the terrible foreboding that is ultimately realized in the appearance of Guido.

6.

Imagination as Ultimate Truth: Book VII. *Pompilia*

Book VII, *Pompilia,* is the imaginative crux of *The Ring and the Book.* It is the poem-within-a-poem by which the integrity of everything else must finally be decided. It is the center that holds everything together and enables it to exist; it is the "center," in William Butler Yeats's extension of Carlyle's metaphor, that *must* "hold" unless "Mere anarchy is [to be] loosed upon the world. . . . "[1] What *The Ring and the Book* means in the larger creative sense, *what it is,* can be determined only by the use of Book VII as the poem's—and hence the critic's—central reference-point.

Efforts to determine what the poem means in the narrower creative sense—to "suppose and state" what general comment on life the poet has attempted to make—have not served *The Ring and the Book* well. The more sympathetic and intense a reader's response to the poem itself is, the more critically dissatisfied he is likely to be with such characterizations of Pompilia's significance as these: "she is the antithesis of fallen Eve. In her, Browning illustrates both the power for good inherent in the pure spirit—she was the divinely chosen means by which Caponsacchi's eyes were opened to true moral and religious values—and the mystic affinity that leads good instinctively to recognize and cling to good."[2] In her, "the miracle of the Assumption is symbolically reenacted."[3] Her call to Caponsacchi "is symbolic of the redemption that can come to all humanity if it heeds the voice of Christ."[4] A reader whose imagination has been exercised to an extraordinary degree by the poem may feel betrayed by such conclusions, like one who has been beguiled into taking "the artistic way" to what turns out to be rather a dreary, familiar, parochial destination. And he may feel more churched than inspired to find "the meaning of Pompilia's story" summed up with such unction as this: "not just that she is innocent, or that she suffered unjustly, but that she to whom it was not given '*to know much,/Speak much, to write a book, to move mankind*' could become a blazing star for those still struggling on earth. She could become this only because the poet, to whom it *is* given to write a book and move mankind, makes her live again and lets us see how good can overcome evil."[5] The reader may find this a dubious improvement on the Sermon on the Mount and wonder why the poet went to so much trouble to shape a "ring," if the ring, "by when it reaches him, looks false,/Seems to be just the thing it would supplant/Nor recognizable by whom it left . . . " (XII, 850–852, paraphrased and adapted).

If the narrower, thematic approach to *The Ring and the Book*'s poetic center has proved so inadequate, it seems appropriate to try the larger, experiential approach by examining, not what the poem says or is said to say, but what it does, how it actually works, "Nor wrong the thought, missing the mediate word" (XII, 857). By examining how Book VII works, we should come as close as possible to seeing how the whole poem works.

Book VII begins "I am" (1) and ends "I rise" (1845); how the speaker gets from the one point to the other is thus the problem of poetic creation that it poses. Since what is made depends to an important extent on what it is made of, a knowledge of the "am" is indispensable to a genuine understanding of the "rise." Further, the fiction of the poem—its "plot"—is a verbal fiction: how the "voice" of someone who, according to "the church's register," lived almost 200 years ago and was named "Francesca Camilla Vittoria Angela/Pompilia Comparini" (VII, 3–7) "endeavoured to explain her life" (I, 1104) is the poem's historical/imaginary drama. By the time we reach Book VII, the transformation of our literary focus is so complete that we hardly notice how little emphasis the speaker puts on the disputed aspects of the case, either moral or legal, that had so absorbed the earlier speakers' attention. She simply declines to play the popular game of "what if" and "yes, but"—the dust-in-their-eyes game that Guido and his sympathizers generate so energetically as a blind for their slippery activities. The question of whether or not the love letters were forged is given no quarter, and the issues of the inevitably compromising appearances of the flight and of the natural assumptions of a romantic attachment are brought out of the closet and dealt with in the full light of day. As a result, our interest, consciously or unconsciously, is wholly riveted on what the persona actually says. She is a language-person, and language is our only access to her.

Pompilia speaks on the last day before she dies. Thus her whole life has been a preparation for what she says. She had been silent, her soul entombed in the Old Yellow Book, for some 170 years; now she has been speaking, through the pages of *The Ring and the Book,* for well into the second century. She "lives," presumably, because "precious [is] the soul of man to man" (XII, 829–830), and the reader's challenge is to identify what it is in her that speaks to him at such a level as to make "soul" its appropriate metaphor. For some readers, this may eventually lead in directions that will make "the antithesis to fallen Eve," "the miracle of the Assumption," and "the voice of Christ" seem relevant, but homelier, more personal, less parochial expectations need satisfaction first.

If Pompilia tells us anything from the beginning to the end of her monologue, it is that she knows who she is. In fact, everything else she tells us is rooted in that clear, firm, functional sense of identity. It is because she knows who she is that she knows what she believes. Not being a self-swindler, she has no need, conscious or unconscious, to swindle others. Self-knowledge is a real and sufficient base on which to erect whatever ideal structure her inner sense of truth, her innermost flow of personal reality, requires, and hence she has no spiritual, moral, or psychological need to lay waste the personal structures of others. At the point at which she begins her monologue, Pompilia is "Formed to rise, reach at, if not grasp and gain/The good beyond" her (I, 715–716). What she has to learn is how to overleap the last barrier that stands in the way of that fulfillment and to have at least the momentary earthly experience of human joy that will enable her to greet death in a spirit that, being different in kind from the "death peace" that comes even to brute beasts when they see the end of life as inevitable—"As eyes the butcher the cast panting ox/That feels his fate is come, nor struggles more . . . " (VII, 578–579)— is peculiarly human. Not to see death as the mere extinction of life or as preferable simply to life's insupportable pain or as a calculation and redress of earthly inequities; but to greet it in a spirit of expectant affirmation, a joy of afterlife, that is validated by a sense of having known, even for that brief moment, the very best this world has to offer.

Those are the stages through which Pompilia's monologue takes us: what she is like at the beginning (VII, 1–583); what happens (VII, 584–1770); what she is like at the end (VII, 1771–1845). Much of the energy behind the movement of the monologue is generated by memory, but her past life, which is history, is not to be confused with her present life, which is poetry. Past events are all converted into present language, and the shape that language gives this "incident in the development of a soul" brings us face to face with a poetic rather than a historical action; its unifying center is there, and that is what enables it to hold together and exist.

The burdens and rewards of self-knowledge—the price one has to pay for it, the infinite growth that it makes possible—is the poet's subject in Book VII of *The Ring and the Book*. On the very face of it, then, it has an Apollonian character that puts it beyond a purely Christian pale. It is in no sense anti-Christian: if, as Christ said, the kingdom of heaven is within one, then self-knowledge is the most direct route to it. But self-knowledge has not been an especially prominent goal of Christian teaching or of Christian practice, and it certainly is not a prominent goal of the historical Christianity portrayed in *The Ring and the Book*. Thus there is a poetic justice at least in the fact that "Know thyself" appears on the wall of the Temple of Apollo at Delphi rather than on the wall of St. Peter's Basilica in Rome.

The influence of Pompilia is a poetic rather than a specifically religious influence. Though many of the metaphors in which she speaks do not have traditional religious associations, many of them do; but even those can be seen as the inevitable legacy of her culture, and they undergo a poetic transformation that gives them a character that the culture was itself unable to give them. "I never realized God's birth before—," she says in the closing moments of her life, "How he grew likest God in being born./This time I felt like Mary, had my babe/Lying a little on my breast like hers" (VII, 1690–1693). She is expressing a poetic dilation of spirit in traditional religious terms, but she uses language in the experientially clear but substantively approximative way of poetry rather than of theology. What she is confirming is not the myth, but the experience of the human spirit out of which the myth sprang. The effect she has on such sympathetic characters as Caponsacchi and the Pope is analogous to this. She renews the flow of currents that, from quite different causes, have become stagnant in them, and they too use familiar religious metaphors to characterize what they feel about her as a result of this renewed flow. But the thoughts that overtake them with such power and surprise are thoughts of what *may be* rather than of what *is,* and, as Plato said, those are essentially poetic thoughts.

Self-knowledge is also organic with the method of Book VII and hence with the poem as a whole. Being the most successful of all the personae in completing her incompleteness through self-knowledge and the magnification of spirit self-knowledge makes possible, Pompilia's monologue becomes the poetic paradigm of *The Ring and the Book*. Behind it is a principle Goethe claims to have taught the German poets, and, we know, it was a principle widely adopted by the nineteenth-century English poets.

"Through me the German poets have become aware that, as a man must live from within outwards, so the artist must work from within outwards, seeing that, make what contortions he will, he can only bring to light his own individuality. I can clearly mark where this influence of mine has made itself felt; there arises out of it a kind of poetry of nature, and only in this way is it possible to be original."[6]

Pompilia rather than the Pope is, from the poet's perspective, the most credible guide to life that *The Ring and the Book* offers. She has not only suffered most; she has also wasted least of the pain she has suffered. She is at once the most self-aware and the least self-conscious persona in the poem. She puts no special premium on herself in comparative terms; she did not even know that other women did not live lives very much like her life until it was almost over and the world rushed in and declared it.

> All the seventeen years,
> Not once did a suspicion visit me
> How very different a lot is mine
> From any other woman's in the world.
> The reason must be, 'twas by step and step
> It got to grow so terrible and strange:
> These strange woes stole on tiptoe, as it were,
> Into my neighbourhood and privacy,
> Sat down where I sat, laid them where I lay;
> And I was found familiarised with fear,
> When friends broke in, held up a torch and cried
> 'Why, you Pompilia in the cavern thus,
> How comes that arm of yours about a wolf?
> And the soft length,—lies in and out your feet
> And laps you round the knee,—a snake it is!'
> (VII, 113–127)

What she learned through her long pilgrimage of pain was that, although endurance has its limits, one can in fact bear infinitely more than those with little knowledge of pain would ever imagine. She learned, too, that there is a difference in kind between being asked to bear and being asked to bear seeing others bear. The former, being acceptable, makes the martyr; the latter, being unacceptable, makes the revolutionary. Martyrdom may be a form of nobility, certainly; endurance carried to heroic heights teaches one an incomparable truth about oneself. But martyrdom, though noble, is essentially passive and, if it is known at all, sets chiefly a passive example. Rebellion, on the other hand, is active. Without any necessary diminution in the nobility of its motive—selflessness—it is purgative, cathartic, setting a public example that may be ennobling to others. At the root of it are, besides the love that would serve others, the faith that one would not be asked to collude in evil and the hope that even in the most imperiled of circumstances there is something yet to be done.

These are the stages through which Pompilia passes on her way to the poetic dilation or transcendent affirmation with which her monologue ends: from a nonperson, to a baby-doll without moral definition, to a passive martyr, to an active person with an all-consuming role in life, to a heroine with a moral clarity and strength that make her tower above the cowardice and confusion around her. Finally she emerges as a physically, morally, and spiritually resourceful woman who, in the wake of a violent catastrophe, has the inner capacity to reenact her personal sojourn in hell, to discover there the experiential bases for affirmation, and to greet with exhilaration the unknown future through a personal history whose ways surpass human understanding but whose results she perceives as surpassing all expectation too. At no point could she have fabricated a future for herself of comparable strangeness and richness as, in retrospect, she recognizes her own life to have, and thus she greets another future in full faith that it will also have a strangeness and richness beyond her wildest dreams.

The only thing that Pompilia "bring[s] to light," then, is "[her] own individuality," but there "arises out of it," as Goethe says, "a kind of poetry of nature." And it is "original," as Goethe also says, in the only way in which it is possible for poetry to be original. By enabling someone not ourselves to tell the truth, it tells us the truth of ourselves. We are not Pompilias and are not meant to be. We are ourselves, but until we strip away all the disguises, all the lifeless masks and mechanicals that distort and neutralize the truth of ourselves, we will never know who we are, what we alone can endure, and what we can make of a life we shall "leave so soon" (VII, 1664–1666).

The identity that Pompilia establishes in the first, domestic movement of her monologue (VII, 1–583) is shaped and textured by what she is ready and able to recall without the austere memorial discipline imposed on her by her confessor, Don Celestine. Therefore, the truly horrid parts of her life are excluded, and she tries to give a retrospective of her first thirteen years. She speaks of them as happy—"each day, happy as the day was long" (VII, 374)—but she tells us almost nothing about them, and what she does tell is hardly proof of childlike happiness—a marble lion "rushing from the wall,/Eating the figure of a prostrate man" (VII, 23–24), a game of make-believe in which a hound is harassing a stag and a girl is being changed into a "brown and rough" tree (VII, 186–196), a predatory owl on a boy's wrist (VII, 397–398), the frightful-looking Master Malpichi with his phial of black bitter if therapeutic medicine (VII, 413–424). What she tells us essentially and unintentionally is that her childhood goal was to "purchase . . . the praise" of those she loved (VII, 408–409) and that her chief anguish was the periods of conflict and grief that they experienced: " 'All is right if you only will not cry!' " (VII, 573). Thus she would like to remember an idyllic childhood, but either none existed or the heavy weight of later events gives her memory no access to it. In a poetic process in which memory is given such a catalytic role, this is a matter which the poet would obviously have treated with great care. The poets, novelists, and autobiographers of the century were fascinated with the role of memory in character *Bildung* or psyche formation, including its input into imagination, and clearly a form of that fascination is manifested here.

Though she would like to, Pompilia simply has no strategy for overleaping the awful period of blight that was concurrent with her years of puberty. Hell and womanhood opened up together, and she was equally unprepared for both. Ignorant alike of the stern realities of the distressed adult world and of the sexual demands of marriage, she had to learn everything on the most abrupt, *ad hoc* basis and to adjust to life seriatim. Had she had a husband who loved her for her childlike innocence and was tender and patient in introducing her to adult responsibilities, her deficiencies might, with proper tending, have been the soil from which happiness of a rare kind grew, but not a single circumstance favored her, and she was left to such physical, mental, and spiritual resources as were native in herself. Subjected relentlessly to mental torture and under perpetual physical threat, she retreated into her innermost spiritual sanctuary and found there whatever solace her life had to offer her.

Violante's role in Pompilia's diseducation has gone unnoticed by the critics of the poem, who have seen Violante only as a restless, meddlesome, misguided manipulator and matchmaker in the myth's external plot line. But Violante's influence is considerably deeper and darker than that, and it is Pompilia who, with poignant irony, exposes it. The enchanted childhood that Pompilia tries quite unsuccessfully to remember as "happy as the day was long" was the deeply flawed fabrication of a would-be fairy godmother who, having made the princess appear out of nowhere, had in due course to produce the prince. In the meantime, the princess had to inhabit fairyland. She had to feed on fairy tales, "purchase . . . the praise" of her enchantress, and fear only her fairy godmother's pain and displeasure. If she was told that someone who looked like an owl, "Hook-nosed and yellow in a bush of beard" (VII, 396-398), was a cavalier, she must believe he was a cavalier; if her fairy godmother said, " 'Girl-brides never breathe a word!' " (VII, 460), then she must believe that; a funeral called a wedding must be accepted as a wedding. Pompilia brings to an end this first false phase of her life with a recitation of Violante's account of why she did what she did. The account begins with a series of attitudes toward young people, men, and priests. Though she has just signed Pompilia's death warrant and consigned her to four years of mental and physical torture, she begins, patronizingly, " 'You are too young and cannot understand' " (VII, 533). Men, she says, don't know what's good for them either. They hate change and must be taken advantage of for their own advantage, which they are likely to reject even while they crave it. In both these matters, priests are women's best allies.

Then Violante articulates the personal myth that was her motive:

'My scheme was worth attempting: and bears fruit,
Gives you a husband and a noble name,
A palace and no end of pleasant things.
What do you care about a handsome youth?
They are so volatile, and teaze their wives!
This is the kind of man to keep the house.
We lose no daughter,—gain a son, that's all:
For 'tis arranged we never separate,
Nor miss, in our grey time of life, the tints
Of you that colour eve to match with morn.
In good or ill, we share and share alike,
And cast our lots into a common lap,
And all three die together as we lived!
Only, at Arezzo,—that's a Tuscan town,
Not so large as this noisy Rome, no doubt,
But older far and finer much, say folks,—
In a great palace where you will be queen,
Know the Archbishop and the Governor,
And we see homage done you ere we die.'

(VII, 552–570)

This is something more than the myth of the matronly female putting a patina of high-mindedness on what is obviously an adamant determination to have her own way, a sort of female equivalent to and extenuation of the virulent male sexism that runs through the poem. This is the peculiarly human myth of old age robbing youth of its chance for happiness to ensure its own comfort. The fairy godmother now becomes the wicked witch who reveals, in silvery tones, her horrible price: " 'In good or ill, we share and share alike,/And cast our lots into a common lap,/And all three die together as we lived!' " Besides its ominous prophecy, it is the closing of the circle by those who have had their youth around those who have not, and though it is fatal to the perpetrator, it is also fatal to the victim.

That Pompilia at least subconsciously understands what she is reporting is suggested both by the fact that it is at this point that "a blank begins" (VII, 574) and by her failure to validate the happiness that, cliché-like, she claims to have known as a child. She may have been " 'very ignorant' " then (VII, 572), but she is sadly wiser now. Though she is generous of spirit to Violante, not knowing how to forgive her while not wanting to blame her, Pompilia has "pierc[ed] straight/Through the pretence to the ignoble truth" (VII, 326–327). Violante, she says,

> Fancied she saw God's very finger point,
> Designate just the time for planting me,
> (The wild briar-slip she plucked to love and wear)
> In soil where I could strike real root, and grow,
> And get to be the thing I called myself:
> For, wife and husband are one flesh, God says,
> And I, whose parents seemed such and were none,
> Should in a husband have a husband now,
> Find nothing, this time, but was what it seemed,
> —All truth and no confusion any more.
> I know she meant all good to me, all pain
> To herself,—since how could it be aught but pain,
> To give me up, so, from her very breast,
> The wilding flower-tree-branch that, all those years,
> She had got used to feel for and find fixed?
> She meant well: has it been so ill i' the main?
>   (VII, 328–343)

Pompilia claims in this connection that "one cannot judge/Of what has been the ill or well of life,/The day that one is dying" (VII, 344–346), even though that is exactly what she will do throughout parts two and three of her monologue. Her motive is generous, but her evasion is false, and we must answer her question for her: yes, it has been very "ill." She has been denied the joy and spiritual elevation of true human love, and this denial, from a purely human point of view at least, may be a crueller cut than all the brutality she suffered in its name.

Pompilia begins her monologue by trying to stretch out her age to the utmost—"I am just seventeen years and five months old,/And, if I lived one day more, three full weeks . . ." (VII, 1–2)—and she is concerned that her son "keep apart/A little the thing" she is from the "Lucias, Marias, Sofias, who titter or blush/When he regards them as such boys may do" (VII, 86–87, 70–71). But as she recalls the memory that must go with this memory, she has "second thoughts":

> I hope he will regard
> The history of me as what someone dreamed,
> And get to disbelieve it at the last:
> Since to myself it dwindles fast to that,
> Sheer dreaming and impossibility. . . .
> (VII, 108–112)

Her whole earthly life has been suspended in a counterfeit medium. Her childhood was a delusion and her marriage a fraud; even her babe, taken from her on the third day, has "withdraw[n] into a dream."

> Thus, all my life,—
> As well what was, as what . . . was not,—
> Looks old, fantastic and impossible:
> I touch a fairy thing that fades and fades.
> (VII, 198–201)

The only reality and permanence things have are endowments given them by her "fancy" (VII, 214), and that is eventually how she comes to see life:

> There was a fancy came,
> When somewhere, in the journey with my friend,
> We stepped into a hovel to get food;
> And there began a yelp here, a bark there,—
> Misunderstanding creatures that were wroth
> And vexed themselves and us till we retired.
> The hovel is life: no matter what dogs bit

> Or cats scratched in the hovel I break from,
> All outside is lone field, moon and such peace—
> Flowing in, filling up as with a sea
> Whereon comes Someone, walks fast on the white,
> Jesus Christ's self, Don Celestine declares,
> To meet me and calm all things back again.
> (VII, 360–372)

Only outside of life does there seem to be any peace for her, and if "Christ" is the "Someone" who comes to meet her there, as "Don Celestine declares," then let it be Christ.

Pompilia would like to forget her four horrid years in that hovel. Life has done all it can to her, and she would like to mirror it back as the "blank" that it now truly is. But if it is blank, she is blank too, and a quarter of who she is has simply vanished. Giving that part of her life—of herself—renewed existence in language is the subject of the second, epic phase of her monologue (VII, 584–1770). It is in this phase that, through knowledge, understanding, and imagination, she takes her final leave of life on earth and turns a vision greatly magnified toward a future that may be called mystical in traditional terms, but is quintessentially real—that is, simply, imaginatively true—in her own.

At first Pompilia resists Don Celestine's psychological-moral-metaphysical therapy to " 'Search and find!/For your soul's sake, remember what is past,/The better to forgive it' " (VII, 596–598). Remembering the horror seems too depleting and futile, too much like the thing itself and therefore, despite all the pain, likely in the end to prove no more than a fantastic dream. Moreover, she already has something to cling to, a bare, skeletal structure through which to compose her mind sufficiently if minimally. The childhood incident of the shuddering she-goat supplies that structure:

> I am held up, amid the nothingness,
> By one or two truths only—thence I hang,
> And there I live,—the rest is death or dream,
> All but those points of my support. I think
> Of what I saw at Rome once in the Square

O' the Spaniards, opposite the Spanish House:
There was a foreigner had trained a goat,
A shuddering white woman of a beast,
To climb up, stand straight on a pile of sticks
Put close, which gave the creature room enough:
When she was settled there he, one by one,
Took away all the sticks, left just the four
Whereon the little hoofs did really rest,
There she kept firm, all underneath was air.
So, what I hold by, are my prayer to God,
My hope, that came in answer to the prayer,
Some hand would interpose and save me—hand
Which proved to be my friend's hand: and,—best bliss,—
That fancy which began so faint at first,
That thrill of dawn's suffusion through my dark,
Which I perceive was promise of my child,
The light his unborn face sent long before,—
God's way of breaking the good news to flesh.
That is all left now of those four bad years.
(VII, 603–626)

But Don Celestine will not accept a pathetic prelapsarian incident as an adequate gloss on a tragic postlapsarian state. He
says with urgent intensity,

> 'But remember more!
> Other men's faults may help me find your own.
> I need the cruelty exposed, explained,
> Or how can I advise you to forgive?'
> (VII, 627–630)

There are two new elements in this version of Don Celestine's
urging that convert resistance to acceptance—the possibility that
a crucial fault may lie in Pompilia herself and the role of the
shriver in the forgiveness act. That is "true," she says:

> For, bringing back reluctantly to mind
> My husband's treatment of me,—by a light
> That's later than my life-time, I review

> And comprehend much and imagine more,
> And have but little to forgive at last.
>   (VII, 633–637)

The language here is too curious not to be crucial. Though
her "husband's treatment" of her is the nearest, most obvious
object requiring forgiveness, she hardly needs such "light" as
she describes for that. The only thing that requires the light
of afterlife is life itself—to know it ("review"), to understand
somewhat of it ("comprehend much"), and finally to attain a
fully satisfying image of it *sub specie aeternitatis* ("imagine more").
Only thus can man the victim, of which Pompilia is the quintessential example, see at last how "little to forgive" there is in
the victimization. More than Guido, she has to "forgive" Guido's maker ("So he was made; he nowise made himself" [VII,
1731]) and forgive herself.

Pompilia begins to take her inventory in a rather literal-
minded, rational way. She was wrong as a wife, she says, in not
doing something to break the chain of recriminations between
her husband and her parents (VII, 638–665). She was also
"blind"—that is, dull and stupid—not to "apprehend" her husband's plan to get her involved with Caponsacchi; hence, she
increased his ire by "thwarting [his] true intent" (VII, 666–712).
She acknowledges that in the world's eyes she was guilty of
withholding her husband's connubial privileges, but this she
refuses to concede. On the contrary, if she was at fault in this
regard, it was in yielding to the Archbishop's prurient instruc-
tions when, in presuming to represent God, he "seemed so stale
and worn a way o' the world" (VII, 713–859). Indeed, her account of the Archbishop's "parable" is one of the most piercing ironies in the whole poem. Its ugly sexuality, a perversion
not only of the spirit of the Christian text of which it is a careless imitation but also of the connubial ideal of which it is an
ignorant travesty, is hard enough to witness; but to have it reported through the mouth of Pompilia in her state of sexual
simplicity and moral panic makes it almost intolerable.

> 'Let's try the honeyed cake. A parable!
> "Without a parable spake He not to them."

There was a ripe round long black toothsome fruit,
Even a flower-fig, the prime boast of May:
And, to the tree, said . . . either the spirit o' the fig,
Or, if we bring in men, the gardener,
Archbishop of the orchard—had I time
To try o' the two which fits in best: indeed
It might be the Creator's self, but then
The tree should bear an apple, I suppose,—
Well, anyhow, one with authority said
"Ripe fig, burst skin, regale the fig-pecker—
The bird whereof thou art a perquisite!"
"Nay," with a flounce, replied the restif fig,
"I much prefer to keep my pulp myself:
He may go breakfastless and dinnerless,
Supperless of one crimson seed, for me!"
So, back she flopped into her bunch of leaves.
He flew off, left her,—did the natural lord,—
And lo, three hundred thousand bees and wasps
Found her out, feasted on her to the shuck:
Such gain the fig's that gave its bird no bite!
The moral,—fools elude their proper lot,
Tempt other fools, get ruined all alike.
Therefore go home, embrace your husband quick!'

(VII, 820–844)

Her bodily temple now brutally desecrated, her spirit re-solved to take counsel only with God, Pompilia suddenly feels a flow of empathy for her unknown, much-abused mother. How can those who speak no truth say what her motives were? Maybe in selling her child she made the most heroic of sacrifices, greater even than any Pompilia has been asked to make (VII, 860–894).

This sudden flow of forgiveness through love of her mother is generated by the three elements to which Pompilia had re-ferred—knowledge, understanding, and imagination—and it leads directly to a recurrence of the highly fanciful idea that she had insisted on before (VII, 92–93) and will insist on again almost with her dying breath (VII, 1762–1765), namely, that her son never had a father, only a mother:

> There, enough! I have my support again,
> Again the knowledge that my babe was, is,
> Will be mine only.
>
> (VII, 895–897)

The implicit connection is a crucial one. Despite its apparent contradiction of both realism and rationality, the idea that only love gives life is taking ever firmer hold on Pompilia. Life comes from the great Creator of Life, and He is Love, not this thing men call procreation. Like everything else in which they invest such realism and rationality, that is the "fairy thing," "Sheer dreaming and impossibility," while this that seems so fanciful has the attribute of permanence that qualifies it as the true truth.

It is the midpoint in Pompilia's monologue, and with it she turns to her real subject, Caponsacchi:

> Then, I must lay my babe away with God,
> Nor think of him again, for gratitude.
> Yes, my last breath shall wholly spend itself
> In one attempt more to disperse the stain,
> The mist from other breath fond mouths have made,
> About a lustrous and pellucid soul:
> So that, when I am gone but sorrow stays,
> And people need assurance in their doubt
> If God yet have a servant, man a friend,
> The weak a saviour and the vile a foe,—
> Let him be present, by the name invoked,
> Giuseppe-Maria Caponsacchi!
>
> (VII, 930–941)

He is her reason for remembering: "I will remember once more for his sake/The sorrow . . ." (VII, 944–945), for his sake and for "people [who] need assurance in their doubt." Forgiveness of Guido is implicit in it of course, but only in a relatively minor way. Pompilia is endeavoring "to explain her life," to discover through knowledge, understanding, and imagination how the poor wounded name of man with his "twenty-two dagger-wounds,/Five deadly" can rise above his sorrow and have faith in the future that is not itself a delusion and a mockery. She is our surrogate, her question our question: what does it all mean? what are the grounds for hope? The answer, she "had thought,/Shot itself out in white light, blazed the truth/Through every atom of" Caponsacchi's act with her (VII, 921–923), but since others do not know the "act," do not understand it or see what it signifies, she agrees to recreate it—for his sake and for theirs.

When the affair began at "a public play,/In the last days of Carnival" (VII, 950–951), the designs of all the parties concerned suddenly coalesced. Pompilia saw "the proper friend" to " 'Throw his arm over [her] and make [her]safe!' " (VII, 972–973); the image of the lady with "the beautiful sad strange smile" "Burnt" itself into the "brain" of Caponsacchi, "as sunbeam thro' shut eyes" (VI, 412, 435); and Guido the trapper set the idea of his trap. For two or three weeks, all parties worked at cross-purposes with forged letters, baitings, couriers, rejections, reports of departures, and thoughts of suicide. Then Pompilia rose one morning to a world that had mysteriously changed its aspect in the most natural way imaginable:

> When, what, first thing at daybreak, pierced the sleep
> With a summons to me? Up I sprang alive,
> Light in me, light without me, everywhere
> Change! A broad yellow sun-beam was let fall
> From heaven to earth,—a sudden drawbridge lay,
> Along which marched a myriad merry motes,
> Mocking the flies that crossed them and recrossed
> In rival dance, companions new-born too.
> On the house-eaves, a dripping shag of weed
> Shook diamonds on each dull grey lattice-square,
> As first one, then another bird leapt by,
> And light was off, and lo was back again,
> Always with one voice,—where are two such joys?—
> The blessed building-sparrow! I stepped forth,
> Stood on the terrace,—o'er the roofs, such sky!
> My heart sang, 'I too am to go away,
> I too have something I must care about,
> Carry away with me to Rome, to Rome!
> The bird brings hither sticks and hairs and wool,

And nowhere else i' the world; what fly breaks rank,
Falls out of the procession that befits,
From window here to window there, with all
The world to choose,—so well he knows his course?
I have my purpose and my motive too,
My march to Rome, like any bird or fly!
Had I been dead! How right to be alive!
Last night I almost prayed for leave to die,
Wished Guido all his pleasure with the sword
Or the poison,—poison, sword, was but a trick,
Harmless, may God forgive him the poor jest!
My life is charmed, will last till I reach Rome!
Yesterday, but for the sin,—ah, nameless be
The deed I could have dared against myself!
Now—see if I will touch an unripe fruit,
And risk the health I want to have and use!
Not to live, now, would be the wickedness,—
For life means to make haste and go to Rome
And leave Arezzo, leave all woes at once!'
                                        (VII, 1222–1259)

She was pregnant, and with this exultant pregnancy epiphany, passivity became activity, morbidity was changed into a vigorous life-flow. She knew what she had to do, how to do it, and did it. " 'Tell Caponsacchi he may come!' " (VII, 1358), she said, and she faced down doubt with simply " 'He will come' " (VII, 1383). She felt like one suddenly rescued from the jaws of hell, and a battle-song filled her thoughts:

An old rhyme came into my head and rang
Of how a virgin, for the faith of God,
Hid herself, from the Paynims that pursued,
In a cave's heart; until a thunderstone,
Wrapped in a flame, revealed the couch and prey:
And they laughed—'Thanks to lightning, ours at last!'
And she cried 'Wrath of God, assert His love!
Servant of God, thou fire, befriend His child!'
And lo, the fire she grasped at, fixed its flash,
Lay in her hand a calm cold dreadful sword

She brandished till pursuers strewed the ground,
So did the souls within them die away,
As o'er the prostrate bodies, sworded, safe,
She walked forth to the solitudes and Christ:
So should I grasp the lightning and be saved!
(VII, 1389–1403)

When Caponsacchi answered her summons, she spoke "on the instant," sweeping away all the " 'dust and feathers' " and challenged him to serve God by saving her (VII, 1416–1442). He replied like one under a spell: " 'I am yours' " (VII, 1447). Later he was caught in a paralyzing conflict of duties, but she only prayed, never doubting, and when he came at last to present his prudent arguments against so " 'rash' " and " 'desperate' " a plan, she cut through everything with " 'I know you: when is it that you will come?' " (VII, 1474). So he came, and they set out.

From the moment their flight begins, Pompilia's monologue assumes a rich metaphoric texture; it soars on lyric wings to an illumination of epic proportions. Their flight to Rome reaches far beyond its chief literary analogues—the medieval legend of St. George and the classical myth of Perseus and Andromeda. The flight to the Eternal City is only the metaphor of a flight to the Eternal Reality of which Rome is only man's grand but ultimately shabby symbol.

Caponsacchi was for Pompilia God's way of showing " 'the way!' " (VII, 1455). First, he rewrote "The obliterated charter" of womanhood. He had

a sense
That reads, as only such can read, the mark
God sets on woman, signifying so
She should—shall peradventure—be divine.
(VII, 1498–1501)

He did not see the marred print other men see; he saw by faith, purged by worship, and so mended what by weakness had been marred (VII, 1502–1510). When bitter thoughts threatened to overwhelm her or old fears to suffocate her or sheer physical and mental weakness to suck her down, he "divined" both the human condition and the human remedy.

These were the manifestations of divine guidance in Caponsacchi—the signs that through him God was showing her the way home—and they not only transformed her but enabled her to transform the most terrifying moment of her life into a supreme moment of selfless affirmation of metaphysical reality. It was the incident at Castelnuovo when "time" was "crushed," between the "tragical red eve" when she had swooned and "the other red of morning" when she had awakened, into one "solid fire":

> When in, my dreadful husband and the world
> Broke,—and I saw him, master, by hell's right,
> And saw my angel helplessly held back
> By guards that helped the malice—the lamb prone,
> The serpent towering and triumphant—then
> Came all the strength back in a sudden swell,
> I did for once see right, do right, give tongue
> The adequate protest: for a worm must turn
> If it would have its wrong observed by God.
> I did spring up, attempt to thrust aside
> That ice-block 'twixt the sun and me, lay low
> The neutralizer of all good and truth.
> If I sinned so,—never obey voice more
> O' the Just and Terrible, who bids us—'Bear!'
> Not—'Stand by, bear to see my angels bear!'
> I am clear it was on impulse to serve God
> Not save myself,—no—nor my child unborn!
> Had I else waited patiently till now?—
> Who saw my old kind parents, silly-sooth
> And too much trustful, for their worst of faults,
> Cheated, brow-beaten, stripped and starved, cast out
> Into the kennel: I remonstrated,
> Then sank to silence, for,—their woes at end,
> Themselves gone,—only I was left to plague.
> If only I was threatened and belied,
> What matter? I could bear it and did bear;

It was a comfort, still one lot for all:
They were not persecuted for my sake
And I, estranged, the single happy one.
But when at last, all by myself I stood
Obeying the clear voice which bade me rise,
Not for my own sake but my babe unborn,
And take the angel's hand was sent to help—
And found the old adversary athwart the path—
Not my hand simply struck from the angel's, but
The very angel's self made foul i' the face
By the fiend who struck there,—that I would not bear,
That only I resisted! So, my first
And last resistance was invincible.
Prayers move God; threats, and nothing else, move men!
I must have prayed a man as he were God
When I implored the Governor to right
My parents' wrongs: the answer was a smile.
The Archbishop,—did I clasp his feet enough,
Hide my face hotly on them, while I told
More than I dared make my own mother know?
The profit was—compassion and a jest.
This time, the foolish prayers were done with, right
Used might, and solemnized the sport at once.
All was against the combat: vantage, mine?
The runaway avowed, the accomplice-wife,
In company with the plan-contriving priest?
Yet, shame thus rank and patent, I struck, bare,
At foe from head to foot in magic mail,
And off it withered, cobweb-armoury
Against the lightning! 'T was truth singed the lies
And saved me, not the vain sword nor weak speech!
                                    (VII, 1585–1641)

It is all there: the cowardice of Guido; the terrible illumination
of Caponsacchi; the heroic grandeur of Pompilia.

Knowledge, understanding, and imagination have now en
abled Pompilia to complete her incompleteness. "Others may
want and wish," she says, "I wish nor want/One point o' the

circle plainer . . ." (VII, 1644–1645). If she had weeks and months to live, she could learn more about life, but she now knows all she needs to know: love is the only author of life; time is a mere mode of consciousness; in God's "face/Is light, but in His shadow healing too" (VII, 1720–1721). Despite the sorrow and the doubt, God yet has servants, man has friends, the weak have saviors, and the vile have foes. Man needs only the will, the way being left to God: "There is no other course, or we should craze,/Seeing such evil with no human cure" (VII, 1099–1100); viewed in the light of "after-time," what "seems absurd, impossible to-day," may yet prove to be true, as "seems so much else not explained but known" (VII, 1765–1767).

This, then, is how Pompilia gets from "I am" to "I rise." The final, glorious movement of her monologue is a magnificent aria of affirmation in which she takes an inductive leap, with the help of the imagination, from one order of experience to another order of experience. It makes no heavier demands upon our credulity than any other inductive leap of a similar magnitude, and it does not even require that we believe it. The only requirement that it makes is that we believe that she believes it, that it is true *for her*. What it affirms is that it is a sensitive and full-bodied rendering in language of the spiritual— even the immortal—meaning of love based on a knowledge of life, some understanding of it, and even more imagination concerning its ultimate significance. But while it does not ask us to accept its particular myth, it does ask us to consider this: if not its myth, then what myth? Because so long as we are human and hence have the imagination as our universally defining characteristic, some myth is unavoidable, and though we may not accept an individual myth, we deny at our peril the universal human process by which myths are made.

Notes

1. William Butler Yeats, *The Second Coming*, ll. 3–4.
2. Richard D. Altick and James F. Loucks II, *Browning's Roman Murder Story* (Chicago: University of Chicago Press, 1968), p. 57.

3. Altick and Loucks, p. 58.
4. Altick and Loucks, p. 359.
5. Mary Rose Sullivan, *Browning's Voices in "The Ring and the Book"* (Toronto: University of Toronto Press, 1969), p. 210.
6. As quoted by Matthew Arnold, "Heinrich Heine," *The Complete Prose Works of Matthew Arnold,* ed. R. H. Super (Ann Arbor: University of Michigan Press, 1962), III, 110.

7.

Wrenching Poetry out of Prose: Books VIII and IX

Browning was never known for setting himself small challenges. His dedication to poetry and to poetry's social function was, like Chaucer's and Shakespeare's, extraordinarily robust, and he pushed both his talent and his medium to the limit. Although *The Ring and the Book* has what one may call a unifying idiom—a canonical subject, structure, and style—the variations within the canon are enormous, so that it becomes in a very real sense an anthology or symphony of styles.[1] Some of these styles, Browning knew, were more popular than others, and he was more than a little concerned in *The Ring and the Book* to gain and hold a more popular readership than he had had in the past. But it was specifically *poetic* popularity that he aspired to; he was not willing to sacrifice the necessary austerity of poetry to the Parnassianism of public taste. Aristophanes was a poet as well as Homer and Sophocles, Chaucer and Shakespeare, and some human realities demanded for their exposure an Aristophanic manner. Books VIII and IX are poetically austere in that sense: their peculiar truth, Browning thought, demanded their peculiar manner.

Of course, the overall structure of the poem required some concession at this point, and the lawyers' monologues provide it in the comic relief that is one aspect of their literary character. To have moved from the transcendent lyricism of Pompilia directly to the Pope would have imposed an impossible challenge on the poet. If he succeeded in excelling the level reached in Book VII, he would endanger the heroic stature of Pompilia; a Pope made so grandly noble could not be critically measured without making his "hidden germ of failure" the source of a tragic catastrophe rather than the sympathetic portrait of a grand but deeply faulted old man that Browning intended. Pompilia's spell had to be broken and a quite different level of reality established before the poet's Pope could be properly placed in the hierarchy of human admiration. Its validity and preferability could then be tested against the counterpointed authoritarianism of the Guido of Book XI.

The tone and imagery of the poet-speaker in Book I are dependable and useful guides to the poet's attitude toward the successive monologuists and to his sense of the levels of complexity at which they function.[2] He tells us a great deal in a relatively few words, and every word, including every substantive word's order and sound, requires careful watching. Among the earlier books, the nearest approximation to the tone the poet-speaker adopts toward the lawyers' monologues is the cutting irony with which he introduces Tertium Quid. But whereas there he had twitted the speaker mercilessly as that "elaborated product" from the beginning, he is stealthier with the lawyers, beginning mildly, gradually building an ironic tendency, shifting to transparent sarcasm, and climaxing with undisguised disgust. Moreover, he but grudgingly grants the lawyers status as individual human beings representative of a human constituency. His emphasis is on "law, the recognized machine,/Elaborate display of pipe and wheel/Framed to unchoak, pump up and pour apace/Truth (I, 1110–1113)—like a vulture puking up half-digested food to feed its own young! Though they surface as two persons with two monologues, they are really two stages in one evolutionary process, "The chick

in egg" incubating (I, 1126–1127) the fully developed "cockerel that *would* crow" (I, 1204, emphasis added) through its
"scrannel pipe that screams in heights of head" (I, 1201).[3] Only
a semicolon separates the two, and the reader has been passed
to the latter before he quite knows that the former has been
dispensed with.

There is still a vestige of nature in the stage represented by
Archangeli comparable to that of a hawk whose entire existence is absorbed into thoughts of food and of feeding and
training his chick so that he will grow up to be the most hawkish of hawks. By the time he reaches the stage of Bottini, however, even that natural vestige is gone; all that is left is the self-
absorbed predator waiting—with sharp eye and ruddy cheek
but with "brow all prematurely soiled and seamed/With sudden age, bright devastated hair" (I, 1196–1199). A sort of hybrid serpent-fowl-hyena, his only interest is to lure the innocent and the hapless to destruction so that he may seize the
scavenger's or " 'wrecker's fee' " (I, 1194). It is horrible to witness nature thus wholly perverted by a role, but it forces the
reader to think feelingly about this dread aspect of reality.[4]

That the comparison of Archangeli with a hawk obsessed with
food and with feeding and training his chick is not fanciful is
clear from the first verse paragraph of his monologue. "Giacinto," "Cinone," "Cinozzo," "Cinoncello" seems to be hawkish
parental cooing, as *"Amo—as -avi -atum -are -ans,"* in addition
to its denotative meaning, suggests the yelping or screeching
of the chick upon the return of the food-gathering parent to
the nest. The child "chews Corderius with his morning crust";
"Look eight years onward, and he's perched, he's perched"; and
he feeds on his father's regurgitated food: "—Trying his milk-
teeth on some crusty case/Like this, papa shall triturate full
soon/To smooth Papinianian pulp!" (VIII, 1–14 passim). This
ritual of food and feeding is the obsession of the speaker's life,
his eye's vision of paradise to which all of life's business is subordinated, including all of life's morals (VIII, 15–59). He
wanders incontinently through the business of the afternoon,
thoughts of food perpetually erupting through his most resolute efforts to attend to the issues at hand. He takes his stom-
ach for his soul (VIII, 1386), perpetually picks the dry bones

of his legal, literary, and Biblical predecessors, models himself after Agur's wish (" 'Remove far from me vanity and lies,/Feed me with food convenient for me!' " [VIII, 1777–1778]), tucks his "inchoated" speech into a pigeon-hole (VIII, 1802), and in his review of Guido's execution, proudly reports that "Cinone" preferred witnessing the beheading to seeing Guido exonerated and that the chick quipped that, had his father not been reluctant to " 'aggrieve his Pope,' " he would have " 'argued-off Bottini's . . . nose' " (XII, 337–338, 353–356)—that is, in a battle of the beaks!

As used here and, the text suggests, as intended by the poet, *hawk* is not meant to designate a particular species of bird, but to include a large group of birds of prey with short, rounded wings, a long tail and legs, and a hooked beak and claws, active by day. Eagles and vultures would not be included, but falcons, buzzards, harriers, kites, and caracaras would be, as buzzard hawks, chicken hawks, and pigeon hawks would be also. Likewise, the poem's network of images associated with these birds of prey has an essentially subtextual and subliminal function, conditioning our imaginative response to the speaker rather than providing a literal, analytical model by which all his verbal actions are to be measured and judged. His spiritual consanguinity with the hawk, so to speak, is not allowed to stand in the way of his silliness, incompetence, pretension, and transparent deception. However, a recognition of the hawkish subtext does give us the critical direction and energy to track him in those human aspects.

The alpha and the omega of Archangeli's life—the sustainer of all of his enthusiasm and the source of all his energy—is domesticity. He begins with a paean to "home-joy, the family board,/Altar and hearth!"

> Well,
> Let others climb the heights o' the court, the camp!
> How vain are chambering and wantonness,
> Revel and rout and pleasures that make mad!
> Commend me to home-joy, the family board,
> Altar and hearth! These, with a brisk career,
> A source of honest profit and good fame,

Just so much work as keeps the brain from rust,
Just so much play as lets the heart expand,
Honouring God and serving man,—I say,
These are reality, and all else,—fluff,
Nutshell and naught,—thank Flaccus for the phrase!
Suppose I had been Fisc, yet bachelor!
                                                        (VIII, 47–59)

His day's work done—"I' the rough, i' the rough!" (1728)—he
concludes with an expression of deep bewilderment that "the
ambitious" so "lightly hold by these home-sanctities."

                                        Because ambition's range
            Is nowise tethered by domestic tie:
            Am I refused an outlet from my home
            To the world's stage?—whereon a man should play
            The man in public, vigilant for law,
            Zealous for truth, a credit to his kind,
            Nay,—through the talent so employed as yield
            The Lord his own again with usury,—
            A satisfaction, yea, to God Himself!
            Well, I have modelled me by Agur's wish,
            'Remove far from me vanity and lies,
            Feed me with food convenient for me!' What
            I' the world should a wise man require beyond?
                                                        (VIII, 1767–1779)

Thus it behooves the critic concerned to penetrate the inherent nature of the man to look carefully into the character and
quality of Archangeli's domesticity.

     That it, too, is shrunken and venal is everywhere manifest.
Like many men imprisoned in a professional role, especially
second-raters who have somehow managed to get promoted
beyond their genuine capacity, Archangeli does not have a son
so much as a clone. Giacinto is the father's best hope of beating his enemies and of gaining the approbation that, despite
all his self-massaging, he knows he has failed to achieve. His
elaborate celebration of domesticity is not disinterested and
genuine, therefore, but a virtue manufactured out of profes-

sional insecurity, an escape from the perpetual and imminent fear of failure appropriately disguised as high-mindedness. Protest against, malign, and belittle Bottini as much as he likes, Archangeli is yet painfully aware that he has been beaten by the Fisc and is liable to defeat at his hands at any time and when he least expects it. He tells himself that his professional duties are a sacrificial intrusion on his domestic tranquility, but the fact is that he reverts to thoughts of domesticity when he feels most inadequate to the relentless demands of his profession, as his thoughts seek solace in the sensuous delights of feeding when they become shakiest as thoughts. Moreover, domesticity does not offer the solace and tranquillity he claims for it. In the guise of affection, admiration, and solicitude, he is perpetually preying on his son; his "good fat little wife" is hardly more than an intermediary between the boy and her father's fortune; his so-called love-feasts are more like carrion-stews to create turmoil in the lives of various members of the larger predatory flock who will face any adversity to try to protect their own interests in the competition over codicils and wills.

As Archangeli sees himself, however falsely, as torn between idyllic domesticity and the demands of his profession—between the "poetry" of his sentiments and the voracious "prose" of "the law" (VIII, 136, 969–971)—so the poet suspends him in a grotesquely mixed medium of horror and humor, despicableness and pathos. Even while we recognize that the *Procurator Pauperum* has, ex officio, inherited a task that would perhaps prove impossible to even the wiliest of advocates and is absurdly beyond his patently limited powers, we can look with amused interest—even with a degree of tempered admiration—on the gusto with which he attempts to manufacture a favor of Providence out of a devilish situation. It is his particular form of whistling in the dark, of protecting himself against the devastating recognition that he is competing in a world of adversarial talents for which he is inadequately gifted. He retreats into the rough-sketching of his defense in the half-realization that his would-be flights of poetic fancy are fatuous absurdities—e.g., "married" becomes "underwent the matrimonial torch," etc. (VIII, 129–135). Instead of settling on the plain fact that no pistol was involved, he tries to do the Fisc one better with such florid extravagance as "igneous engine," "sulphury arms," and "popping-piece" (VIII, 202–209). Having failed at style, he turns to law only to find Bottini, the mastertrickster, in his path. Distressed beyond measure by a plight he cannot afford to face frankly, he indulges in a fury of ad hominem abuse of the Fisc and hoists himself on his own petard. His only real hope is in the yeoman work of Spreti, his assistant, but he disparages that as the effort of a mere "Pedant and prig" (VIII, 276) and for himself aspires to "the new, the unforeseen,/The nice bye-stroke, the fine and improvised,/Point that can titillate the brain o' the Bench/Torpid with over-teaching by this time!" (VIII, 259–262).

The pathos of Archangeli is a real dimension of the poet's imaginative vision, but of course the advocate's venality must not be rescued through the pathos of his floundering incompetence. Therefore the body of his defense *"P-r-o-pro Guidone et Sociis"* (VII, 128) is presented as an absurd, incontinently rambling, putatively learned, pretentiously farfetched improvisation tenuously held together by a schoolboy's understanding of classical rhetorical structures.[5] When his besieged ingenuity in answering Bottini's six "aggravations" prematurely collapses after the fourth aggravation, he again resorts to an inverted ad hominem technique, namely, a rhetorically inflated ceremony of flattery.

> We do ask,—but, inspire reply
> To the Court thou bidst me ask, as I have asked—
> Oh thou, who vigilantly dost attend
> To even the few, the ineffectual words
> Which rise from this our low and mundane sphere
> Up to thy region out of smoke and noise,
> Seeking corroboration from thy nod
> Who art all justice—which means mercy too,
> In a low noisy smoky world like ours
> Where Adam's sin made peccable his seed!
> We venerate the father of the flock,
> Whose last faint sands of life, the frittered gold,
> Fall noiselessly, yet all too fast, o' the cone

And tapering heap of those collected years,—
Never have these been hurried in their flow;
Though justice fain would jog reluctant arm,
In eagerness to take the forfeiture
Of guilty life: much less shall mercy sue
In vain that thou let innocence survive,
Precipitate no minim of the mass
O' the all-so precious moments of thy life,
By pushing Guido into death and doom!

(VIII, 1427–1448)

Then, after a mop-up foray, including a so-called peroration, characterized by fantastic logic, questionable fact, and a barrage of putative learning (VIII, 1511–1727), Archangeli concludes with a haughty slap at the Court he has been so quick to flatter (VIII, 1736–1745), a renewed celebration of the glories of domesticity (VIII, 1749–1779), and a chuckling revelation that he has acquired Pompilia's pawned necklace very cheaply and intends to use it as a white ruff around his henwife's neck if she can get her father to alter his will in favor of *"Hyacinthus,"* father *and* son.

Though the poet-speaker does not specifically refer to the lawyers' monologues as "sample-speeches" in Book I, it is clear even in their exaggerated form that Archangeli and Bottini do represent large if specialized slices of life. The legal profession to which they belong gets a severe buffeting, of course, as it has since the days of Aristophanes, and that certainly is a transparent part of the poet's intention here. But the metaphor is larger than that; it includes the familiar tendency of men (and women too, especially in the modern period) to subordinate themselves so completely to the professional machinery of a competitive, even an adversarial, society that they gradually become spiritually dehumanized and spend most of their creative energy rationalizing as a virtue what they half-recognize as a swindle of the self. Though Archangeli represents a stage not quite so complete and irremediable as that represented by Bottini, he is nonetheless far advanced in self-deceit, and despite the ruse of high-mindedness with which he claims the joys of domesticity as the real character of his life and self, it is clear that the external pressures and internal inadequacies that have led him to sacrifice his genuine identity to the lure of a public profession for which he is at once supremely and doubtfully qualified are also dominant in the private life to which he makes such reiterative professions of devotion. At one level, he is one of man's—especially modern man's—most pathetic representatives: a hedonist without any real understanding of or capacity for pleasure.

If the observation that the two lawyers were conceived by the poet both as distinct individuals and as different stages on a continuum is apt, then it is fair to see their conflict of roles as the internal grindings of a distressed spirit against itself. Both are comic asses, though Bottini is more advanced in subtlety and is more terrifying. Neither has a real audience, but manufactures an adversary out of the case, the Court, and his official counterpart; Bottini, especially, makes law an enclosed world, a power in itself without external reference points. Neither is sincere in his function, but uses it for self-glamour and to serve increasingly narrowing self-interests. Each blames his client for making his job too hard (Archangeli) or too easy (Bottini), and both are fixated on showmanship at the cost of truth. Each distrusts the other, Archangeli being fearful of Bottini while Bottini is contemptuous of Archangeli. Neither has any respect for the society he presumably serves, nor is there any honor among thieves.

Taken together and seen in this double perspective, their monologues provide a superb illustration of the enormous imaginative resourcefulness of the dramatic monologue form and a reminder that at the center of our dissatisfaction with the world around us is often an unrecognized or unacknowledged dissatisfaction with ourselves. Seen in this way too, the lawyers' monologues suggest the highly unorthodox critical conclusion that though the refined distinctions that we customarily make between such similar formal techniques as the soliloquy, the dramatic monologue, and the monodrama are real distinctions and cannot be swept either together or away, they are choices of the poet, not necessities of the subject. So when we say, as we often do, that *form is meaning,* we need to make provision for the fact that, though marvelous poets are marvelous, they are not infallible. Their use of form is always experimental, and its inherence in the subject is a metaphor, not a fact. Like the ideas poets have, their forms seem true to them, and we regularly accede to their choices, but had they made a different choice, we would have acceded to it too. This does not mean that we have a critical obligation to deconstruct them, but only that we should not expose them to the need for deconstruction by allowing our own reverence for *what is* to lead us to overdraw our imperatives and to speak of *what is* as *what must be*. This in turn puts quite a different burden on deconstruction than it has thus far been challenged to assume, namely, to subject deconstruction to the test of reconstruction—to show how the poet might have succeeded where it is thought that he failed. Though more to be hoped for than expected, success in that challenge would make criticism truly creative and could lead to a literary, a critical-creative, renaissance.

The process that the poet has been cultivating throughout *The Ring and the Book* has become fully operative when we reach the lawyers' monologues. What side each is on is of little importance except as a familiar machinery of self-exposure. We pick up with ease such gross errors of fact as, for example, Bottini-the-meticulous's assertion that Guido took seven hirelings with him instead of four, but we know that neither of the lawyers can be trusted to do anything but sniff out and track his own self-interest according to the style of each and that we must look through the style—mental, moral, linguistic, rhetorical, spiritual—to see the man as he truly is. In this way, we discover, I think, that, of all the characters in the poem, there is the widest discrepancy between the person Bottini thinks he is and the person his style tells us he is and that, concomitantly, he is the most thoroughly horrifying creature in the poem.

For a quick preliminary confirmation of the validity of this judgment, one can cite the poisoned condition of women in Bottini's psyche. Half-Rome as a brutal woman-whipper and Other Half-Rome as a mythicizer and de-creator of women are, by comparison with Bottini, bland and recognizable participants in an all-too-familiar sexist game. The eunuch-like Tertium Quid, though worthy of our cutting and dismissive irony, is neutralized and ineffectual, and we may find some plausible explanation for his distorted views in the shadowy origins from which he seems to have come and which he is trying so desperately to mask. Even Guido—who, as we have seen in Book V and will see more fully in Book XI, has so shattering a moment of insight into the truth of Pompilia and of himself that it sends him screaming like a tiger into eternity rather than change his male stripes—carries terror to its outer edge, but he does not, except in the deeply troubled mind of Caponsacchi and, to a lesser degree, in the noble but overstructured and romantically naive soul of the Pope, slip into horror and the deadening disgust that horror induces in our souls. Bottini, on the other hand, deals in poison gas. Into his hands is entrusted the reputation of the one person in the poem, a woman, whom even Guido has for an instant recognized as worthy of "the epic plunge" (IX, 217), and, in the name of praise, he drags her through the pollution of his own mind, "wily as an eel that stirs the mud/Thick overhead, so baffling spearman's thrust . . ." (IX, 1417–1418). Bottini is compounded of many disguised hatreds, of course; he is anti-Christian, anti-Jewish, anticlerical, anti-idealistic, even antisecular, and his idea of Paradise is one eternal, universal lawsuit with himself in the starring role. But in this monologue, his duty is the celebration of the tragic grandeur of a young woman, and he uses it, through the most cowardly of strategies, to demean her in every aspect of her life from childhood to the grave and with her what he sees as her whole wily, deceitful, prurient, treacherous sex.

The poet-speaker in Book I had warned us of something like this, but the event is much heavier and more focused than the promise.[6] Bottini, he had suggested, is a consummate pretender and opportunist who uses would-be "eloquence" to smooth out good and evil until they are indistinguishable and combines calculated "rashness" with calculated "caution" to lure the unfortunate and the unwary to a doom in which he sees a profit for himself. His physical appearance is consistent with his moral condition, masks of juvenility mixed with "soiled and seamed" and "devastated" signs of age, a megalomaniac masquerading as a musician of the soul and imaginative minion of the judiciary. His official role, the poet-speaker reminds us, is to make the "last speech against Guido and his gang," but we will discover that all of his monstrous energy goes into the sleazy defamation of Pompilia and the sex of which she is an exquisite flowering in a male atmosphere of such virulent enmity and predation that only the rarest and most favored survive it with their integrity intact. Thus there is consistency between the promise of Book I and the realization of Book IX, but the imaginative difference between the former and the latter is so explosive that it clarifies and confirms quite magnificently the difference in kind between thought and action and between rhetoric, however precise and useful, and poetry.

We know from the very beginning of his monologue that Bottini is obsessed with the self-love of self-contempt: "Had I God's leave, how I would alter things!" (IX, 1). But we cannot know how ominous the portent of those nine words is and tend, in emoting the line, to let our voice rise rather than fall with the word "alter," hearing in it an imprecation rather than a hiss or a growl. Then, as Bottini choreographs the world as *he* would have it, we are naturally amused by the fantastic staging he creates before our very eyes (IX, 2–16), being as yet unaware how morally and psychologically systemic is his dissatisfaction with reality and his own place in it. Even the ceremonious flattery, the opportunistic cuts at Jews, Turks, and Molinists, the flashes of prurience, and the unction of the next two verse paragraphs (IX, 17–70, 71–118) are not enough to detract seriously from our interest in the extended art analogy he draws and the thoroughly respectable aesthetic theory he articulates through it. Also, we may not immediately perceive that the poet is allowing the speaker to hoist himself on his own petard:

> For in that brain,—their fancy sees at work,
> Could my lords peep indulged,—results alone,
> Not processes which nourish the result,
> Would they discover and appreciate,—life
> Fed by digestion, not raw food itself,
> No gobbets but smooth comfortable chyme
> Secreted from each snapped-up crudity,—
> Less distinct, part by part, but in the whole

Truer to the subject,—the main central truth
And soul o' the picture, would my Judges spy,—
Not those mere fragmentary studied facts
Which answer to the outward frame and flesh—
Not this nose, not that eyebrow, the other fact
Of man's staff, woman's stole or infant's clout,
But lo, a spirit-birth conceived of flesh,
Truth rare and real, not transcripts, fact and false.
                                                    (IX, 92–107)

Bottini and the poet have very different purposes in this passage. Bottini wants to show how urban and sophisticated—how very Roman—he is; the poet wants to allow him to articulate the very method and metaphors by which he will be measured and be found to be so "eximiously" false (IX, 109), so "splendidly [i.e., audaciously, deceptively, terrifyingly] mendacious!" (IX, 836).

At the very end of his impressive "exordium" (IX, 119), a sudden crack appears in the highly polished surface of Bottini's self-presentation: his aesthetic theory renders up the negligible Ciro Ferri at the expense of Michelangelo and Raphael; his facts wobble; and his identification of himself with "Ciro's self" (IX, 121) shows that his motive for inflating contemporaneity is self-reflexive (IX, 109–121). From this point on, the poet becomes more aggressive as the self-satisfied speaker, intoxicated with the grand effect of his beginning, becomes careless. Bottini's "artistic" designs fall apart, his use of rhetorical color is outrageously tasteless, his appeal to the exclusive authority of antiquity is both inconsistent and inept, his claim to being the easy master of his artistic medium, language, is repeatedly ridiculed through false notes, and the calculated humility of "dares my feebleness" reveals rather than hides his arrogance (IX, 121–195 passim).

Bottini's fundamental distrust of Pompilia and of female honor, virtue, and integrity generally now takes over in the guise of the "great theme" of "A faultless nature in a flawless form" (IX, 191, 195); in the inflated rhetoric of turgid euphuisms, he makes his "epic plunge" into moral filth. To catalogue the instances of defamation, variously sly, oblique but patent, clumsy and heavy-handed, would be to belabor the obvious: they are legion.[7] What seems more critically serviceable is to remind ourselves that Bottini's monologue is a "sample-speech" and to examine its larger implications.

We know from experience that each of the speakers, particularly each of the nonprincipals, has a generic as well as an individual role to play in the poem, and we have speculated on a special, progressive relationship between Bottini and Archangeli—that Bottini is the full flower of a mechanical system of which Archangeli is an intermediate growth. Considering, too, the gross abuse of language that is a chief mark of his monologue—the use of florid euphuisms in the underhanded assassination of a youthful heroine and her sex—Bottini becomes the most emphatic proof of what the poet-speaker in Book XII calls the "one lesson" that the poem "should teach":

> This lesson, that our human speech is naught,
> Our human testimony false, our fame
> And human estimation words and wind.
> (XII, 834–836)

Viewed from that perspective, Bottini's monologue is a summary and climax of all that has gone before—the quintessence of falsehood masquerading, through rhetoric, as truth. That is an important consideration, certainly, having a crucial relevance to the poem as a whole. So is another function of this monologue as a summary and climax of all that has gone before. It is by now quite clear that "the great constringent relation between man and woman"[8] is "A great theme" (IX, 191) of *The Ring and the Book*. It has been a persistent presence in every earlier monologue, being mirrored from separate angles of vision according to each character and the importance he or she attaches to it, and it will continue to be an important theme in *The Pope* and in Guido's second monologue. But the Pope is hardly qualified by experience to give it full-dress exposure in his troubled apologia, and though it is "the thing itself" in Book XI, it is locked into Guido's individual character so idiosyncratically and dramatically that, without the risk of considerable dissipation of the monologue's dramatic or "scenic" emphasis, Guido cannot be the agent of the broadest generic or "panoramic" reflection of the theme. So Bottini's monologue becomes the poet's last opportunity to pull all the sexist threads together and see their monstrous totality, and that is one of the important functions the poet gives it. In turn, one of the most important critical opportunities it provides the reader is to see, en masse, the great variety of ways in which male sexism surfaces and does its dirty work in a culture profoundly infected by it.

These two climactic themes—the rhetoric of falsehood and the cunning masks of sexism—repeatedly merge into one in Bottini's monologue. Conspicuous among the instances of this fusion are the following seven passages: 229–238, 298–326, 350–366, 539–550, 886–923, 1192–1205, 1235–1247. Other passages that qualify will serve to illustrate other strategies of sexism, and, for reasons of economy, of the seven cited above only three will be quoted and commented on here.

The first example occurs soon after the exordium, when the poet is just putting into high gear the process of exposing the significance of the double entendre in Bottini's phrase "my picture's self!" (IX, 159).

> And what is beauty's sure concomitant,
> Nay, intimate essential character,
> But melting wiles, deliciousest deceits,
> The whole redoubted armoury of love?
> Therefore of vernal pranks, dishevellings
> O' the hair of youth that dances April in,
> And easily-imagined Hebe-slips
> O'er sward which May makes over-smooth for foot—
> These shall we pry into?—or wiselier wink,
> Though numerous and dear they may have been?
>   (IX, 229–238)

Behind this cavalier and would-be ingratiating celebration of a nymph-like girl's early discovery of the warming sun and gentle breezes of youthful passion wrought with multiple rhetorical devices—alliteration, assonance, allusion to the freshness of the early world and to the benignest moments of the pagan gods, a tone of amused and indulgent permissiveness—are the premises of indictments of Pompilia and her sex as inherently deceptive tricksters in an endless warfare against men, employing a deadly "armoury of love" with such wiliness that only men who are eternally vigilant and have steeled their hearts against them, never winking a foolish eye, have any chance of survival. Thus both the Pompilia and the Bottini of the piece are stationed in this seemingly gay, rhetorically stylized vignette that has no correspondence at all in the actual life of the poem's heroine.

The second example will do double service, not only showing how Bottini's devilish intent is disguised in high-flown rhetoric but also revealing what the crucial incident at Castelnuovo means to him:

> But virtue, barred, still leaps the barrier, lords!
> —Still, moon-like, penetrates the encroaching mist
> And bursts, all broad and bare, on night, ye know!
> Surprised, then, in the garb of truth, perhaps,
> Pompilia, thus opposed, breaks obstacle,
> Springs to her feet, and stands Thalassian-pure,
> Confronts the foe,—nay, catches at his sword
> And tries to kill the intruder, he complains.
> Why, so she gave her lord his lesson back,
> Crowned him, this time, the virtuous woman's way,
> With an exact obedience; he brought sword,
> She drew the same, since swords are meant to draw.
> Tell not me 'tis sharp play with tools on edge!
> It was the husband chose the weapon here.
> Why did not he inaugurate the game
> With some gentility of apophthegm
> Still pregnant on the philosophic page,
> Some captivating cadence still a-lisp
> O' the poet's lyre? Such spells subdue the surge,
> Make tame the tempest, much more mitigate
> The passions of the mind, and probably
> Had moved Pompilia to a smiling blush.
> No, he must needs prefer the argument
> O' the blow: and she obeyed, in duty bound,

Returned him buffet ratiocinative—
Ay, in the reasoner's own interest,
For Wife must follow whither husband leads,
Vindicate honour as himself prescribes,
Save him the very way himself bids save!
No question but who jumps into a quag
Should stretch forth hand and pray one 'pull me out
By the hand!' such were the customary cry:
But Guido pleased to bid 'Leave hand alone!
Join both feet, rather, jump upon my head,
I extricate myself by the rebound!'
And dutifully as enjoined she jumped—
Drew his own sword and menaced his own life,
Anything to content a wilful spouse.

                                        (IX, 886–923)

The critical significance of the passage justifies, I think, quoting it at such length. It may at first glance seem strange to cite these lines as particularly euphuistic since the metaphors, classical allusions, and conceits, though farfetched, seem rather hard-hitting than florid. But though such a characterization of the rhetoric of the passage is fair, it should be noticed that at its center is a reprimand of Guido for not having used the language of allure—euphuism—instead of the language of confrontation and attack: "gentility of apophthegm," "Some captivating cadence still a-lisp/O' the poet's lyre" to "mitigate/The passions" and move even a hostile audience "to a smiling blush" (IX, 900–907). Bottini emphatically claims that he knows the dangers of such confrontation and attack—"Tell not me 'tis sharp play with tools on edge!" (IX, 898)—and since his preference throughout has been for the language of allure, it is reasonable to accept his defense of euphuism as a personal rationale and to see this passage as relevant in its very inversion of a euphuistic style. What Bottini tries to demonstrate thereby is that he can play with logical argument as well as with "gentility of apophthegm" and "captivating cadence"; like Guido, he says, " 'I extricate myself by the rebound!' " (IX, 920)—regain feet on solid ground by standing Pompilia on her head! That is, in fact, the self-saving technique Bottini uses. He suddenly (acrobatically) portrays Pompilia as having taken "the virtuous woman's way,/With an exact obedience" and thus "Crowned him" "lord" and husband. He brought the sword, she used it, and this vindicates Guido's own prescription of "honour" (IX, 912–914). Thus her action was a rational statement ("buffet ratiocinative" [IX, 910])—blow for blow.

The argument is without persuasive merit, but it is agile and shows a complexly calculated design. It satisfies Bottini's need to appear to be always on top of the situation. It enables him to keep his male sexism intact—virtue in a woman is to crown her husband with absolute obedience. By making Pompilia the instructress of her erring husband in the matter of the sword, it makes her share any guilt he may suffer in the use of it and points to the conclusion that his later use of the sword against her bore her sanction. Most importantly, Bottini uses it to sidestep entirely the issue of Guido's cowardice in this crucial incident while at the same time subverting Pompilia's credit for heroism. It was not a moral failure, but a momentary failure in judgment for which he deserved the quick rebuff she gave him and, fortunately, was duly instructed by it.

In the third example, Bottini lends his euphuistic talents to the Court. This is his way of reinforcing the argument of the pro-Guido advocates that the Court's original judgment meant that Pompilia, not being wholly innocent, was therefore guilty, but besides interpreting the Court's judgment, he actually puts his own peculiar style into the Court's mouth:

> 'Quit the gay range o' the world,' I hear her cry,
> 'Enter, in lieu, the penitential pound:
> Exchange the gauds of pomp for ashes, dust:—
> Leave each mollitious haunt of luxury,
> The golden-garnished silken-couched alcove,
> The many-columned terrace that so tempts
> Feminine soul put foot forth, nor stop ear
> To fluttering joy of lover's serenade,
> Leave these for cellular seclusion; mask
> And dance no more, but fast and pray; avaunt—
> Be burned, thy wicked townsman's sonnet-book!
> Welcome, mild hymnal by . . . some better scribe!

For the warm arms, were wont enfold thy flesh,
Let wire-shirt plough and whip-cord discipline!'
(IX, 1192–1205)

That the flowery tropes and tone of pastoral exhortation ("Go thou and sin no more!") are patently absurd does not negate the fact that the choice of rhetorical strategy suits Bottini's purposes admirably. Throughout, his basic goal has been to assert his own mastery by obfuscating all issues rather than by using "sharp play with tools on edge!" Therefore, even if the Court is disdainful of the style he visits on it, its members may react to it subconsciously as one reacts to flattery, not quite so unequivocally as one thinks or says he does, and even a degree of ambiguity serves Bottini well. The content of the passage is analogous to its style. It further strengthens the speaker's systemic distrust of and antagonism toward women: the "Feminine soul" is a guilty thing requiring penance, and feminine "flesh" needs to be ploughed with the "wire-shirt" and disciplined with the "whip-cord." With particular reference to Pompilia's case, the formula he uses is analogous to congratulating a man for having stopped beating his wife. Unctuous exhortation takes the place of established fact, and guilt is the implicit assumption behind the praise. In addition, there is in this passage a clever shift of emphasis. Previously, Pompilia had been used as a basis for generalizing about women. Here, a general attitude toward women is used as the net to catch Pompilia in: consideration of the merits of the individual case is simply lost in the wholesale condemnation of the class. That the condemnation is nothing more than a rhetorically stereotyped cliché that ultimately numbs the ingenuity even of the speaker (" 'Welcome, mild hymnal by . . . some better scribe!' ") will not, he hopes cynically, prevent its doing its subterranean dirty work.

This fusion of the rhetoric of falsehood with a cunning male sexism may be the most distinctive mark of Bottini's monologue, but it is by no means the only one. To poison the world against women is such an obsession with him that he provides a virtual handbook of antifeminist techniques, a guide to female defamation. Translated into "rules," with only one or two

clarifying examples out of many, Bottini's example would lead
to the following:

(1) Introduce wherever possible diminishing tropes to stress,
   perhaps in the form of a lamentation, the inadequacy of
   women: "The weaker sex, my lords, the weaker sex!" (IX,
   225)—such seemingly ingratiating tropes, for example, as
   frisking lambs (IX, 220–224) or the "heifer [that must]
   brave the hind" (IX, 251).
(2) Insist upon the fundamental principle that the male is "lord
   and king" by immutable "natural law" (IX, 252–254).
(3) Give your male sexism a patina of grandeur by calling it
   "the philosophic mind," meaning a man who accepts sto-
   ically the universal recalcitrance of women (IX, 261–275).
(4) If you want to slur the reputation of a woman, cast it as a
   rumor that "foes allege" and then give it full elaboration
   (IX, 298–326); or grant for argument's sake any calumny, however patently false, and play brinksmanship with
   the lady's reputation (IX, 328ff., 445ff., 635–638, 651,
   682ff., 706–707, 798–836, 1250ff., 1275)—"Anything,
   anything to let the wheels/Of argument run glibly to their
   goal!" (IX, 471–472).
(5) On the general principle that the end justifies the means
   (IX, 516–517), assign the woman the highest motive and
   then undercut it with the most incriminating method (IX,
   527–534, 539–551). The moral: "Grime is grace/To who
   so gropes amid the dung for gold."
(6) Since people are always ready to fall for an old saw and
   smoke is the easiest thing on earth to see, use some version of *where there's smoke, there's fire* (IX, 560ff.).
(7) If there's a second man involved, make him romantically
   irresistible—young, "potent," with "complete equipment"
   (IX, 598ff.); people's romantic fantasies will do the rest.
(8) If the woman is well-reputed, make her at least "Prepared
   for either fortune" (IX, 657ff.); ambiguity is very serviceable.
(9) If the facts resist your insinuations, "Nature" won't. A
   woman in a deathlike swoon from physical and emotional
   fatigue can be taken with natural impunity by a tender,
   virile male half mad with love (IX, 730–766).
(10) Using the universal axiom that no one is perfect, convict
   the woman of imagined duplicity—"Feint, wile and trick"—

and then appear to rectify it by calling her mendacity splendid (IX, 767–836).

(11) Reject the gross charge in favor of the lesser charge—not pitch black but only black and blue; the seeming defense, like faint praise, is an effective smear tactic (IX, 979–1013).

(12) There's nothing like a little levity to dissipate an emotion-charged situation. If the wheels of justice have turned too slowly, redeem the good intentions of the authorities and thereby make the unorthodox actions of the victim seem impatient and precipitate (IX, 1107–1127).

(13) Convert the monster-husband into a reformed saint imploring the truant wife to return to his loving solace before it is too late and she be lost forever to others' "nocturnal taste of intercourse" (IX, 1228ff.).

(14) If the woman has succeeded in exonerating herself, lavish her with poisoned praise, making her saving testimony appear to be the grandest and most applaudable of simulations (IX, 1412–1444). This pinking of the white, so to speak, works best as a final resort, but it helps one save face and at least may take some of the radiance out of her victory (IX, 1445–1503).

(15) Insist that your purpose throughout—past, present, and future—is "To draw the true *effigiem* of a saint,/Do justice to perfection in the sex . . ." (IX, 1397–1398), insinuating that womankind never had a truer friend than you.

If Bottini's monologue is a "sample-speech" in that it is a summary and climax of all that has gone before in *The Ring and the Book* in the rhetoric of falsehood and in the monstrous reality of male sexism, it would perhaps be futile to try to identify a group of real individuals for whom he is a representative stand-in. He becomes a metaphor of the whole rather than of its individual parts, and to see a whole Bottini in ourselves or in individuals we know would itself be a defamation. On the other hand, it should not be difficult to see fragments of ourselves in Bottini or fragments of Bottini in ourselves, and that is sobering enough. He is those fragments pulled together and pushed to their ultimate extreme, but horror of the whole cannot, for conscientiously engaged persons, provide an escape from the relevance of the parts. Most people can say *Bot-*

tini c'est moi without meaning the whole *Bottini* or the whole *moi*, and in that there is both moral astringency and moral relief.

It is perhaps futile, too, to search for a specific explanation for the way Bottini is, considered individually. A thousand speculations would not constitute an adequate explanation. Like evil, he is beyond rational understanding. But metaphorically he is frighteningly clear: sexism looked at whole, looked at in all its horrible length and breadth, is a moral cancer in any culture, and unless steps are taken to eliminate it, even our finest phrases and most elegant feints will not be able to disguise the moral rot it really is.

Notes

1. The fullest study of this aspect of the poem is Donald S. Hair, *Browning's Experiments with Genre* (Toronto: University of Toronto Press, 1972).
2. I cannot improve on the excellent chapter in Richard D. Altick and James F. Loucks's *Browning's Roman Murder Story* (Chicago: University of Chicago Press, 1968), " 'Here's Rhetoric and to Spare!': The Lawyers and Classical Oratory" (Chapter 6, pp. 151–183). The authors show in considerable detail the lawyers' observance of the rhetorical principles enunciated by "Aristotle, Cicero, and Quintillian" (p. 152). I certainly agree that the lawyers are not "mere buffoons." What I do not accept quite so readily is the implication of conscientiousness in the suggestion that the lawyers have been busily conning their rhetorical guidebooks and applying their lessons (p. 153). These rhetorical formulae may be esoteric to us, but they were probably schoolboy stuff to them, as routine as the conjugation of *amare*, handbook paradigms long since committed to memory. It is also likely that they had commonplace books, private or public, of familiar and useful quotations from the classics and the Scriptures that they could draw upon quite routinely. So while they were not buffoons, they were also not devoted students of the law. The deadly, dehumanizing aspect of the legal situation was that they had to use the same material day after day throughout their professional life, and the Court had to listen to it.
3. Also, the "worm" in the "cabbage-bed" becomes "some finished butterfly" (I, 1108–1171), and the conceiver and inchoater of "the argument" and conceiver of the exordium becomes the "composite" successor who frames the "full-grown speech"—at least in the self-amorous fancy of the cock-

erel-butterfly, whose *soi-disant* epic poem turns to dusty prose as soon as pen touches paper (I, 1155, 1165, 1174, 1208).

4. It also prepares the reader to recognize, on quite a different plane, the conflict between the natural hero and the Papal role-player in Book X, *The Pope.*

5. See note 2, above.

6. This is characteristic of the "promise" of Book I. The poet-speaker expresses an implicit evaluation that we can then test, but he does not indicate the particular imaginative strategies that will be used in the various monologues.

7. Some representative examples can be found in the following passages: 224–225, 231–237, 251–275, 356–366, 393, 410–415, 435–443, 457–458, 501–506, 527–534, 540–546, 624, 652–656, 671–676, 711–713, 730–766, 772–777, 791–793, 802, 804, 821–822, 937–938, 982, 1002–1008, 1192–1205, 1237–1242, 1274, 1412–1424, 1464–1474.

8. Henry James, "The Novel in *The Ring and the Book*," in *Notes on Novelists* (New York: Scribners, 1914), p. 409.

8.

"*Quis pro Domino?* . . . I": Book X. *The Pope*

That the Pope in his monologue provides one model for reading *The Ring and the Book* is clear. Such is the unmistakable conclusion implied at a near-explicit level by the language in which he introduces us to the procedure he has followed "through this sombre wintry day" and his motive for reflecting further on the significance of his labor and his conclusion. First, the procedure:

> I have worn through this sombre wintry day,
> With winter in my soul beyond the world's,
> Over these dismalest of documents
> Which drew night down on me ere eve befell,—
> Pleadings and counter-pleadings, figure of fact
> Beside fact's self, these summaries to-wit,—
> How certain three were slain by certain five:
> I read here why it was, and how it went,
> And how the chief o' the five preferred excuse,
> And how law rather chose defence should lie,—

> What argument he urged by wary word
> When free to play off wile, start subterfuge,
> And what the unguarded groan told, torture's feat
> When law grew brutal, outbroke, overbore
> And glutted hunger on the truth, at last,—
> No matter for the flesh and blood between.
> All's a clear rede and no more riddle now.
> Truth, nowhere, lies yet everywhere in these—
> Not absolutely in a portion, yet
> Evolvable from the whole: evolved at last
> Painfully, held tenaciously by me.
>
>   (X, 211–231)

Then the motive:

> Therefore I stand on my integrity,
> Nor fear at all: and if I hesitate,
> It is because I need to breathe awhile,
> Rest, as the human right allows, review
> Intent the little seeds of act, the tree,—
> The thought, to clothe in deed, and give the world
> At chink of bell and push of arrased door.
>
>   (X, 275–281)

These two passages are so well known to every close student of *The Ring and the Book* that it would be quite unnecessary to quote them here at such length except for one fact: almost all the commentators on the poem have adopted the Pope's model as the "authorized" model for reading the poem—that is, they have assumed that the Pope "speaks for Browning" and have used these and correlative passages to justify the mind-set that enables them to read the poem in that way. At stake, then, is the largest critical issue imaginable—how to read not only *The Ring and the Book* but also whatever *The Ring and the Book* is a way of reading—and that cannot be reexamined too often. Indeed, the very spirit of the poem demands that it be examined afresh by every conscientious reader so long as the poem is read.

One of the transparent reasons for being skeptical of the Pope's authority over the poem is the obvious care with which the cards are stacked in favor of that authority. As Other Half-Rome says, "That were too temptingly commodious . . ." (III, 1674) in a poem whose very raison d'être is an exposure of the infinite if not always subtle ways in which truth is manipulated by language.

On the positive side, the poet-speaker in Book I introduces the Pope's as "the ultimate/Judgment save" the reader's, emphasizes the possibility that this may be the Pope's last moment of truth before his own death and accounting, describes him as "Grave but not sad," stresses his exemplary conscientiousness, his need "for respite and relief" after a job thoroughly done, his quiet, humble fellowship with God through prayer, and the "clear conscience" with which he goes to supper directly after issuing the fatal order (I, 1220–1271 passim). In point of fact, this is only a sympathetic characterization of a grand old man, not a subscription to a judgment that is ultimate only in being last, but it *appears* to be an endorsement through character delineation. The same is true of the elaborate and wholly ingratiating way in which the Pope seems to dissociate himself from the doctrine of Papal Infallibility. After reading the macabre narrative of Formosus and Stephen, he says with irresistible simplicity, " 'Mankind is ignorant, a man am I:/Call ignorance my sorrow not my sin!' " (X, 257–258). Ignorance as one of the wounds of man is a perfectly orthodox assertion, and in the criminal case at hand, the Pope has absolutely no doctrinal presumption of infallibility. Moreover, he plays his Papal role to the hilt throughout the monologue, humanely but unswervingly, and when one considers the horrifying alternative and what such horror would do to the tragic integrity of *The Ring and the Book,* it cannot be considered grudging to see even the splendid daring with which he looks at the stark jeopardy in which Christianity stands as no more than the duty of a courageous Pope who thinks. Still, in the poet's treatment, the Pope *seems* to sacrifice orthodoxy of both thought and action to the awful truth, and that appearance wins over both our hearts and our minds.

The negative side is perhaps even more psychologically persuasive. We come to the Pope's monologue from Bottini's, and the Fisc may be, both as a result of his inherent nature and the role in which he is cast, the most truly horrible character in the whole poem. He is so deep in self-corruption that his touch disfigures loveliness far more intolerably even than Guido's Genoese dagger; he is an Abate Paolo carried to the ugliest imaginable extreme, and we reach the atmosphere of the Pope's simple, dutiful, reverential integrity like persons on the verge of suffocation, having witnessed even Pompilia reduced through Bottini's advocacy to a slippery eel. Moreover, Bottini is only the climax to a general drift toward Guido's acquittal. Half-Rome (II) and Archangeli (VIII) are outright Guido advocates; Other Half-Rome (III), though an advocate of Pompilia, is a literary cousin of Bottini, a hollow man who flounders onto Pompilia's side and attempts or pretends to fill the vacuousness of his own inner self with pathos, melodrama, and romantic fabrication—"gilding the lily" in the most falsifying sense; Tertium Quid (IV) is so morally neutered that he may not even perceive the tilt toward Guido of his *soi-disant* objectivity and so morally distasteful that no genuine admirer of Pompilia's hard-won heroism would want him as an ally; and Caponsacchi, though he understands at last something of Pompilia's "glory" and "beauty" and "splendour," is susceptible to such emotional muddle that, even at the end, he endangers her reputation by the manner in which he goads her judges, sings her praises, and pronounces anathema on her enemies. As a result, we come to the Pope's irrevocable resolution as to terra firma after a long struggle with quicksand and to his pronouncement of Pompilia as "Perfect in whiteness" as to the blessed light at the end of a dark, circuitous tunnel. What they are *not* greatly enhances both what he is and what, in such company, he appears to be.

Much more evidence of positive as well as negative ways in which the reader is predisposed or pushed in favor of the Pope's authority could be adduced if it were not supererogative, like taking a score of syllogisms to demonstrate what two or three make sufficiently conclusive. The point is not to strip the Pope of authority, a goal that, even if it were successfully accomplished, would be grossly self-defeating. The critical premise that needs to be reestablished in the face of its near-universal dismemberment by the commentators is that the Pope's *degree of authority,* like that of every other "sample" speaker, must be drafted, qualified in detail, revised to fit all the facts, and tentatively concluded according to the principles of the inductive method whose stages are outlined in these four predicates. In short, the Pope's "reading" must be subjected to our reading uninhibited by a predisposition that would enable case-making to parade behind the mask of honest investigation in the service of truth.

But the most binding reason for discountenancing the Pope's authority to speak for Browning is the integrity of the poem and the poet. The poet-speaker in Books I and XII is Browning genericized, *a* poet metamorphosized into *the* poet, and he makes a promise that cannot be forfeited with integrity: the final judgment is ours, and to be deprived of that judgment's privileges and responsibilities, for whatever grand purpose and by whatever sleight of hand, is to strip us of the worth of reading (seeing or knowing, understanding or comprehending, imagining or transforming), a deprivation that, in the enveloping metaphor of the poem, is equivalent to denying us the worth of life. The integrity of the poem is correlative to that of the poet. *The Ring and the Book* is a massive poem about the games, specifically the word games, all people play. Those word games are given a panoply of manifestations—forms, moods, ad hoc goals—but all, in relative degree, are made relevant to the ultimate meaning of life through the elevation given them by classical poetic means: a life-and-death subject or action; an architecture or construction that, while it accommodates a modern outlook, maintains the grandeur and solemnity traditionally held to be appropriate to a drama of epic proportions; a language or diction that adapts a modern expressionism to an ancient sense of literary decorum, each speaker being highly individualized by a fusion of character and genre and his language appropriated accordingly. The commitment all this literary high seriousness makes to the reader is a solemn one: it is worth any investment we are willing to make in it. But the promise is even more specific than that. If we were simply to eliminate Books I and XII from *The Ring and the Book* and relieve the generic poet of all explicitly stated obligations, the implicit contract of form and idea would remain, including the following specific terms. This is the fatal truth, winnow it out of these grim givens as best you may. The grimmest given of all is the impossibility of finding the whole truth in any one view of it, including your own view. But out of the multiple examples of manipulation so elaborately dramatized, three hope-restorative perceptions do suggest themselves: there is, among the tumbled fragments and not to be pressed too dogmatically, a wide but observable spectrum of worst to best. The characters in the general field of better-to-best seem, again in varying degrees, to have in common a will to believe in a higher order of reality, a capacity, though in some cases a threatened or deteriorating capacity, to convert the lower to the higher, and a catalyzing experience that enables them, on the strength of their will and their capacity, actually to make the conversion. Though success at this conversion spares them none of the vicissitudes of life, it increases their ability to deal with those vicissitudes constructively, to hold steady in their reinforced will to believe rather than to become the powerless victims of circumstantial buffetings.

The Ring and the Book being a modern quest poem, therefore, and the invitation to the reader being to participate in its dynamic process with courage, care, and such hope as his inner resources working on these sample circumstances can purify and strengthen, it would be a serious breach of contract if, at the eleventh hour, one of the most distasteful games people play were suddenly played on him. It would collapse the presumed representativeness of the poem's myth, since none of the "poor weak trembling human wretch[es]" who play their parts in the poem and with whom we variously identify has any such *deus ex machina* advantage; and it would convert literary high seriousness to farce, participation to passivity, and literary tragedy to ingenious triviality in the manner of the popular quiz show or the family magazine that says, "See Book X for the answers."

It is impossible to believe that Browning intended that result or that he would have been either blind to or careless of it as a likely consequence of placing an authorial stand-in and mouthpiece within the poetic text in the teeth of a multitude of explicit and implicit disclaimers. Indeed, the very untenableness of such a position points strongly toward a quite contrary thesis—namely, that the Pope's monologue is the ultimate test of the poem's whole manner. In other words, as *Pompilia* models the poetic process of personal redemption through exemplary imaginative mythmaking, *The Pope* challenges to the nth degree the reader's critical-creative maturation—the capacity, developed through the reading of this and other serious literary texts, so to keep his critical mind and his sympathetic emotions in creative balance as to detach himself with love from the Pope's gloriously well-intentioned but untenable "way" (I, 772) and to see that the model he represents for resolving an admittedly terrifying problem may be negatively evaluated without giving up the deep and genuine affection he merits as a man.[1] In short, Book X is our test in critical reading as Book VII is our test in creative mythmaking, and, I suggest, once one begins, however tentatively and experimentally, to follow this line of thought, the Pope emerges in a light very different from the customary one. He seems not only fallible but deeply faulted, and the discrepancy between the conclusions he arrives at and the manner in which he reaches them appears to be at least as great as that in any other of the poem's monologues. Moreover, to the critical question that inevitably comes of seeing the Pope's monologue as a "sample-speech"—what would be the result of a general adoption of the Pope's "way" of problem-solving?—the answer that emerges is as critically terrifying as his own terror when one remembers that the motive does not necessarily go with the method.

Finally, the judicious critic, seeing such a radical and explosive view of the Pope beginning to take shape and wishing perhaps to scotch it before he himself gets deep in self-corruption, may move quickly from the Pope's motive to the poet's: why, if that was his true intention in his treatment of the Pope, did Browning disguise it so thoroughly that for more than a century his intention has been misconceived? Though a century is not long to wait in the history of the Papacy, as the Pope himself points out in introducing himself, or in the longer history of man's search for truth, as his imagined pleading of Euripides makes clear (X, 1676–1790), two plausible answers suggest themselves: one, that this was his subtle, oblique way of dealing with the most subtle and oblique problem that any truly ambitious poet faces, namely, challenging the reader to the utmost; and two, that this was the most satisfactory way he thought he could devise for being true to his own perception of the peculiar role the Roman Church, particularly the Roman Papacy, was beginning to play in the battle of modernism and at the same time avoid an outcry so violent that his most broadly relevant and imaginatively gratifying poetic labor would be lost in the furor. It was wiser, he may have thought, to await time's slow vindication than to be damaged by an anathema that, like Pope Stephen's over Pope Formosus, eight centuries could not wholly repair.

Respect for the poet's processive method suggests the desirability of beginning with the Formosus question to see how it prepares us for the "reading test" and the view of the Roman Church that the monologue is supposed to embody. Browning had no *donnée* from the Old Yellow Book other than the fact of his decision to monitor his choices in dealing with the Pope, so there are no accidents to extenuate those choices. Thus the Pope's habit of reading daily from a history of his Papal predecessors and his choice for this particular day are purposeful calculations, and the tendency to see the some 150 lines devoted to them as merely establishing historical grounds for a disclaimer of infallibility on a matter in which he has no claim to it seems grossly disproportionate. No serious poet would use to such a limited if significant end so many crucial initial lines in a poem-within-a-poem that gives the whole poetic effort its greatest philosophical depth and most extended historical parameters. It is in such passages that a speaker is made to reveal his unconscious mind and a poet plants seeds that will grow the largest plants. Browning uses them in those ways.

Despite the muting frame given it—a quiet, serious old man with well-worn habits faced with an official duty of great consequence that, however absolute his judgment and however fatal its import, will never bear the mark of infallibility in this world and may be called mistaken in the next—the sequence on Formosus, Stephen, Romanus, Theodore, John, and Sergius, six Popes, is stunningly modern in that it is genuine theatre of the absurd. It takes a solemn subject and makes it so horrifying that it is wildly comic, and nothing in the poem's central myth equals it in that respect. And yet, Innocent seems remarkably immune to the comic horror of his Papal predecession, moving without so much as a raised eyebrow to the solemn, deadpan questions, "Which of the judgments was infallible?/Which of my predecessors spoke for God?" (X, 150–151), though the very idea of the questions has been made ridiculous by a history just as official as that of the Old Yellow Book. When we look at the Roman Church as reflected in the poem's own myth, with its Cardinals, Archbishops, Bishops, Abates, Canons, Confessors, Priests, and near-Priests, it seems just as absurd that it should claim to be the Mystical Body and Bride of Christ as that, in the history of the Papacy, the Popes should claim to speak infallibly for God. But Innocent sees none of the absurdity of the latter at the beginning of his monologue, and we are thereby alerted to study exactly how he comes to terms with the former as his monologue opens up to face that question.[2] In the meantime, the manner in which he introduces himself makes it clear that, despite his ingratiating humanness—his mental fallibility, his physical fragility, his moral courage—he is systemically Papal, every inch a Pope, and when, later on (X, 382–397), he so charmingly summons Antonio Pignatelli, his "ancient self," to a self-critical colloquy, we are not to assume that the Pope, like the man, is "inquisitive and dispassionate," but are warned that the procedures of this "after-me, this self now Pope," require very careful watching lest the hero half-smothered in the Papacy be confused with the Pope himself.

From beginning to end, the Pope sets courage at the forefront of conscience—"Have I to dare" (X, 13) and "how should I dare die, this man let live?" (X, 2133). It is a noble virtue, certainly, the stuff of heroes. But in the Christian hero at least, courage must be tempered with mercy, and as Innocent takes Christ's "staff with [his] uncertain hand" (X, 164), he exudes mercy:

> I sit and see
> Another poor weak trembling human wretch
> Pushed by his fellows, who pretend the right,
> Up to the gulf which, where I gaze, begins

From this world to the next,—gives way and way,
Just on the edge over the awful dark. . . .
                                    (X, 169–174)

Though the tone is quite different, the language echoes the judgmental ferocity of Caponsacchi's "creation's verge" speech. That the ferocity is potentially real becomes more thinkable as the Pope's sense of his solitariness strengthens (X, 193) and his imagery darkens—"either hold a hand out, or withdraw/A foot and let the wretch drift to the fall" (X, 195–196)—until the very idea of reprieve is perceived as only a strategy for protecting his "calm" from the "passion" of the mob and hence but "nature's craven-trick" (X, 197–206). Resolution, not discretion, is the better part of valor to the Pope:

A mere dead man is Franceschini here,
Even as Formosus centuries ago.
                                    (X, 209–210)

It is a curious correlation. Either it means nothing, since there is no connection between the actual deaths of Guido and Pope Formosus, or the terms of the correlation seem to be these: I, Innocent, am to the condemnation of Franceschini as Stephen was to the condemnation of Formosus. Such a reading tends to confirm the observation that the Pope takes the divine status of the Papacy quite literally even though he has disclaimed infallibility for himself in the present case and thus was not struck by the shocking absurdity of Stephen's language and actions. It is also relevant to the general statement, which comes soon after, about how truth is discovered:

All's a clear rede and no more riddle now.
Truth, nowhere, lies yet everywhere in these—
Not absolutely in a portion, yet
Evolvable from the whole: evolved at last
Painfully, held tenaciously by me.
                                    (X, 227–231)

These lines are often quoted by the commentators with unqualified approval and are regularly used to suggest that their

clear applicability to the method of *The Ring and the Book* itself
demonstrates that the Pope speaks for Browning.

The difficulty with such a reading of the passage is that it
does not account for the contradiction at the center of it. The
Pope takes back with one hand what he gives away with the
other. The truth lies everywhere but not absolutely in a portion; however, it is (absolutely) evolvable from the whole and
is held (absolutely) by him. Such absoluteness assumes that he
is not a "portion" but is "everywhere," and that assumption
seems to reinforce the notion that the Pope transcends the other
characters in *The Ring and the Book*, has a "whole" view, and
therefore speaks for Browning. But only God is "everywhere"
and has a "whole" view, and therefore the "Pope" in essence
takes back the infallibility that the "man" has given away. Faced
with that reading of the case, a commentator might be reluctant to make a Pope who speaks for God speak for Browning.

It is in this sense that the Pope seems profoundly faulted:
there is a deep fissure or crevasse in the dramatic character
Browning is developing, and to the degree that that character assumes those prerogatives and functions as the spokesman for the Roman Church, it is being portrayed as deeply
faulted too.

The parable of the man bitten by a poisonous snake is relevant here. This parable leads to one of the speaker's most
graceful, endearing, and oft-cited remarks. It begins with
" 'Mankind is ignorant, a man am I:/Call ignorance my sorrow
not my sin!' " (X, 257–258) and ends with what is generally
seen as a doctrine repeatedly endorsed by Browning:

> For I am ware it is the seed of act,
> God holds appraising in His hollow palm,
> Not act grown great thence on the world below,
> Leafage and branchage, vulgar eyes admire.
> (X, 271–274)

But these lose much of their human warmth and doctrinal validity once the "whole" context out of which they are "evolved"
is scrutinized. The speaker imagines himself as a recognized
" 'Lord of the land and counted wise' " by "Peasants of mine."
The peasants describe as best they can the symptoms of a

stricken brother and challenge their Lord to " 'prove [his] worth!' " He "presume[s]" to "pronounce" a cure from which the patient dies. The peasants then discover a serpent crawling from the dead man's breast and confess their mistake in describing the symptoms and charge him with a bad prescription, thus killing the man. To this, he replies with the confession of ignorance and goes on to say that God gave him only so much talent, instructing them to " 'Ask Him if I was slack in use thereof!' "

There are some difficulties presented by the "ignorance" and "limited talent" defenses themselves since they obviously lead to moral chaos in unscrupulous or incompetent persons, as is suggested by the fact that most systems of justice have had to adopt the principle that ignorance or misconstruction of the law is no excuse. Their kinship with Guido's "So am I made" defense in Book XI (2098), for example, is obvious. Also, while one may cheerfully yield to God the capacity to hold "in His hollow palm" "the seed of act" and appraise it, he may be more reluctant to grant it to the "at best imperfect cognizance" of man, "Since, how heart moves brain, and how both move hand,/What mortal ever in entirety saw?" (I, 827–829). So our applause of the Pope's admirable principle of personal integrity—"Therefore I stand on my integrity" (X, 275)—may not wholly sustain itself when we perceive that he means to set *his* integrity against the integrity of another.

Even if one can resolve his difficulties over these principles by accepting them as sufficiently sound working principles in an imperfect world, such a resolution is undermined to the degree that they are espoused so tenaciously as to assume a character of practical infallibility, and that, contextually, is the character the Pope gives them. Throughout the parable and the gloss on it, he is the "wise Lord," and they are the "vulgar peasants." He "presumes" to "pronounce" a "prescription" on the basis of testimony proved untrustworthy by being wrong, and then he defends himself against a fatal error of judgment *both* on the plea of his share in universal human ignorance *and* on his unshakable confidence that *he knows* that *God knows* that he did the best *God enabled him* to do: " 'Ask *Him* if I was slack in use thereof!' " (emphasis added). There is the crevasse: a good, old, learned, experienced, holy, fallible man of the world, on the one hand, and, on the other, a Pope in whom the presumption of infallibility, of speaking absolutely for God, has become systemic, operative at a subliminal, subconscious level.

Thus it appears that the doctrine of Papal Infallibility, which was the most hotly debated topic in Christendom at the time *The Ring and the Book* was being written and has always been recognized as having an obvious topical relevance to the poem, has in fact been so deeply, so metaphorically, integrated with its subject and apparatus as, in a real sense, to monitor both its form and its idea.[3] It is the largest and clearest anti-proposition to the poem's proposition of the relative relativism of truth. As the poem places a profound and urgent emphasis on the elusiveness of truth, its dependence on the purity and strength of the consciousness seeking it, and the primary importance to it of the difficult, essentially imaginative, and enormously rewarding process of perpetually purifying and strengthening that consciousness, infallibility tends in the opposite direction—solidifies truth, assumes its absolute and unchanging nature, places a higher premium on acceptance than on understanding, makes conscience rather than consciousness its chief instrument, and, in its rage for orthodoxy, prefers dogmatic literalism to dynamic imagination. Of course, Papal Infallibility as such was only the most impressive, current, well-defined example of an approach to truth in one of truth's largest and most encompassing arenas—faith and morals—infallibility in the archetypal sense being inherent in that statuesque example. But Browning was too fine an aesthetic empiricist not to take hold of that colossus which, through the "miracle" of the Old Yellow Book, God had seemingly delivered into his hands. Here was infallibility institutionalized in the Roman Catholic Church, which Macaulay had characterized as the "work of human policy" most "well deserving of examination" in the whole history of man on this earth,[4] and it gave him the opportunity to explore with historical guidance and poetic license the workings of even the unconscious presumption of infallibility on the human mind through the imagined character of a wise, conscientious, courageous, admirable old man. The critic should remind himself throughout that this is not history or journalism but poetry and that what we are offered for study, therefore, is a *poetic* Pope who is head of a *poetic* Church in which a *poetic* doctrine of infallibility is a distinguishing characteristic. No part of Browning's motive in writing *The Ring and the Book* can be assumed to have been to attack the historical or contemporary Roman Church, though the view of the poem being developed here effectively explodes the argument put forth by some that he was compensating for such previous instances of unfriendliness as *Bishop Blougram's Apology.*

But while we should not literalize the use the poet makes of the Pope, his Church, and the doctrine of infallibility officially promulgated by that Church in 1870, we should not wink it away either since, metaphorically perceived, it is of enormous importance. The subject of his poem was poetry and truth, and not only had the two been linked by many people in religion historically, but there were also strong tendencies abroad in the nineteenth century both to reduce religion from doctrine and history to myth and to save religion from the shipwreck of literalism by emphasizing its richness as metaphor. Hence it was impossible to consider truth in any adequate way without considering the truth of religion and its relationship to man's way of conducting himself in the world. The Roman Church was, of course, a large part of the *donnée* of the Old Yellow Book, but it was also the most universal, coherent, well-defined, and, perhaps, ancient form of institutional religion in the world with an active and successful philosophy and apparatus of self-propagation. Its central relevance both to the struggle of religion to survive and flourish in the modern world and to the increasingly interesting question of how it affects how the minds of those who come under its influence do their work was obvious. So acknowledging that Browning was using the Roman Church as a metaphor does not erase the fact that it was a particular metaphor about which he did a great deal of conscientious research or that his motive for so much careful work was an interpretive judgment of his particular metaphor. His purpose was larger than an implicit or poetic interpretation of the Roman Church and its influence on the mind of man, but it included that.

The Pope begins the next sequence, the last preliminary to the long brief of blame and praise that completes the first half of his monologue, by establishing the mood and pattern of what will follow through a poetic characterization of the dying February day:

> O pale departure, dim disgrace of day!
> Winter's in wane, his vengeful worst art thou,
> To dash the boldness of advancing March!
>   (X, 282–284)

His all-absorbing self-consciousness colors everything: the death of the day, his own imminent death, the death of the Church and of Christianity, the inevitable birth of the new age, all are inherent in his images, and he takes it upon himself to do "his vengeful worst," seemingly for the honor of "paleness" and "disgrace," "To dash the boldness of advancing March!" It is a rather conventional idea of the heroism of old age, and it could have been put differently—as Tennyson's Ulysses puts it, for example: " 'Tis not too late to seek a newer world" or "One equal temper of heroic hearts,/Made weak by time and fate, but strong in will/To strive, to seek, to find, and not to yield."[5] But that is not the way the Pope puts it; he speaks of doing his "vengeful worst" against the bold new age, and in the awful solitariness of his official role, he seems to see himself as singularly responsible for avenging the past. If one is right in seeing an oblique allusion to Shelley's *Ode to the West Wind* hidden in the Pope's images, it is a very disquieting inversion that the poet imagines him as endorsing: not a desperate hope for, but a violent disgust with, the future. How pervasive that disgust is and how much it shapes the Pope's judgment and the manner of his final action is a valid critical question for the reader of the whole monologue.

Solitariness itself critically conditions the Pope's reflective and dramaturgical responses. He sees himself and Guido as the only two self-evident presences in the grey consciousness of Rome, and then he allies the world with Guido and against himself in a minidrama featuring Swedenborg ("the sagacious Swede") and his theories of mathematical probability.[6] In fact, of course,

Swedenborg was not an ominous threat to Christian stability and wholeness in the manner of the brilliant and relentlessly critical Voltaire (1694–1778), who would dominate the next age. Swedenborg was basically sympathetic to religion, as Voltaire was not, but he did cast doubt upon some of its traditional tenets, and it is that incipient doubt that the Pope sets up and knocks down. " 'It is not probable, *but well may be* '"; " '*That, possibly*, this in all likelihood' " (X, 316, 333, emphases added). The Pope's rebuff is that of unequivocal authority to quite mild and innocent dissent: "I thought so: yet thou tripp'st, my foreign friend!/No, it will be quite otherwise . . ." (X, 334–335). Even the term of address, "my foreign friend," tingles with a sarcasm that is alienating and patronizing.

The creation of the minidrama itself is as significant critically as its content. In his monumental solitariness, the Pope has cast himself in the role of adversary to the world. He has taken his circumstances—old man, judge, Pope—and created out of them the role of an eponymous hero under siege—the last in a lineage of Christian heroes who fought to the death with wild beasts in pagan amphitheatres and who carried the red cross on a white field as a standard in the Crusades against the encroaching infidels. Perceived in one way, it is exhilarating, analogous in spirit to Ulysses' noble perseverance: "Old age hath yet his honour and his toil . . ."[7]; but seen in an equally legitimate but different way, it is excruciatingly sad, the symbolic leader of a monumental past turned adversary to the future and spending the last remnant of his pontifical energy glorifying what was and calling down anathema on what will be. Again it is a case of the miscast hero, the epic protagonist caught in a sterile, noncreative antagonism, a living man imprisoned in a dying fact.

But Don Quixote must have his windmill, and the Pope creates his. He takes the characteristics of the times—young, brisk, irreverent toward the past and its institutionalized arrogances and abuses, self-interested in a secular rather than a religious sense, disdainful of a supernaturalist faith in shambles, ebullient over a naturalist knowledge and reason in the ascendant, blind to its own inherent limitations—and out of them shapes a monstrous adversary with whom to do gladiatorial battle. He

yields no quarter to such emergent tendencies as legal leni-
ency ("clean escape by leave of law/Which leans to mercy in
this latter time" [X, 301–302]), popular rule, social discretion,
extenuating individual circumstances (" 'So was I made, a weak
thing that gave way" [X, 357]). They are only ingenious word
games people play to make black look like white and falsehood
seem truth, a game that has become such an acquired characteristic of men that they even recognize the lie and call it truth:
" 'it is the method of a man!' " (X, 369). The situation is beyond human "renewing," says the Pope, "too contaminate for
use" (X, 374–375), and he takes his stand on "The Word" that
is "the Truth" that is God. No arguments, no arbitration, no
words; just an instantaneous illumination that men will have
"there" despite any so-called enlightenment they may think they
have "here"—"That I am I, as He is He,—what else?" (X, 375–
380).[8] It is a marvelous simplification of the human problem,
and it has the luminosity of original truth, like "the Word" that
was "In the beginning" of St. John's Gospel. But while one can
thrill to its magnificent clarity as an expression of private faith,
one has to wonder how it has weathered the infinity since that
beginning or even the centuries since St. John so phrased it;
and how one can be so officially certain, in light of its carriage
in a language contaminated beyond the possibility of renewal,
that it is *the* "Truth," that that Truth exists, and that we will
know it instantaneously "there" after having shown so little
evidence of such knowledge "here." Only by restoring to the
"Pope" the infallibility that the "man" had so graciously yielded.

But the Pope's condemnation of Guido (X, 398–867, X, 868–
1002, *inter alios*) provides our first expansive dramatic illustration of the way the role he has chosen to play and his consequent need to create a monstrous adversary affect his judgment and of the deep crevasse in his character that the
contradictions reveal.

First, the Pope not only creates a particular character for
Guido; he also makes repeated efforts to consolidate that particular character.

> I see him furnished forth for his career,
> On starting for the life-chance in our world,

With nearly all we count sufficient help:
Body and mind in balance, a sound frame,
A solid intellect: the wit to seek,
Wisdom to choose, and courage wherewithal
To deal with whatsoever circumstance
Should minister to man, make life succeed.

(X, 399–406)

Guarded from the arch-tempter, all must fight,
By a great birth, traditionary name,
Diligent culture, choice companionship,
Above all, conversancy with the faith
Which puts forth for its base of doctrine just
'Man is born nowise to content himself
But please God.'

(X, 429–435)

I find him bound, then, to begin life well;
Fortified by propitious circumstance,
Great birth, good breeding, with the Church for guide.

(X, 477–479)

Although it is true that as readers of *The Ring and the Book* we have been conditioned by the very cultural attitudes that the Pope has earlier nipped in the bud and therefore are disqualified from making sound judgments, not many of us would have seen Guido "furnished forth" in the same way the Pope does. So while it is reasonable to concede that a Guido with a balanced personality, a "solid intellect," a "diligent culture," wit, wisdom, courage, "choice companionship," and genuine "conversancy with the faith" might be expected to play the moral game fairly, those are not exactly the qualities of the character with whom the reader actually has to deal. They are largely inventions of the Pope's need for a certain kind of adversary, not self-evident facts but fancies of a determined case-maker.

A later passage confirms them as, if not fictions, at least strongly fictionalized. One hardly needs to be a rigid behaviorist to doubt that the elder Countess Franceschini of the Pope's beast fable, Guido's mother, would have nurtured the privileged young nobleman of the Pope's description:

>   Then comes
> The gaunt grey nightmare in the furthest smoke,
> The hag that gave these three abortions birth,
> Unmotherly mother and unwomanly
> Woman, that near turns motherhood to shame,
> Womanliness to loathing: no one word,
> No gesture to curb cruelty a whit
> More than the she-pard thwarts her playsome whelps
> Trying their milk-teeth on the soft o' the throat
> O' the first fawn, flung, with those beseeching eyes,
> Flat in the covert! How should she but couch,
> Lick the dry lips, unsheathe the blunted claw,
> Catch 'twixt her placid eyewinks at what chance
> Old bloody half-forgotten dream may flit,
> Born when herself was novice to the taste,
> The while she lets youth take its pleasure.
>   (X, 909–924)

It is a chilling creature of the Pope's fancy, invented out of the "facts" he knows or thinks he knows about the Countess's three sons, and if it is fair for the Pope to assume "like sons, like mother," it is fair for the reader to assume "like mother, like sons." If she is the "hag" the Pope says she is and her three sons "abortions," this proves that the princely, privileged, favored Guido of the Pope's description is "furnished forth" only in his imagination and according to his own dramatic need.

Further, the character equation by which the Pope justifies calling Guido's moral struggle or probation "a trial fair and fit" may not persuade everyone of its own fairness.

> So, Guido, born with appetite, lacks food,
> Is poor, who yet could deftly play-off wealth,
> Straitened, whose limbs are restless till at large:
> And, as he eyes each outlet of the cirque,
> The narrow penfold for probation, pines

> After the good things just outside the grate,
> With less monition, fainter conscience-twitch,
> Rarer instinctive qualm at the first feel
> Of the unseemly greed and grasp undue,
> Than nature furnishes the main mankind,—
> Making it harder to do wrong than right
> The first time, careful lest the common ear
> Break measure, miss the outstep of life's march.
>   (X, 413–425)

"[L]ess monition, fainter conscience-twitch,/Rarer instinctive qualm"—this seems to be the Pope's way of hedging a suspicion which, if accepted outright, would tumble his whole philosophy of life as a moral struggle, a perpetual contest in this "narrow penfold for probation"—namely, that Guido lacks a conscience and therefore cannot be tried by the usual tests of conscientiousness. That evil is systemic in Guido to an extraordinary degree can hardly be denied, and the Pope's preemption of the "So am I made" argument of Book XI (2098) is an inverted admission of its plausibility. Admittedly that argument seems too commodious and self-serving coming from Guido, facing "Mannaia"; but when Pompilia first enunciated it—Pompilia whom the Pope pronounces "Perfect in whiteness," wholly praiseworthy (X, 1005, 1047)—it had an axiomatic cogency:

> Nothing about me but drew somehow down
> His hate upon me,—somewhat so excused
> Therefore, since hate was thus the truth of him,—
> . . . .
> So he was made; he nowise made himself. . . .
>   (VII, 1725–1731)

At the very least, then, the reader is faced with the facts of Guido as they are reflected in the total myth of the poem and with a choice between Pompilia's simple, perfectly clear moral syllogism and the Pope's use of the equivocal comparative ("less," "fainter," "rarer") in building his case against Guido as the "midmost blotch of black/Discernible . . ." (X, 868–869).

Moreover, since it must be recognized that the poet has used the issue of "how we are made" to tie Books VII, X, and XI together in a special way that makes it central to an understanding of just what degree of development Guido finally does achieve and how that is to be evaluated, we are forced seriously to admit the possibility that the Pope's strong sense of his office and its obligation to rationalize an infallible and uncompromising moral system cripples his willingness (and his ability) to entertain freely alternative possibilities that the man behind the Pope's mask perceives, as his hedging the matter in comparatives also suggests.

That the Pope's inventory of Guido's corruption as mirrored in his relentlessly predatory actions is a lurid, detailed, epic-dramatic catalogue of domesticated evil, all readers of *The Ring and the Book* will attest. They will attest, too, that the voice in which it is rendered, despite the careful scrutiny of detail with which he makes his Table of Discovery, has none of the scientific objectivity or detachment associated with the ancient Greek or the modern post-Renaissance European mind. The Pope's "science" is that of the mystical Middles Ages, a deeply emotional recital of the innumerable evidences for a *contemptus mundi* that has gotten so deep into his soul, mind, and body that it has reached the level of actual physical disgust. Guido, of course, is the focus of it—the "midmost blotch of black"— but he is by no means its singular object. The Pope's impassioned moral editorial is shot through with a disgust for mankind in general that has reached an abstract and hence virtually irreversible level. "All say good words/To who will hear, all do thereby bad deeds/To who must undergo; so thrive mankind!" (X, 517–519). "What does the world, told truth, but lie the more?" (X, 672).

The Pope's images give the truest revelation both of the level his disgust has reached and of his peculiar nature, the innermost imperative of himself that accounts for his intensity of feeling. In his character as Pope, he is driven to large historical, philosophical, and moral generalizations, to *sententiae*, piercing summations, dogmas or first principles severely honed and absolutely pronounced. But these seem grafted onto the man, and we can easily quarrel with them because of the very pluralism or openness that philosophy nurtures as a corrective to infallibility and absolutism, i.e., to the closed system that the Pope is officially bound to defend. But in his character as a man—his natural character, so to speak—the Pope has the most thoroughly visual imagination of any persona in the poem. He is a *born* naturalist as, in his character as Pope, he is a *made* supernaturalist. He has the keenest eye and liveliest attraction for natural phenomena—living things with their own individuating "inscapes," significant forms, ontological definitions. There is a poet under this priest who, as it were, hears the grass grow and sees through the dark, has observed a female leopard with the practiced attentiveness of a painter or a scientific naturalist and knows with the precision of one who habitually and minutely notices such things as the healthy autumnal mood of the farmer when his crops are all harvested, his fields all plowed, his wood all chopped and stacked, his beasts all housed, and he can welcome the frost with buoyant contentment. Such imaginative power of seeing in a man is an Apollo gift, of course, making his ecstasies more intense and his agonies more profound, enabling him to appreciate the graces of nature with a godlike joy but causing him to perceive its disgraces with almost intolerable pain. The man Antonio Pignatelli, under the spell of this tragic myth, is made by the Pope in him to convert the glories of the naturalist's eye into the horrors of the moralist's vision,[9] and this, too, takes a medieval form: his inventory of beasts is transformed into a series of beast fables, and since the human types with which he must deal are mostly bestial in the degraded sense of that term, he draws upon the lowest, most treacherous, most violent animal images to articulate his revulsion against the depravity that these human beings exhibit to his imaginative-moral eye.

Guido is a "parasite," an "ambiguous fish" that uses its shell as armor against misfortune, pretending it is himself, a man-at-arms in coat of mail, while he, a slug, pursues his "carrion-prey" with the "Sand-fly and slush-worm at their garbage-feast," "Prostrate among the filthy feeders" (X, 453, 485–509). He is a reptile-like creature, covered over "scale on scale" with falsehood (X, 514); he sinks manhood below the "level of the brute," even his brutishness being a falsehood (X, 540–541). He lives like a "toad," in slime and excrement, feasts on his "lamb-like" prey like a wolf (X, 548–549, 557–558). First he is a gor-crow to the Comparini bramble-finch and then, in the trick of "the tricking lying world," the bramble-finch's moth, a change that in turn transforms him into "the fiercer fowl" or hawk (X, 575–588). He degrades even the fowlers' sport of hawking, shooting, or snaring and employs the poacher's "vile practice" of jacklighting or use of the owl as lure (X, 721–723). He revives the steel trap abandoned by all fair-minded hunters who know from personal experience its deceit and cruelty because an overplus of pain is integral to his goal (X, 724–743). He and his murderous hirelings were, like the Gadarene swine, driven headlong to destruction by the devil in each of them (X, 848–851). In his bestial Franceschini cave or kennel, next in line after Guido the wolf is Paul the fox, more disgusting still, and after him the hybrid pup of the brood, Girolamo, who adds lust to craft and violence and may prove to be "hell's better product," a horror as yet not fully known. Deeper in the cave is the hagbitch Countess, with no more motherliness, womanliness, or compassion than a "she-pard" dreaming of her own first bloody lusts while her "playsome whelps" try their teeth "on the soft o' the throat/O' the first fawn, flung, with those beseeching eyes,/Flat in the covert" (X, 868–924).

These images, which constitute a concrete naturalist subtext to the Pope's ethical arguments and give a physical anchorage to his moral disgust, seem to be drawn from the pre-priestly period of Antonio Pignatelli's life, from his boyhood on the coast and among the surrounding farms and wildernesses. But to the fascination that he presumably felt then, an editorial or judgmental quality has been added that is alien to the mentality of the objective scientific observer, who would look at the wolf, the fox, the gor-crow or even the slush-worm and say, "So [it] was made; [it] nowise made [itself]," a position which the Pope cannot entertain despite his persistent recurrence to animal imagery to illuminate his ethical responses.

The quality in a man or a woman that the Pope admires above all others is courage. It is for him the special mark of human worthiness, the divine insigne, the proof that a person is not wholly the servant of time. He begins and ends with the word *dare* on his lips, and in the second half of his monologue, he steadies himself in the face of the awful terror with which his vision of the modern world, the world his own death will usher in, threatens to overwhelm him by repeated reminders that he, too, must "dare." He largely ignores the Church contemplative in favor of the Church militant; the touchstone of Christian heroism is the *miles Christianus gloriosus,* its glory days the age of the martyrs, renewed in Pompilia, and the age of the Crusades, renewed both in Pompilia and in Caponsacchi. The only hope he has for Guido's salvation is an act of God, administered by him, that will suddenly strip away the compacted scales that have blinded Guido and seemed to make him fortress-safe and enable him, perhaps, in death's very instant to see the truth and be saved. This is the ultimate, the quintessential, contest from which all human knowledge is excluded except that of the creature and the Creator.

The imaginary construct by which the Pope reconciles himself to the terrifying future is that of a walled city exposed by an earthquake to primitive dangers that force its inhabitants, like the early Christians, to do combat with wild beasts.

> What if it be the mission of that age,
> My death will usher into life, to shake
> This torpor of assurance from our creed,
> Re-introduce the doubt discarded, bring
> The formidable danger back, we drove
> Long ago to the distance and the dark?
> No wild beast now prowls round the infant camp;
> We have built wall and sleep in city safe:
> But if the earthquake try the towers, that laugh
> To think they once saw lions rule outside,
> Till man stand out again, pale, resolute,
> Prepared to die,—that is, alive at last?
>
> (X, 1851–1862)

Finally, his last act is framed in the metaphor of the haughty, bullying, world-class challenger and the courageous, solitary acceptor of the challenge:

I will, Sirs: for a voice other than yours
Quickens my spirit. '*Quis pro Domino?*
Who is upon the Lord's side?' asked the Count.
I. . . .

(X, 2098–2101)

To one so all-devout in his reverence for courage, Guido can hardly appear as anything but the blackest of human blotches, and the Pope condemns him in a relentless litany of anathematizing tropes that charge essentially one thing: "Coward!" But that conclusion, if not absolutely prima facie, is too transparent to require such endless and ultimately dreary reiteration. Even if we have a contrary judgment, it is clear almost immediately what the singular basis of the Pope's condemnation is, and it is on the basis itself or a weighting of its moral significance that we might divide with him. By contrast with the some 500 lines he devotes to Guido's direct indictment, he concentrates his paean of praise of Pompilia into 91 lines and his full exoneration of the much more ambiguous Caponsacchi into 117 lines.

Part of what appears to be judgmental prolixity is the inevitable result of the Pope's use of Guido as the focus of his review of the sequential facts, as the structuring device for the narrative portion of his rhetoric. That accounts for the "facts," but not for the "tenor," and since the facts are given, it is to the tenor that we must look for individuation of character. From it, two conclusions seem luminously self-evident: the Pope is fascinated with evil, which seems to have the conventional charm of the snake—magnetic repulsion; and he is obsessed with the need to give vent, even in private, to his disgust with the fascination evil has for him. Thus two questions require examination: why does the Pope feel this need so imperiously? what is the effect of his satisfying *the* need on the impression of evil he leaves?

The answer to the first question is inherent in the question itself and is universally applicable rather than peculiarly applicable to the Pope: evil is inexplicable; the grosser the evil, the more inexplicable; the fairer the inquirer, the less satisfactory the explanation. One may, like the Pope, adopt a touchstone and accept its results implicitly; one may, again like the Pope, be positively ferocious in one's condemnation of those who, like Guido, fall completely foul of the results; one may even accept the Pope's touchstone as, on the whole, as fair and workable a touchstone as any known. That is a practical, conscientious, trustworthy way of proceeding so long as one admits that he is in fact being practical, conscientious, and trustworthy rather than right in any absolute or exclusive sense. Like the Pope, most people decline to do that.

On the issue of evil, the inductive method is ultimately unsatisfactory; it never quite brings us to the point of safely making the inductive leap to an all-encompassing generalization. Thus we are driven to the deductive method, of which the syllogism is the primary operating tool. But all students of philosophy know that, in value judgments such as good and evil, different world-class philosophers develop systems from very different premises, no one of which is more than relatively dependable. Therefore, if one requires an absolute system of ethics, he must make what may be called the "intuitive leap"— from human reason to divine inspiration. Only then can one call his system infallible. If, however, one has, like the Pope, disclaimed infallibility while still desiring absolute certainty— resolute, irrevocable, without the shadow of a doubt's shadow— then, like the Pope, one will "need to breathe awhile"; indeed, he will need not just to "review," but to reiterate, reaffirm, reassert, protest with increasing passion to compensate for the "hidden germ of failure, shy but sure" (I, 850) that fallibility imposes on the man.

The issue is not the number of one's "evil" actions or the unmistakable "evil" of one's motives, which the Pope emphasizes. After both have been conceded, the issue persists. It is a question of one's *responsibility* for one's actions and motives, and although the Pope categorically assigns responsibility to the agent of the act and motive, the question lingers on in the consciousness of the man. In the severe Manichaean terms that the Pope implicitly observes rather than in the flabby sociological terms that he dismisses, the question might be put in forms like these. If only the grace of God can effect salvation, is one responsible for the actions he performs in a graceless state? If it is a contradiction in terms to be proud of one's spiritual successes, is it not also a contradiction to be ashamed of one's spiritual failures? If the instinct for good versus evil is innate in most people, what are we to say of people who are deficient in this essential instinct—that they are evil or that they are deprived? Are people with vastly different moral capacities to be judged by fixed moral standards?

The question of the effect of the Pope's satisfying of his need to ventilate his disgust with evil on the impression of evil he leaves is a relevant but different question. Here the issue is one of strategy rather than of philosophy, and it supplies another instance of the discrepancy between the character's perception and the poet's. As the Pope consciously disavows infallibility while he unconsciously assumes it, so he ferociously builds the case for Guido's guilt in such a way as to dismantle it—makes, in a reversal of one of his own metaphors, a stepping-stone a stumbling-block (X, 412). First, he deprives Guido of a representative conscience (X, 419–425). Then he asserts as the foundation doctrine of the Church " 'Man is born nowise to content himself/But please God' " (X, 434–435) without any acknowledgment that, to one handicapped with a deprived conscience, the Church's doctrine as exemplified by the Church's representatives did not make a very dramatic distinction between contenting oneself and pleasing God. In fact, one would hardly need to look beyond the Canons Conti, Guillichini, and Caponsacchi to see that contenting oneself and pleasing God made for a thoroughly comfortable combination as deserving as Guido himself of the mean, prejudicial metaphor "ambiguous fish."[10] Further, he singles Guido out for ferocious abuse as one who makes of "Honor and faith,—a lie and a disguise" (X, 515), while in the very same breath he concedes that it is true "Probably for all livers in this world": "All say good words/To who will hear, all do thereby bad deeds/To who must undergo; so thrive mankind!" (X, 516, 517–519).

The whole catalogue of charges the Pope makes against Guido is put together on this same ambivalent pattern, the charge being undermined by the way it is phrased. Since the Pope as a dramatic character is the poet's primary focus here—*as dis-*

tinct *from the guilt or innocence of Guido as a different character—*
the conclusion seems unavoidable that the poet is perceiving
him quite differently both from the way he perceives himself
and from the way a reader too quick to accept the infallibility
of his moral premises would perceive him. The Pope's use of
the gor-crow, bramble-finch, hawk analogy, extending it to include the Comparini with Guido in the struggle for existence
(X, 572–588), overlays the calculus of natural selection on the
calculus of moral responsibility to the considerable equivocation of the latter. His epic simile of the torched "peasant house"
that in the burning reveals "Some grim and unscathed nucleus
of the nest,—/Some old malicious tower, some obscene
tomb/They thought a temple in their ignorance" cuts both ways
equally, suggesting that there is or may be something "grim,"
"malicious," "obscene" at the center of our most sacred human
illusions (X, 619–639). The impact of the moral outrage he
expresses over the forged love letters—"craft should supple-
ment/Cruelty and show hell a masterpiece!"—has already been
weakened by his introduction of the marriage theme with a
generalization that all men thrive by saying "good words" and
doing "bad deeds" (X, 510–530) and by the attitude, especially
rife at the time, that forged sentiments are the universal expectation of the love-letter convention; and when he adds to
this the grotesquely fascinating idea of offsetting the cherubic
image of love and marriage contained in the missal with the
pornographic image of marriage reflected in such fabliaux as
the oft-cited *Hundred Merry Tales,* he suggests a "masterpiece,"
not of "hell," but of salty truth worthy of Rabelais (X, 652–
655).

That the Pope's sexual morality is in fact unrealistic, subli-
mated, highfalutin to the point of absurdity is the unambigu-
ous if genial import of the next verse paragraph. The subject
is the rendezvous between Pompilia and Caponsacchi in which
they worked out their arrangements for the flight, and we know
their own testimony of what went on as well as having our own
idea of what their respective motives were. Here is the Pope's
version.

> Pompilia, wife, and Caponsacchi, priest,
> Are brought together as nor priest nor wife

Should stand, and there is passion in the place,
Power in the air for evil as for good,
Promptings from heaven and hell, as if the stars
Fought in their courses for a fate to be.
Thus stand the wife and priest, a spectacle,
I doubt not, to unseen assemblage there.
No lamp will mark that window for a shrine,
No tablet signalise the terrace, teach
New generations which succeed the old,
The pavement of the street is holy ground;
No bard describe in verse how Christ prevailed
And Satan fell like lightning! Why repine?
What does the world, told truth, but lie the more?

                                            (X, 658–672)

It is star-struck in the manner of a romantic schoolgirl, inflated, melodramatic, cliché-ridden: no lamp, no tablet, no bard, but why "repine"? After all, "What does the world, told truth, but lie the more?" One can be as sympathetic as possible to the motives of Caponsacchi in that balcony scene without confusing the "truth" of what actually happened there with some hieratic opera replete with "spectacle," "unseen assemblage," stage lighting, a heroine enshrined in a window, and an odor of sanctity suspiring from the pavement!

As we read on from this point in the Pope's condemnation of Guido, we are suddenly aware of a pervasive and curious characteristic of his language that had not been present before and that might have gone unnoticed without so pointed a signal from the poet. It contains a substantial portion of clichés, conventional ideas clothed in conventional phrases. For example, the next thirty lines, which lead up to the critical scene between Pompilia and Guido at Castelnuovo, are a network of clichés like "plot is foiled," "blot is blanched," "Champion of truth," "a thorn . . . completes the rose," "Courage to-wit," "Courage . . . I' the crisis," "might . . . vindicating right," "the strong aggressor, bad and bold," "how fares he," "quails," "armed to the . . . teeth," "the chattering teeth," "But anon of these!"

This is obviously a fact of large critical significance in a poem about language as the chief index to character, but obviously too it is a fact that must be interpreted with critical circum-spection. One plausible explanation is that the Pope, being the spokesman for a traditional moral point of view, a view that has become "conventionalized" in the very language with which traditional moralists talk about ethical issues, uses conven-tional language as a mirror of that point of view, a significant variation on that explanation being that, after almost 2000 years, Christian morality defies real distinction of thought and orig-inality of discourse. A less friendly but still reasonable theory might hold that, having yielded to the domination of feeling over thought, of outrage over objective analysis, the Pope hur-tles along on overridden phrases. Or, if it is true that clichés assume a quite new dominance in the Pope's monologue at this particular point, perhaps he has used up his originality of phrase and has begun to show the fatigue of incessant reiteration. The most unsympathetic hypothesis—one that Guido himself might use if, in the high tide of his second monologue, he had any knowledge of the Pope's extended indictment—would be that a fustian mind on a fustian topic, especially a mind that claims to be a direct reflex of God's mind, can hardly be expected to be other than a transparent mask of hollowness, concealing nothingness in language-puff. It seems likely, in the Pope's own words, that "Truth, nowhere, lies yet everywhere in these—" (X, 228) and that the poet is being implicitly critical of the Pope while remaining fundamentally sympathetic and loyal to him. The heart of the man is in the right place, but the official has undertaken a task that is not susceptible to the absoluteness of judgment he demands of it. Hence, the poet gently undercuts him by making him a language-man whose language, while it is not false, has an "uproar in the echo" that does not quite ring true.

When the Pope turns from the condemnation of Guido, his hellish brood, the ignoble savages who were his accomplices,[11] and the seconds in his troupe, to praise of Pompilia, a new en-ergy and freshness reinvade his language (X, 1003–1093). It is as though he has been infected by the life-force that carried her through—the mother's obligation to save her unborn child, the Bride of Christ's duty to "stay the . . . arm/ . . . of the wicked" (X, 1074–1091). But again it is not in familiar phrases like the foregoing that the power of his language shows—purity, patience, faith, forbearance, long-suffering, "the good and faithful servant"—but in the images that reach back to his boyhood close to nature. At the center of these is the gardener "heart-sick" with the poor results of all his painful labor and despite all his sanguine expectations ("made fat/By the master's eye") who suddenly comes upon "earth's flower/She holds up to the softened gaze of God!" (X, 1017–1018). It is a rogue-plant, the product of a "mere chance-sown, cleft-nursed seed," that received none of the tendance of the horticulturalist nor any of the warmth of his expectation; and yet, it "Spreads itself, one wide glory of desire/To incorporate the whole great sun it loves/From the inch-height whence it looks and longs" and becomes the fairest of all flowers on earth, "My rose, I gather for the breast of God . . . (X, 1040–1046). There seems to be, moreover, an image from animal husbandry half-hidden behind the moment of Pompilia's greatest exaltation as perceived by the Pope:

> Thou, patient thus, couldst rise from law to law,
> The old to the new, promoted at one cry
> O' the trump of God to the new service, not
> To longer bear, but henceforth fight, be found
> Sublime in new impatience with the foe!
> (X, 1055–1059)

The image is that of the mongrel bitch, cuffed, beaten, unvalued, half-starved, who, after a long period of submissive obedience, suddenly rears up in the name of natural justice, fights back, and takes her whole world by surprise. She it is who claims common cause with all natural things and, having fought for motherhood, also has the intuition to fight for "Life."

Here as elsewhere in the monologue, a tension is created between what the Pope asserts and what his manner of asserting it seems to imply. He speaks of the Christ-like virtues, the instantaneous response to the "trump of God," and the election to defend "that trust of trusts,/Life from the Ever Living" (X, 1079–1080). But his images from horticulture and animal husbandry—the rose seeking the sun, the law of universal motherhood to protect its unborn, the ultimate tendency of life to fight for life's existence—draw into the consciousness an alternative explanation, namely, sun worship and the basic natural laws of reproduction and survival. For his own part, the Pope resolves the tension with the remark about the "prompting of what I call God,/And fools call Nature," but while the reader can accept this as inevitably the Pope's official position, he may not accept it as singularly conclusive of the issue. Natural law may be God's way of lending his mind out, but it also may not be, and no one who holds a contrary view will be converted by the Pope's dogmatic and haughtily phrased assertion: all those who reject Paley's natural theology in favor of Darwin's natural selection are not fools!

Most readers will find it easier to accede to the Pope's lyrical applause of Pompilia than to his more rationally qualified but still mythically awesome admiration of Caponsacchi. Even if one personally opts for a naturalistic alternative, he still may feel that the Pope's reading of Pompilia is on his terms not only justified but exhilarating. But Caponsacchi's own testimony makes it clear that the Pope has romanticized his actions and his motives into a model of Christian heroism analogous to that of the early Christians and the medieval Crusaders that outstrips both ordinary reason and known reality. It may be ingratiatingly generous in an old man who is the head of a vast institution that is rapidly crumbling into a grotesque mockery of its former grandeur to see in a courageous young maverick in that institution a glimpse of what it was and what, in imagination at least, it still might be, and so to identify with the young man's reversal of empirically based expectation as to excuse him even his conspicuous faults, shifting their burden to the institution or even to himself. It may be, too, that the "terror" to which the Pope first gives voice in this laudation ("He who made/The comely terror, He shall make the sword/To match" [X, 1108–1110]), being imaginatively intense, requires an imaginative antidote bolder than the more strictly rational, judging mind can generate. But the reader may accept these as faithful descriptions of what the Pope does and why he does it without conceding that he tries Caponsacchi by the same judicial rules by which he has tried Guido. In one sense, he treats them similarly—he is drawn by his estimate (vision) of the *character* of one, and he is repulsed by his estimate (vision) of the *character* of the other; but in the case of Guido, he squeezes the maximum of disgust out of each exemplary action, while in Caponsacchi's case, he rather good-humoredly sweeps aside what he concedes to be "amiss,/Blameworthy, punishable" and chronicles instead the glories of the new-minted hero—warrior-priest, Christian athlete and champion, knight-at-arms, angel of light battling the dragon of darkness—with such uncontrolled gusto that he is even drawn to revise the Lord's Prayer to accommodate his enthusiasm:

> O Thou whose servants are the bold,
> Lead such temptations by the head and hair,
> Reluctant dragons, up to who dares fight,
> That so he may do battle and have praise!
> (X, 1188–1191)

Some new impetus is obviously at work here, and the reader's excitement and eagerness to follow it up and see how it works its way through the second half of the Pope's monologue may make him a bit impatient with the pursuit of such an obvious fact as that there is an enormous discrepancy between the view of Caponsacchi that is established (for the reader) by his own monologue and that taken by the Pope. But its very obviousness increases the need to emphasize it for several quite critical reasons. It means that the Pope is not an entirely dependable judge, whatever else he may be; it suggests that, having shown himself to some degree untrustworthy in his judgment of Caponsacchi, the Pope's judgment of Guido may, in degree, be untrustworthy too; it raises the question of just where the Pope's peculiar strength lies if, as seems apparent, it does not lie in ordinary reason and known reality; and, most important of all, it proves that, though the poet has "disappeared," he is working under and through every vein, sinew, and feature of the piece more consciously and demonstrably even than the supernatural presence at work in the universe as envisioned by natural theology.

At the end of his celebration of Caponsacchi, the Pope defines the "use of soldiership" as "Self-abnegation, freedom from all fear,/Loyalty to the life's end!" (X, 1208–1209). From this, he immediately deduces the irreducible elements of a life-plan consequent upon such an initiation ceremony [12] as Caponsacchi's: "Ruminate,/ . . . /Work, be unhappy but bear life" (X, 1209–1211). It is the program of a creative stoic—thoughtful, active, enduring without any expectation of worldly happiness—but as he states it, it is not specifically Christian, and this is significant. The Pope is, of course, the Christian *par excellence,* and his language is saturated with Christian metaphors as his mind is fully furnished with Christian doctrines, Christian analogues, Christian images and points of reference. But he must now "dare" let rise a vision of a post-Christian world and, despite the "terror" of the vision, attempt to deal with it. Creative stoicism may be the line of retreat to which he will be driven back, and in that eventuality Euripides will be the spokesman for a faith that, though not doctrinally Christian, is yet thoughtful, active, and nobly enduring. As the reader knows, Guido will "succeed" the Pope (a metaphor of terrifying significance) and will attempt to topple not only whatever residual Christianity the Pope may salvage, but also the Euripidean vision of a noble, non-Christian alternative. In this, however, there is a remnant hope of some magnitude: far better a product of paganism like Euripides than a product of Christianity like Guido. Inherent in it also is the consoling thought that the death of Christianity's "God" does not spell the death of those innate human qualities that gave him birth and that, 500 years before St. Paul, were evident with considerable luminosity in Euripides. How courageous the Pope will be and by what procedure to what end he will deal with his vision are the chief questions to which the reader, excited by the new impulse visibly at work, must be attentive in the second half of the monologue.

The Pope makes the transition from his role as condemner of criminals and canonizer of saints to his role as broad culture analyst by reasserting his absolute certainty in the particular matter that he has thus far had under review by recognizing afresh that, unless he would abandon the larger obligations of his "post" (X, 1299), he must have the "courage"

(X, 1298) to face "the doubt/I' the sphere above [him], darkness to be felt" (X, 1282–1283), and by elaborating the religious premise upon which he will operate in facing that larger, more doubtful, more ominous sphere that also requires reconciliation (1307–1428). There is an analogy between this premise and the premise with which he had begun the earlier, more particular review (X, 228–230), but the latter is immeasurably larger and resists the very idea of tenacity and resoluteness that had characterized the Pope's mind in regarding the former; this is not the case of a ghastly Roman murder, of men and women in a narrow penfold of moral probation, but of the human mind itself and its capacity to know—to deal, at some level of satisfaction, with the great metaphysical questions of the existence, nature, and manner of God.

On the first two questions—the existence and the nature of God—he reaches relatively quick and perfect contentment. Neither question is susceptible to absolute proof of either the empirical or the syllogistic kind. Induction and deduction both reach a partial way toward what is ultimately incomprehensible, but neither is capable of absolute proof. Still, properly conceived and properly argued, both yield the satisfaction that he as our surrogate in the endeavor needs. Undergirding this satisfactory construction of a proper conception and a proper argument are two mutually inclusive modes of procedure, both of which have relevance in an all-inclusive way to the constructive procedures of the whole poem. One is the mythmaking process that succeeds in different but positive degrees in Caponsacchi's and Pompilia's monologues: a will to believe, an imaginative capacity to convert or transform one order of reality into another order of reality, and a miracle of experience that triggers the capacity and satisfies the will. The other is the frank but buoyant recognition that language ("the Word"), despite the filthy raggedness given it by our daily misuse of it, despite the fact that it shows man's mendacious touch and wears man's mendacious smell, is our chief instrument of imaginative, soul-satisfying construction. At the boundary between human comprehension and the incomprehensible, a sacred, awful silence necessarily intervenes, but within the bounds of the comprehensible the soul rides language.

The seeming elusiveness of this second point requires that it be clarified first. The Pope begins with the creation, and in language that is both devout and highly imaginative (X, 1307–1340), he builds an "old" idealist philosophy of design[13] in the natural universe as a way of enabling the creature, large or small, to "know" the Creator by the creation. Such cogency or persuasiveness as the Pope achieves in this "natural creation" of his own depends on the beauty of his language, on the imaginative precision with which he uses language. But what it needs to enable it to break out of its beautiful but tautological enclosure, its closed circle of thought, is other language to confirm its truth, and that "other language" is supplied by revelation.

> There is, beside the works, a tale of Thee
> In the world's mouth which I find credible:
> I love it with my heart: unsatisfied,
> I try it with my reason, nor discept
> From any point I probe and pronounce sound.
>   (X, 1347–1351)

Revelation—a "tale" or mythos naturalized in language—enables the Pope to confirm the tale or mythos about the natural universe that he himself had given a habitat in language. His argument from design had been magnificent to the degree that "strength" and "intelligence" contribute to magnificence, but man requires "goodness" or love too, and his "isoscele" had been "deficient in the base" (X, 1362–1365). This deficiency is supplied by Revelation's account of God's "transcendent act/Beside which even the creation fades/Into a puny exercise of power" (X, 1338–1340). Others may exercise themselves over the intricate language of scholastic philosophy that wrangles over truth "Absolute, abstract, independent," "historic," "reverberate," and so forth (X, 1387–1391), as others may knit the brows of their souls about such details of Biblical Criticism as "certain riddles set to solve" or "aught hard/Dubious in the transmitting of the tale" (X, 1407–1409), but the Pope is satisfied: "the tale [is] true and God shows complete" (X, 1371) through the agency of language.

The first point now needs no clarification; being mutually inclusive with the second point, it has clarified itself in the process just completed. The Pope wanted to believe; he had the imaginative capacity to convert the natural order of reality into the supernatural; the miracle of Revelation triggered the capacity and satisfied the will. Not only "God shows complete," but the Pope also, and the poet, each being "full" within the limits of his capacity.

God's "manner" is an altogether darker, more dreadful question. Even to those who, like the Pope, have achieved perfect contentment with their idea of God's existence and God's complete character as omnipotent, omniscient, and benevolent, God's conduct toward man—his invisibility, his strange timing—can try the soul with a terror almost unimaginable to those who have not hung there. That terror is the Pope's final subject.

He begins with the overwhelming recognition that men fully cognizant of the authenticity and value of faith immediately treat it as of little consequence in their lives by turning to the lowest, most vulgar sensuous satisfactions. He draws upon his experience as a coastal youth and compares such actions to those who, having been graced with the priceless pearl, dredge "for whelks,/Mud-worms that make the savoury soup" (X, 1446–1449). Though that reality is almost too painful to contemplate, the Pope in fairness turns from the deprived to the privileged members of the so-called "faithful few"—the Archbishops, Confessors, and members of canonical institutions—and acknowledges their haughty time-serving, their cowardice, the venery by which they, as vowed members of the Church, the Mystical Bride of Christ, betray the Bridegroom. The very idea they embody, being "unrealized" in action, is de-created, and being trained in cleverness, they outdo even such legendary malefactors as the soldiers who, being unenlightened, diced for Christ's coat. This is altogether more terrifying than the negligence of the unfaithful many, and the Pope faces its dread implications with courage:

> Can it be this is end and outcome, all
> I take with me to show as stewardship's fruit,

> The best yield of the latest time, this year
> The seventeen-hundredth since God died for man?
>   (X, 1531–1534)

The Pope's third level of recognition brings yet another increase in terror because of the awful irony at its center; it is a terror confirmed and magnified by the divine revelation by which he has just been immeasurably graced. If he could lay the fault at man's nature, a thing of ice the moon may gild not melt, or a stone the sun may warm not "make bear flowers," then he might have greater ease of the reality he perceives. But the instance of Caponsacchi proves man's nature is not at fault, that the ice does melt and the stone does bear flowers today as "in old time." "This," he says, "terrifies me" (X, 1536–1546).

"Where are the Christians in their panoply?" (X, 1565) the Pope cries out, desperate for some solace in his nigh-intolerable pain. The response to his agonized question is a choric "Hubbub of protestation":

> 'What, we monks
> We friars, of such an order, such a rule,
> Have not we fought, bled, left our martyr-mark
> At every point along the boundary-line
> 'Twixt true and false, religion and the world,
> Where this or the other dogma of our Church
> Called for defence?'
>   (X, 1571–1577)

But the claim of religious militancy is self-indicted by the very imagery in which it is framed. To defend the "national borders" against invaders is no more than anyone would do; it is merely " 'an instinct of the natural man' " and is no defense at all for those who claim the "wings" of faith. Such disputes on the frontiers of dogma, which have so often involved such divisions of the Church's troops as the Jesuits and the Dominicans in sharp controversy but which all have seen as matters of life and death for Christendom, have been little more than trivial distractions from the real work of Christianity[14]—to bring temporal succor and divine consolation to the plague-struck masses of its people. They, too, follow a natural rather than a supernatural pattern (X, 1588–1612).

The next question is both inevitable and the most terrifying of all. Is this the "immeasurable metamorphosis" that has been so long awaited? Is this "thing we see" the "salvation" promised by that "transcendent act/Beside which even the creation fades/Into a puny exercise of power"? It is the question toward which the Pope has been courageously, heroically moving since he acknowledged that to "dare try the doubt" was a duty that, as incumbent of the Papacy, he could not honestly shirk. His answer? "I/Put no such dreadful question to myself . . ." (X, 1630–1631).

It is a stunning moment in the dramatic evolution of the poem and was obviously calculated to be such by the poet. From the beginning of this sequence on the terror of doubt, our sympathy with the Pope has been steadily mounting as his human vulnerability and his human courage rather than his official dutifulness have dominated his character. However, now we are suddenly faced with a crisis of confidence of unprecedented proportions. Has the Pope's courage collapsed at the testing point of greatest pressure? Have we here, in the critical language of tragedy, catastrophe unredeemed by heroic insight and acceptance—pity and fear not vicariously purged but compacted into a strangulating pathos? Or has the Pope astutely and nobly sidestepped the alien, secular, systemic appetite for self-destruction implicit in the question and, by yielding not just the last shred of infallibility, but the very presumption of objective, empirical knowledge, taken sanctuary in an irrefragable faith in the existence and nature of God, leaving God's manner entirely to God? Has he, ironically, been forced to assume the higher courage of living with doubt that agnostics have always found to be their only honorable position? Those who insist upon putting the "dreadful question" will presumably read the results in the former fashion; those who reject the question as presumptuous, in the latter. But one conclusion common to both is unavoidable: once one begins to apply the argument from design to the ethical creation (man) rather than just to the physical creation (nature), then he has embarked upon a journey toward complete solipsism so predestined that only Revelation implicitly believed in can save its Christian character.[15]

In the first half of his monologue, the Pope had acknowledged no degree of doubt in making his moral judgments, not allowing even the patent ambiguities in Caponsacchi's history to make him hesitate. In the second half, he has been brought by his own procedures to an acknowledgment that God's ways with men are incomprehensible. While that does not mean that his earlier judgments were wrong, it does have the effect of returning both the judge and the judgments to solution and of particularly reminding us that everything the Pope says from this point to the end must be scrutinized with the uninhibited clarity that all the other characters should have received and that Guido in his second monologue deserves as well.

Having returned to faith as his only and sufficient foundation, the Pope returns also to his philosophy of the imperfect: life is a proving ground, an arena of contest and moral exercise. But this is not a peculiarly Christian philosophy and demands admission into the circle of consideration non-Christians like Euripides and all those for whom he is a proper spokesman (X, 1669–1789). Assuming, like the Pope, that man is to be judged by " 'inward work and worth/Of . . . mind' " (X, 1669–1670) and that only the Creator can judge the true character and intention of his creature, Euripides challenges the Pope to account for the doctrine of baptismal exclusivity that makes the salvation of persons like himself " 'impossible' " (X, 1688). By that criterion, all their "felicity" was made "sterile" and all their " 'word[s] of weighty counsel for man's sake,' " such as the Apollonian dicta " 'Know thyself' " and " 'Take the golden mean!' " so much dry dust (X, 1689–1699). By such a standard, they were no better, maybe even worse, than the brutes and should have lived brutishly. But they were instead supremely cultured, and though they were not faced with the " 'adverse circumstance[s]' " assumed by the Pope's penfold of probation philosophy, they took " 'virtue as [their] rule of life' " and not only practiced it but also taught it with a " 'strong style' " that spared neither the creature nor the Creator (X, 1709–1722). Yet that took place 500 years before St. Paul preached, and even if Paul later corrected their doctrine of duty or if

Galileo even later corrected their doctrine of the planets, are they not to be credited with filling in the blanks in ethics and physics as truly for themselves as Paul and Galileo, centuries later, did for themselves? They saw what they saw courageously and as exactly as their instruments and stage of development would allow. Since then, readjustments have been made in their imperfect knowledge—" 'the small/Proportioned largelier, parts and whole named new' " (X, 1777–1778)—but are those bold originals to be punished as sterile, brutish, and unworthy of salvation " 'For not descrying sunshine at midnight,' " while modern Christian teachers are rewarded who cannot find their way at high noon and, if they were not wallowing in " 'cowardice and slush of lies,' " could follow " 'a sure path across the bog' " laid out by their pre-Christian forebears (X, 1780–1789)?

It is a serious, hard-hitting brief, not only for Euripides and classical Hellenism, but also for all the individuals and eras that have left intellectual, cultural, and humanitarian monuments not circumscribed by the Christian circle. "How shall I answer this Euripides?" asks the Pope, but it is difficult to see that he answers him in any carefully correlated sense at all. The Pope seems to perceive the modern equivalent of a genuinely admirable classicism as nothing like its early counterpart, just as the modern equivalent of a heroic primitive Christianity described so painstakingly already bears no resemblance to its original. But despite its current corrupt state, Christianity is, he feels, redeemable in a way classicism is not. The "torpor of assurance" that has made Christianity so "sluggish, curdled at the source" (X, 1853, 1549) may be awakened as by an "earthquake" and Christians even yet made to "stand out again, pale, resolute,/Prepared to die,—that is, alive at last" (X,1861–1862). But what hope can there be for this to happen to the modern heirs of classicism? It is they who have enabled "the light of earth" to encroach upon "the light from heaven" until man's motive has become to "serve God/For man's sole sake, not God's and therefore man's" (X, 1816–1821); theirs is the "politic, the thrifty way" that inspires an "ignoble confidence,/Cowardly hardihood, that dulls and damps,/Makes the old heroism impossible" (X, 1834, 1847–1849); they are the ones who "Rest upon human nature, take their stand/On what is fact, the lust and pride of life!" (X, 1890–1891). Finally, their latest manifestation is "the educated man's" "new tribunal," resonant with a haughty eloquence and frenetic to push the Christian era offstage forever. Its spokesman is "the brisk junior," and whereas the dying Pope hopes desperately that it will be "the mission" of the new age to usher in the earthquake, "Re-introduce the doubt discarded" (X, 1854), and bring back the "danger" that will bring back the hero too, the "brisk junior" fancies that it will " 'see the golden age return!/Civilization and the Emperor/Succeed . . . Christianity and [the] Pope' " (X, 2027–2029, 1997–2097 passim).

It is surely not unfair for the critical reader to see the Pope's final vision as both enormously powerful and severely limited. The piercing quality of his "view of modernism" does not hide the fact that it is a deeply jaundiced view, and his reduction of the Golden Age of Greece, with its social enlightenment, its clear-headed fortitude, its respect for knowledge and reason, and its grand tragic vision, to the petulance, arrogance, and supercilious disrespect of a bullish adolescent is a *reductio ad absurdum*. His private transformation of the writ condemning Guido into a God-like gesture of apocalypse to a world made despicable, in part at least, by the imaginative fury of his own language is at once disproportionate and a highly self-dramatizing exercise in futility. It is to make Guido a colossal, a universal, scapegoat, and its psychological power is purchased at the price of, at best, irrational and equivocal justice.

There is in the Pope's monologue a network of what commentators have traditionally seen as Browning's own value judgments or philosophical predispositions, though it may be more precise to see them as personality metaphors of a type of character Browning admired—warm, strong, faithful, outspoken people who front life courageously and creatively and who see its meaning as intense and good, people like Fra Lippo Lippi, Karshish, and Rabbi Ben Ezra. It has been customary to enroll the Pope among these Browning favorites, but the case for doing so is only about as strong as the case against it. Pope Innocent's warmth is boundless but specialized; his faith works too wholly within circumscribed parameters; he is courageous only to a point; his creativity does not enable him to establish grounds for reconciliation with the pre-Christian past, the extra-Christian present, or the post-Christian future; life has for him a meaning that is intense and good only if it is subjected to a regimen of self-sacrifice that denies life an independent felicity. The Pope has the genius of a severely limited man, and, to adapt his own misgiving about his Archbishop, Browning has made a Pope and almost undone a hero.

Notes

1. A passage in Book I that particularly displeased British Catholics when the poem first appeared and has since seemed somewhat capricious to most readers takes on new relevance in this critical context. The words are spoken by a representative of the Roman Establishment in response to the poet-speaker's request for help in getting at the truth:

   > 'Content you with your treasure of a book,
   > And waive what's wanting! Take a friend's advice!
   > It's not the custom of the country. Mend
   > Your ways indeed and we may stretch a point:
   > Go get you manned by Manning and new-manned
   > By Newman and, mayhap, wise-manned to boot
   > By Wiseman, and *we'll see or else we won't!*'
   >   (I, 440–446, emphasis added)

2. In concluding the Formosus matter, the Pope quotes Christ as saying, " 'Fear not those whose power can kill the body/And not the soul . . . but rather those/Can cast both soul and body into hell!' " (154–156) without acknowledging its applicability to a priesthood that claims the power to forgive or retain sins.

3. Commentators on the poem have generally skirted this issue. Altick and Loucks, who are more forthright and conscientious than most, approach it, circle it, and then back away from it. See Richard D. Altick and James F. Loucks II, *Browning's Roman Murder Story* (Chicago: University of Chicago Press, 1968), pp. 327–331.

4. Review of Leopold Ranke's *The Ecclesiastical and Political History of The Popes of Rome, during the Sixteenth and Seventeenth Centuries*, in *Miscellaneous Works of Lord Macaulay*, ed. Lady Trevelyan (New York: Harper & Bros., 1880), I, 614.

5. *Ulysses*, 11. 57, 68–70.

6. Swedenborg was only ten years old at the time, and therefore Innocent could have known nothing of him. However, the kind of scientific spiritualism that he represented in the next century was already gaining advocacy as an alternative to Christian orthodoxy, and it is this tendency that the Pope challenges and chides.

7. Tennyson, *Ulysses*, 1. 50.

8. In the *Apologia*, Newman speaks of resting "in the thought of two and two only absolute and luminously self-evident beings, myself and my Creator. . . ." See John Henry Cardinal Newman, *Apologia pro Vita Sua*, ed. A. Dwight Culler (Boston: Houghton Mifflin, 1956), p. 25.

9. Of course, like the young Newman of the *Apologia* or the Marius of Pater's *Marius the Epicurean*, the boy Antonio could have begun early to translate natural data into morally freighted perception, though we are given no hint of that. The exact detail with which he has actually seen fish, birds, and animals suggests objectivity of observation.

10. Clearly these three would not have been the youthful Guido's models, but the Bishop who indoctrinates Caponsacchi and the Archbishop who instructs Pompilia might have served.

11. The Pope brutally "Saturnizes" the poet-advocates of the cult of the Noble Savage (X, 776–781).

12. The Pope's phrase is "initiatory spasm," a further use of the loss-of-virginity metaphor that Caponsacchi had magnified so sensuously. Consistent with his more chaste use of the trope, the Pope implies that a man does not deserve the experience unless, through reflection, he also penetrates its suprasensuous meaning and recognizes the new order of responsibility it introduces into his life.

13. As contrasted, that is, with the "new [scientific] philosophy" of line 1334.

14. The Pope's example of this doctrinal hairsplitting and the disproportionate fulminations occasioned by it in the Church is not quite precise historically, but it is nonetheless brilliantly chosen.

15. Tennyson's tragic protagonist in *Idylls of the King* is forced to face the same issue at the beginning of *The Passing of Arthur*. For a commentary on the relevant passage, see William E. Buckler, *Man and His Myths: Tennyson's "Idylls of the King" in Critical Context* (New York: New York University Press, 1984).

9.

Condemned to the Hell Within: Book XI. *Guido*

One can never hope to know conclusively Browning's imaginative reasons for giving Guido a second monologue and situating it as he did in the poem's structure:[1] that is a value judgment that the poem itself makes as inconclusive as it makes all the value judgments it introduces. But the critic can expect the poet's reasons to have been at least as large, serious, and complex as his own respect for the poem—larger, more serious, and more complex, for example, than focusing simply on the final lines of Book XI, calling them Guido's noblest, deducing from them "a strange sparkle," and concluding that Guido "bears out" the Pope's prophecy by showing "signs of regeneration."[2]

Guido is not a different character in Book XI from the one who spoke in Book V, not a liar in the one and a truth-teller in the other, not hopelessly craven there and sentimentally repentant here. He is a character-in-motion like all the other fully developed characters in the poem. He tries many ruses, experiments with many postures, responds expansively or constrictively to implicit feedback from his listeners, is a practiced if unsuccessful dissembler. He does undergo a moment of insight in the middle of Book V that threatens him with a serious loss of nerve, but he survives it and ends his first monologue with what he calls "returned health" and "sanity of soul." Clearly, that reading of his first monologue makes both redemption and self-strangulation possible, but it by no means guarantees the former, and it makes the latter seem highly likely. From the judges' point of view, that middle passage in Book V spells an end to the plausibility of Guido's defense; it is the structural midpoint that makes his condemnation inevitable.

But the very subject of the poem has as one of its inherent propositions that there are far worse things than mere physical death. Pompilia's murder proves that, as does the imminent death of the Pope. It can even be cogently argued that Caponsacchi has to pay for his own sins by a fate far worse than a quick physical death—namely, "be unhappy but bear life" (X, 1211), awake to "the old solitary nothingness" (VI, 2103), "Do out the duty" (VII, 1843). That proposition supplies one good organic reason for Book XI: it prepares us to read the monologue from the beginning with an acute interest in which version of "health" and "sanity of soul" will finally work itself out in Guido's case, that which threatens a complete loss of nerve and makes him available to the grace of redemption or that which puts his soul on ice and enables him to escape the pain of self-knowledge that, by the simple test of Caponsacchi's pain, would have to be colossal to be equitable. That is the demand of tragedy, and although *The Ring and the Book* makes adequate provision for something beyond tragedy in the more-than-Christian promise that is so magnificently exemplified in Pompilia, it does not violate the integrity of the tragic vision as grounded in the purely human lives of its characters. In Guido's case, there is a third possibility. Neither mere physical death nor ultimate redemption is the price demanded by his character, but something in between, a recognition of the truth of Pompilia that is strong enough to poison his self-image but not strong enough to purge his soul, a fire that scorches him but does not burn out his impurities. Such a possibility would not only carry pathos as far as it could go without either reaching authentic tragedy or falling into sentimental bathos; it would also be a poetically apposite solution to the problem of Guido's just deserts—an eternal purgatory without terminus in heaven or hell,[3] a cosmic validation of free will, and an exoneration of God from the scholastic (and, we hope, playful) obligation to remake a product that insists so adamantly on being forever its incorrigible self:

> Unmanned, remade: I hold it probable—
> With something changeless at the heart of me
> To know me by, some nucleus that's myself. . . .
> (XI, 2391–2393)

Then, the "strange sparkle" of Guido's "noblest utterance" casts quite a different light—or shadow—and we have another thoroughly organic reason for Book XI.

Some critical readers of *The Ring and the Book* may also find in Book XI proof of an aesthetic boldness and integrity that set aside formal symmetry and a mechanical accommodation of the principle of poetic indirection in favor of a higher aesthetic courage and a higher aesthetic truth. For them, Guido's second monologue is not only justified but imaginatively mandated. It exists as testimony to a magnificent modern poet's capacity to overstep the usual expectations of traditional ethics and traditional aesthetics and create an imaginative consciousness that does not depend for its poetic affectiveness on either the heaven-hell, saved-damned dichotomy of a remnant but persistent Manichaeanism or the allegory-literalism, idealist-realist division of a remnant but persistent aesthetic medievalism. Book XI is the ultimate confirmation of Browning's break with these two interwoven traditions. To a measurable degree, Book XI remakes *The Ring and the Book* as, to a comparable degree, *The Ring and the Book* remakes English poetry.

A few points of contrast between *The Ring and the Book* and *Idylls of the King* may make this point both clearer and stronger. There is nothing odious about the comparison because no suggestion is being made that one is a better poem than the other or that Tennyson did not have as good reasons for his aesthetic decisions as Browning had for his different decisions. Moreover, the contrasts would not be so telling if the two poems did not have so very much in common—analogous experiments in overall narrative method, the creation of full-bodied images of "the mighty world," a sense of history that envelops pagan, Christian, and post-Christian epochs, the probing of particular moral, religious, epistemological, and aesthetic atmospheres that, despite their different metaphors, position comparable issues and supply fresh grounds for their contemplation.[4]

Tennyson chose his subject matter from the Middle Ages and drew frankly upon previous literary texts that were either known or would become known as the growing interest in Arthurian subjects specifically and medieval subjects generally intensified. Browning chose his subject matter from the late-seventeenth and early-eighteenth centuries when the seeds of historical (as distinct from mythic) modernism had been broadly sown and the forces hostile to the medieval world view released by the Renaissance were taking firm hold in every aspect of life. Also, he drew upon a contemporaneous set of documents—a book—that was not only not known, but in principle at least could not be known except through his poem and, eventually, the book upon which his poem was based. Tennyson's Arthurian material was neither strictly historical nor strictly legendary but a combination of the two, and that middle ground suited his poetic purposes perfectly—new-old, elusive, multivalent, paradoxical. Browning's material was absolutely historical, a compendium of documents that gave contemporary testimony both to the facts and to the persons reporting the facts, and their poetic significance depends on the *reader's perception* of the *poet's perception* of the *personae's perception* of them. Though it made Tennyson very uncomfortable for people to read his poem "too allegorically," he attested to the fact that "there is an allegorical or perhaps rather a parabolic drift in the poem."[5] *The Ring and the Book* is as far from formal allegory as serious narrative literature with representative human characters can be, and though one can be reasonably comfortable with an application of the term parable to the poem, a distinction needs to be made: it is not a parable to be interpreted but a parable to be found, much of the reader's co-creative energy being focused on the discovery of the integral marks of representativeness, and hence the parabolic value, of the *dramatis personae* both as individuals and as part of a whole.

Though few serious readers would fault the universality of Tennyson's subject or action in *Idylls of the King* and its continuing relevance, most would agree that it makes a very large use of retrospection; consciously employs strategies of archaic language, incident, character, and literary structure; and regards the human prospect with a pervasive sense of belatedness, a nostalgia for a fairer time that, being lost, will never again be known with anything like its original freshness. Whether one focuses on the cycles of history, of the year, or of an individual man's life, the ultimate vision of the poem is memorial, remorseful, resolute in degree but sad. Browning uses history to give the action of his poem factual validity and a necessary element of imaginative detachment, but the future is regarded from *now,* not from *then.* The passing of certain qualities of the past are regretted, but the regret is tempered by the recognition that those qualities were mixed with other characteristics that few would wish to return to. The Pope is an exception to this, but he is terrified by the future and is solitary among members of his own hierarchy in living a plain, simple, exemplary life and in finding his touchstones of human grandeur in the Crusaders of the twelfth and thirteenth centuries or, more vividly, in the Christian martyrs of the first, second, and third. Moreover, against the Pope's lamentation over a lost Christian past, the poem sets Guido's confused contempt for the social leveling going on all around him and his ugly rage against the passing of a time, parallel to that which the Pope remembers with such affectionate admiration, when the privileges of hereditary nobility constituted one of the most virulent of social diseases.

There are many points of contact between Tennyson's and Browning's world views, but our interest here is not in world views but in poems and the way a poet's artistic decisions influence the terms and conditions under which we reflect co-creatively with him about life's possibilities. Over and above the

decisions already reviewed, there is the issue of honest alter-
natives—the degree to which the poet, in addition to structuring a poem's experiences in such a way as to make reconciliation and redemption seem possible or even likely, acknowledges
the reality of an alternative view. We know that Tennyson
thought of adding to *In Memoriam* a section that would show
that the arguments against reconciliation and redemption were
just about as strong as those for it,[6] but he never did add it.
We know too that he held off publication of *Balin and Balan,*
the last of the idylls to be written, for more than a dozen years
(from 1872 until 1885). Read in the order of composition and
first publication rather than in its place in the final sequence,
the myth of irreconciliation in *Balin and Balan* seems to offer
one grim alternative to the myth of Guinevere and Arthur, but
Tennyson's decision to place *Balin and Balan* early in the structure of the poem (fourth in the Round Table idylls) diminishes its dramatic impact as an alternative view. *The Last Tournament,* both in its Tristram story and in its ghastly conclusion
to the story of Pelleas, is a frontal attack on Arthurianism, but
the violent resolution of both of its revenge tragedy myths and
its placement before *Guinevere* in the final order shrink its effect as an alternative world view which a reversal of the order
would have magnified.[7]

Guido is, with appropriate allowances, the equivalent in *The
Ring and the Book* to *The Last Tournament* in *Idylls of the King,*
and the fact that Browning places it after *The Pope* and last
among the principal monologues is a fact of major significance. That significance is considerably blunted, of course, if,
in deference to the idea that the Pope speaks for Browning,
one reads it as the fulfillment of a Papal prophecy and allows
Guido to get his scorched soul out of the fire at the last moment.[8] But the Pope makes no such prophecy; he says that he
has "no hope" for Guido "Except in such a suddenness of fate"
as being promptly forced to lay his neck in the half-moon cra-
dle of Mannaia (X, 2116–2117). Of that "one instant" (X, 2127),
we can know nothing, and the palaver of a systemic liar who
wants to go into eternity with "something changeless at the
heart" of him, "some nucleus that's [himself]"—perhaps the
"hate" that, according to Pompilia, is "the truth of him" (VII,
1727)—is hardly enough to sustain such minimalist orthodoxy

as "no hope/Except" and certainly does not justify finding in it a highly romantic reversal. That, I suggest, is a trap laid by a poet ever sensitive to ways in which people choose, if they possibly can, to turn away from the terrifying truth.

Like Tristram in *The Last Tournament,* Guido makes some cogent arguments that are not made false by his personal falseness. They may be the overwrought dogmas of modernism, and modernism may have to pay an awful price for them, but, objectively compared, they are no more extravagant than the dogmas of the Christian Middle Ages, which took an awful toll too. The hedonism, secularism, neopaganism, determinism, relativism, and naturalism that constitute Guido's chief heresies as well as the chief currents of the new age—its global Pelagianism—are not the mental progeny of a den of devils or a coven of warlocks, but, variously, the deeply considered theories of such men as Bacon, Descartes, Hobbes, and Locke in the seventeenth century and, in the eighteenth and nineteenth centuries, of persons like Voltaire, Rousseau, Hume, Bentham, Winckelmann, Godwin, Comte, the Darwins, Walter Savage Landor, John Stuart Mill, Thomas Henry Huxley, Swinburne, George Eliot, Leslie Stephen, and many others of lesser and greater importance. The fact that Guido pronounces them in his snarling character as a self-proclaimed wolf at bay inevitably makes them seem grotesque, but the frightful absurdity is inherent in the man, not in the ideas. From this perspective, much of Guido's monologue has an analogy in that moment at Castelnuovo when Caponsacchi suddenly perceives for the first time the true character of human life as a grotesque marriage of good and evil:

> how splendidly
> Mirthful, what ludicrous a lie was launched!
> Would Molière's self wish more than hear such man
> Call, claim such woman for his own, his wife,
> Even though, in due amazement at the boast,
> He had stammered, she moreover was divine?
> (VI, 1485–1490)

By placing *Guido* in such a crucial position, letting it stand as the "last word," so to speak, Browning redeemed, not Guido, but *The Ring and the Book*. Gently but consistently, he further undercut the noble untenableness of the Pope's position; he implanted a host of ideas that, taken together, do in fact constitute the broad character of a modernism in full flow, a modernism that cannot be dealt a deathblow by even the most heroic defiance or deflected by a romantic retreat into a past that to some may seem nobler; and by putting those ideas into the mouth of a cruel, manipulative, violent character, he suggested to what evil uses they could be put without passing a hopelessly prejudiced verdict on the ideas themselves.

Thus Browning turned poetry away from a persistent Manichaeanism of moral blacks and whites and away from an equally persistent aesthetic medievalism of thematic or allegorical primacy. Instead, he insisted on the essential complexity and ambiguity inherent in moral issues despite the tendency of all but a few to misconceive their own motives and to dogmatize their judgments in the name of high-mindedness; and by subjecting argument to character, thought to the experience of thought, he reversed the usual order of priorities in both the creation and the usability of poetry by showing that the identity of the thinker is organically related to the authority of the thought, what a man believes being essentially an expression of who the man is.[9]

In Book V, Guido attempts to persuade the Court that he is not the person certain facts and interpretations identify him as being. In the process, he fabricates a self that is true to his essential falseness but false to the essential reality until, midway in this activity, he remembers the spontaneous defiance of Pompilia at Castelnuovo and recognizes there an image of human grandeur that momentarily shatters his faith in himself and threatens him with a loss of nerve. However, after a brief interval of self-abasement during which he frantically grasps at straws, he survives his identity crisis and completes his process of self-fabrication very much in the manner in which he had begun it. The reader thus comes to Book XI with the earlier fabrication, crisis, and recovery still fresh in his memory and the conviction that Guido has not forgotten it either.

The factual difference between Book V and Book XI is that

Guido's appeal to the Pope to exercise his special privilege and overturn the judgment of the Court has failed and he is in the middle of his execution vigil attended by Cardinal Acciaiuoli and Abate Panciatichi, who have come to shrive his soul. Thus Guido's second monologue is the last word of a man who has nothing to lose but his soul and will lose that unless he makes a full confession of his sins, is "heartily sorry" for having committed them, and is sincere in his resolution to sin no more. Those are the normal expectations of a "good confession," which is the Church ritual by which the monologue is being shaped. Implicit in the act of confession is the testimony of faith that one has a soul, that it is immortal, and that God will redeem it if he is humbly asked to do so.

The first verse paragraph seems to put beyond hope the notion that Guido feels any genuine contrition or any capacity resolutely to struggle against temptation. He appeals to his confessors' Tuscan bloodlines to collude in freeing him, declares his innocence to be immaculate, condemns the Court as the toadies of a "sneaking burgess-spirit," damns the Pope to hell, denies the reality of Christianity, says the Pope is a sick old animal who devours him just to satisfy his final hunger (makes a Last Supper out of him), claims immunity on grounds of the achievements of his noble ancestors, cites with pride his grandfather's stabbing of a peasant for making a slighting remark, and declares himself the unlucky victim of a sudden change in the rules of the game (XI, 1–142). But the energy behind Guido's furious tirade has a curious and crucial source: he is determined to put down at any cost a repetition of that momentary weakness he experienced under the influence of Pompilia. That was the "folly" that must never again be allowed to threaten his male soul:

> I knew that just myself concerned myself,
> Yet needs must look for what I seemed to lack,
> In a woman,—why, the woman's in the man!
> Fools we are, how we learn things when too late!
> Overmuch life turns round my woman-side;
> The male and female in me, mixed before,
> Settle of a sudden: I'm my wife outright

In this unmanly appetite for truth,
This careless courage as to consequence,
This instantaneous sight through things and through,
This voluble rhetoric, if you please,—'t is she!
Here you have that Pompilia whom I slew,
Also the folly for which I slew her!

(XI, 164–176)

He has never before "had the words" to say it (XI, 160), but the rhetoric has come with the recognition. An insatiable "appetite for truth," a "courage" "careless of consequence," "instantaneous [in]sight"—these were the "folly" of Pompilia, he says; they were "woman" stuff that his maleness, being threatened, "slew."

The fact that Guido immediately afterwards recalls himself to reality—"Fool!/And, fool-like, what is it I wander from?" (XI, 177–178)—draws an implicit parallel between this passage and that moment of truth at the center of Book V when he felt the influence of Pompilia so precariously. This, together with the peculiar applicability of what he says here to Pompilia's motives and actions in the earlier episode, shows that he is still having to deal with her influence, even the words "Fool!" and "fool-like" being echoes of the terrible self-abasement he had felt at that time. More importantly, it comes very near the beginning of Book XI and is an implicit explanation of why Guido adopts so furious a tone in his second monologue. This is the "nucleus" of himself that Guido will refer to at the end (XI, 2391–2395); this is the identity that must be kept intact and dominant if he is going to hold together in this life and continue to exist hereafter. Finally, like that moment in Book V, it is a "true" truth, not a ruse: it is "the word" he never could find before; it emerges when his mind is wandering into self-communion; and it is the key to his second monologue.

The level at which this theme of male dominance is operating in *The Ring and the Book* can perhaps be made clear through consideration of a short passage in the Pope's monologue, that in which he pronounces Pompilia "First of the first" (X, 1003–1093).

Regardless of the disproportion one may find in various aspects of the Pope's manner of supposing and stating fact or truth and the degree of freedom from the Pope's authority such discovery may give one, he remains intact as a warm, engaged, dutiful, admirable old man. His competitiveness is a function of his office, not of his private person, and his grandfatherliness liberates him from the close-range male-female stresses that, in different ways and degrees, hold Caponsacchi and Guido hostage. He bills and coos over Pompilia, and that raises the ghost of the woman stereotyped as baby-doll: "stoop thou down, my child,/Give one good moment to the poor old Pope" (X, 1005–1006); but his imprecation "stoop thou down," coupled with his sense of limitless wonder that one so young and tender should be "first of the first" in his long, varied, ever-attentive experience of life, makes it an act of genuine adoration, not of patronage. She is even more than the *"flos regum"* ("flower of kings") of Alberic's characterization of King Arthur;[10] she is the Pope's *flos omnium hominum, flos humanitatis* ("flower of all humankind, flower of humanity"). But Pompilia's glory as a human being is, in the Pope's praise, inextricably interwoven with her glory as a woman in a world dominated by men. Thou hast, he apostrophizes her,

> having been obedient to the end
> According to the light allotted, law
> Prescribed thy life, still tried, still standing test,—
> Dutiful to the foolish parents first,
> Submissive next to the bad husband,—nay,
> Tolerant of those meaner miserable
> That did his hests, eked out the dole of pain,—
> Thou, patient thus, couldst rise from law to law,
> The old to the new, promoted at one cry
> O' the trump of God to the new service, not
> To longer bear, but henceforth fight, be found
> Sublime in new impatience with the foe!
> Endure man and obey God: plant firm foot
> On neck of man, tread man into the hell
> Meet for him, and obey God all the more!
>   (X, 1048–1062)

This is one of the crucial evaluative passages in the whole poem, as carefully and delicately phrased by the invisible poet as is, in *Idylls of the King,* Arthur's evaluation of Guinevere at their final parting: the integrity, coherence, and purgative power of the central myth is at stake.

What that phrasing does is move the victory and significance of Pompilia to a far more generalized level than is encompassed by the literal story line of her tragic transcendence over Guido. The forces against which she had to struggle long preceded any knowledge of Guido or even of her "foolish parents." Guido and her parents were merely reflections of the "light allotted," realities of the "law/Prescribed." Those realities were the system, the way things were; that was the "law" for which a new law must be found, a "new service" promoted. "God" plays a part in this more generalized, more encompassing level to which the Pope's phrasing points in that he is exculpated from the authorship of *this* law, *this* disposition of things. The real author and hence the real "foe" is "man." *He* must be endured as life itself must be endured, but God must be obeyed, and in this situation—in the current state of "enlightenment," the current state of morals and legislation—to "obey God" means to "plant firm foot/On neck of man, tread man into the hell/Meet for him, and obey God all the more!" Guido as an isolated monster is not the foe; the real foe is all the moral, legal, political, social, psychological "dole of pain" that women in a male-dominated society of which Guido is the monstrous epitome have had to endure in obedience but which they will endure no longer except with a "sublime impatience" that will break up the old law, tread the old lawmaker into the hell he deserves, and promote the new law of the new lawmaker.

Where Guido begins, he ends—in a fury of self-assertion underpinned by his philosophy of the male animal with a "hasty hunger" for the blood of his victims. Right up to the moment of his cowardly collapse at the sight of the Brotherhood of Death, he is one fiery eruption of faith in maleness: "I lived and died a *man,* and take *man's* chance,/Honest and bold: right will be done to such" (XI, 2410–2411, emphasis added). The fact that Guido's mind and soul are saturated with this view of man in his universe—so deeply dyed with a philosophy of male domination that he cannot be cleansed except in some grossly sentimental fashion—raises fundamental questions about individual versus social, cultural, political, even anthropological responsibility, but it does not justify equating the craven cowardice with which he panics in the wake of his own haughty bravado with something so positive and crucial as repentance and redemption. Even his penultimate utterance, which Professor Langbaum sees as Guido's noblest and I see as merely an instant of superficial self-deception when one has rationalized dying to the momentary exclusion of its horror, is the conclusion to a unit of thought, a verse paragraph, that begins with a sudden rupture of silence and then moves to a sense of having found "something like a foothold in the sea." That "foothold" is Guido's "proper instinct of defence" against just such an "instant" as that of which the Pope had spoken, and Guido becomes "Careless, gay even" when he "taste[s]" the strength of his "wolf-nature" cutting through the flesh and breaking the backbone of his "lamblike wife" (XI, 2288–2329). That is the joyous thought that momentarily reconciles Guido both to the "untimeliness" of death and its "rude and rough" manner, and so far from being a fulfillment of the Pope's so-called prophecy, it is a mockery of it.

Just two verse paragraphs before that, Guido had given voice to a full-dress fantasy of his ideal of the male-female relationship. It, too, is a kind of climax, a climax of rottenness at the core of a drab, deprived, menopausal monster desirous only of glutting himself on evil and teasing himself into a state of solitary sexual frenzy by imagining himself not only as wholly dominant, but dominant over the indomitable (XI, 2181–2208). From the depraved Olimpias and Biancas, he moves to Delilah, Circe, and Lucrezia Borgia, bringing under absolute service to his will and making traitor to "king, priest, father, mother, stranger, friend" in absolute service to him women who in reality would have looked upon the unkempt, incompetent, unprepossessing little loser as beneath the notice of their contempt. The patent sickness of Guido's megalomaniacal fantasy introduces the idea of psychological and moral accountability, but it offers no credence whatsoever that he is on the verge of reaching into his soul, finding grounds there for nobility, and suddenly repenting and being saved. It does something far more organic, however; it gives the reader a new basis for understanding the recurrent images of Pompilia with which his monologue is punctuated.

Pompilia is a pervasive presence in the monologue. Guido is throughout haunted by her image. His killing of her is the one action he must defend while it is his one wholly indefensible act. Pompilia has become a popular legend by virtue of the miracle of her four-day survival of so many fatal wounds and the deathbed story of her tragic life. She has served as the poet of her own presence in this vale of tears and has been adopted as a popular saint. Guido knows this, and his unacknowledged despair of dislodging it is one explanation of why he rages so furiously and why he seemingly goes so far afield for his arguments. But his despair of countering the world's opinion of Pompilia is greatly complicated by his inability to flush out of his mind's or soul's eye endless images of her that perpetually rise and, without being themselves judgmental, confront him with the threatening necessity of judging himself. That, however, is the one thing Guido is adamantly determined not to do; the devastating effects of such a self-measuring at Castelnuovo are still fresh in his memory. He believes that he cannot again make that mistake and survive. Whether or not the reader credits Guido with a full and genuine understanding of his awful plight—the plight of a man who *cannot* save his head and *will not* save his soul—he himself understands it. That is the soul-grinding condition Guido is in in his second monologue and, if his willful determination is prophetic, the condition in which he will continue to exist for all eternity. It is both the justice and the pathos of his situation.

Of the two dozen or so passages in the monologue that reveal the peculiarities of Pompilia's relentless, torturing presence in Guido's imaginative memory, five seem richest in their overall resonances and therefore to have been intended by the poet to bear the chief weight of this crucial dimension of his intuition: XI, 976–983, 1371–1378, 1723–1731, 2074–2097, and 2098–2155.[11]

The first passage is a characterization of Pompilia at the wedding ceremony:

She eyes me with those frightened balls of black,
As heifer—the old simile comes pat—
Eyes tremblingly the altar and the priest:
The amazed look, all one insuppressive prayer,—
Might she but be set free as heretofore,
Have this cup leave her lips unblistered, bear
Any cross anywhither anyhow,
So but alone, so but apart from me!

(XI, 976–983)

It is a recollective emotion that Guido is describing, but he casts it in the present tense as though it were taking place at the moment, and the vividness, empathy, and hieratic imagery in which he remembers it suspend for the moment his fury of argumentative self-justification and enable us to see the scene and feel its emotional content or tenor with the clarity of vision with which we might view a painter's representation of it. Immediately thereafter, he offers it as sufficient reason for hating Pompilia forever, as he thinks he must. But the reason for what he calls hatred, and indeed acts out as hatred, is the intolerable discomfort of a recognition that he does not dare articulate: in that first instant, she had looked into the terrifying truth of him, and he had seen something of himself in her mirror. He "hates" her for it, but he cannot erase any part of it from his memory.

To understand fully the impact of the second passage, one must note that Guido is at his wits' end trying to find some way of punishing Pompilia in a manner that will make domination over her psychophysically stimulating to him. Even the sex act, to which he has made her succumb, is totally without pleasure:

Then, she lay there, mine:
Now, mine she is if I please wring her neck,—
A moment of disquiet, working eyes,
Protruding tongue, a long sigh, then no more—
As if one killed the horse one could not ride!

(XI, 1358–1362)

Pompilia has so far de-created herself, doing everything according to his rules and waiting for the new rule to come, that he can hardly find in her an enemy worth torturing without torturing himself even more.

> I advise—no one think to bear that look
> Of steady wrong, endured as steadily,
> —Through what sustainment of deluding hope?
> Who is the friend i' the background that notes all?
> Who may come presently and close accounts?
> This self-possession to the uttermost,
> How does it differ in aught, save degree,
> From the terrible patience of God?
>
> (XI, 1371–1378)

Again Guido shifts into the present tense, but this time it is not a visual mirror but a spiritual mystery that possesses him. He does not believe in God, except as Jove Aegiochus, and his stance throughout his monologue is to snap his fingers at all questions not consciously positioned by him as rhetorical strategies, refusing to ponder imponderables. But the solidity of things so threatens to dissolve in the aura which Pompilia's intact endurance radiates about her that every effort to despoil her is frustrated, her very solitariness being inexplicably companioned and her long-suffering evocative of thoughts of "the terrible patience of God." This fascinating phrase is not to be taken as even an oblique revelation of faith; "God" is used throughout the monologue as a purely conventional metaphor, as part of Guido's inherited word-baggage. What it shows is that Pompilia has induced in him a strong if remnant reminiscence of the psychology of religion, of that state of mind, long since abandoned, in which terror of the supranatural found its natural expression in the feelings and language of religion. It is the mental or spiritual state opposite to that which he is so ferociously fabricating, and though he unconsciously despairs of ever returning to or acquiring it and would consciously mock the very idea of doing so, Pompilia yet puts him in mind of it and thus increases while undermining the satisfaction of his ferocity.

The motifs of the first two passages—the painter's unforgettably penetrating eye and the mystic's impalpable mystery—become interfused in the third passage and make it a turning point in Guido's progress toward *either* recognition, acceptance, and tragic redemption *or* evasion, rejection, and pathetic damnation.[12]

> What's disputable, refutable here?—
> Save by just one ghost-thing half on earth,
> Half out of it,—as if she held God's hand
> While she leant back and looked her last at me,
> Forgiving me (here monks begin to weep)
> Oh, from her very soul, commending mine
> To heavenly mercies which are infinite,—
> While fixing fast my head beneath your knife!
> 'T is fate not fortune! All is of a piece!
> (XI, 1723–1731)

The painter's image is still there, like a Dürer illustration of a passage in Dante, of the ghostlike figure of Pompilia on the margin of eternity regarding for the last soulful instant the lost soul of Guido, but the mystery, which is there too, is rendered in a tone of irony that converts awe to bitterness. Guido's perception of himself as a victim of the irony of fate deflates a healthy sense of terror (mystery perceived in terrifying magnitude) to something slightly more than petulance: "While fixing fast my head beneath your knife!" It is more than bad luck ("not fortune!"), it is evil destiny ("'T is fate") that he blames for his undoing; and since he will not or cannot, in the face of the awful aftershocks, blame himself, even "heavenly mercies which are infinite" are unequal to his moral metamorphosis. Thus all genuine hope of Guido's tragic redemption—that he will see the stark truth, admit his complicity in it, and face the consequence with a degree of moral grandeur—is lost, and no false dawn, however "strange" its "sparkle," will save Guido's myth from ending shabbily—both pathetic and damned. "All is of a piece!" he cries. It is all of a piece, of course, if one can only externalize blame, if one cannot even go so far toward moral realism as to say "I am more sinned against than sinning," but must fall back upon such a moral fantasy as "Innocent as a babe, as Mary's own,/ As Mary's self" (XI, 30–31). No one—not "Mary's self"—can make such a moral claim; for Guido to make it is the absurdest of absurdities and puts him beyond any comprehensible idea of redemption.

Though this passage is an important turning point in Guido's response to the influence of Pompilia in the monologue as a whole, it bears a climactic relationship to the individual sequence in which it occurs. That is the long sequence (XI, 1518–1908) in which Guido argues that his whole debacle has been the result, not of his "fault" or even of Pompilia's, but of "the luck that lies beyond a man" (XI, 1565), so many manifestations of which are "of a piece" that he calls it "ordained just so" or "fate" rather than willy-nilly "luck" or "fortune." In introducing this sequence and this argument, Guido refers to

> that particular devil whose task it is
> To trip the all-but-at perfection,—slur
> The line o' the painter just where paint leaves off
> And life begins,—puts ice into the ode
> O' the poet while he cries "Next stanza—fire!"
> Inscribes all human effort with one word,
> Artistry's haunting curse, the Incomplete!
>   (XI, 1553–1559)

Guido then goes on to challenge his auditors, if they will use a "fair unjaundiced eye," to fault his "masterpiece" of planning and execution except for his bad "luck" in not discovering the fleeing pair in flagrante delicto and then goes on to invite them to review the entire sequence from the perspective of the "poor obstructed artist." It is obviously a crucial challenge in such a poem as *The Ring and the Book* as articulated by such a character as Guido in the final phase of his defense. It connects the central incident of his first monologue (the discovery and what it led to) with the climactic incident of his second (the murder and its ultimate consequence).

It is a worthy challenge because it puts Guido's auditors—in the present context, his readers—in a real dilemma. On the one hand, there is no denying the ingratiating attractiveness of the line "Artistry's haunting curse, the Incomplete"; on the other hand, Guido's actions must not be allowed so ingratiating an excuse. So unless the poet is to be accused of simply teasing the reader through his use of a patently fascinating but ultimately trivial analogy, one must take the argument seriously. The subtle significance seems to be that the perniciousness is inherent in the attractiveness. Guido is talking about the perfect crime, "perfect" in and of itself without any regard to its moral content—a crime perpetrated in such a way as to relieve the perpetrator of all judicial accountability and even earn him praise. That is what the two crucial incidents of the two monologues (i.e., the two apologias) have in common. Had he caught Pompilia and Caponsacchi in the middle of lovemaking, he could have run them through with impunity from the law and applause from the crowd, however hypocritical, cruel, calculating, and cowardly his part in the incident may have been. Had he not overlooked the little matter of the permit for horses, he could have reached the Tuscan border after committing the triple murder and, being beyond the reach of Roman authority, escaped punishment and received homage as a local hero who had upheld the honor of Tuscany. In either case, he would have authored a "masterpiece" of rare device rather than having to suffer the consequences of failure.

Viewed from the other side of the analogy, it would mean that a work of art, if it were "perfect" in and of itself without regard to its moral content—a poem, symphony, or painting executed in such a way as to be above critical exception and conducive of critical acclaim—would achieve the completeness which is success. It could preach the meanest of motives, celebrate the most despicable of heroes, trace the most devious of strategies, evoke the most prurient of emotions, and incite the most violent or blasphemous of attitudes and still be called completely successful if the perfection of its execution (art for art's sake), like the perfection of a crime's perpetration (crime for crime's sake) were its goal and its test.

The "poor artist's" obstruction, then, is in himself, as is the "poor criminal's," not out there in "the luck that lies beyond a man." The key to both is attitudinal, and the attitude specified by the language of the artist-criminal analogy is that of perceiving the incompleteness with which "all human effort" is "inscribed" as a "haunting curse." It is a curse only if one so literalizes his quest for perfection as to consider himself cursed—haunted by failure—if he does not perfectly succeed. That is to make oneself the devoté of the pride that seeks the fall and then to curse one's "luck" or one's "fate" because it did not make one rise. Hence, it is not man's imperfection—be he artist or criminal—that is his "haunting curse," but a presumption of perfection, a philosophy, that makes his imperfection a curse rather than a blessing and haunts him with the fear of failure in undertakings that, if they succeeded, would do him unimaginable harm.

The fourth and fifth passages are two parts of a single continuity that breaks naturally in the middle. In the fourth passage or first half of the continuity (XI, 2074–2097), the visual image has become concentrated into a synecdoche, Pompilia's "eyes"—"those detested eyes"—having become a maddening metaphor of all she represents to Guido. What was formerly a source of mystery to him has become polarized into a mighty opposite against which he sets all his aggressive energy. As she had recognized "hate" as "the truth of him," he recognizes "no touch . . . of hate" as the truth of her; as heaven would "prove her hell" if she knew he had reached his, he would give up heaven to secure his revenge against an enemy, crying out in animal fury against her "abnegation of revenge!"

The fifth passage, which completes the continuity, is short and conclusive:

> So am I made, 'who did not make myself:'
> (How dared she rob my own lip of the word?)
> Beware me in what other world may be!—
> Pompilia, who have brought me to this pass!
> All I know here, will I say there, and go
> Beyond the saying with the deed. Some use
> There cannot but be for a mood like mine,
> Implacable, persistent in revenge.
> (XI, 2098–2105)

Pompilia has stolen all of Jove's strength—his need for a polar opposite to hate, torture, humiliate, ravage, and utterly destroy—and has ended even by stealing his thunder: "So he was made; he nowise made himself" (VII, 1731). In the maddening frustration of his powerlessness to avenge himself on the unlikeliest person in the whole world to "have brought [him] to this pass!" Guido projects himself into the world beyond, with his threats and fulminations still exploding and rumbling through eternity. Perceived with minimalist realism, it is a grand mockery, the puffing and blowing of a psychotic pygmy with delusions of grandeur on a cosmic scale! What in a man of heroic stature might have inspired tragic terror collapses in Guido's case into pathetic horror. Endowed with just the degree of mystery inherent in metaphor, however, it becomes a satisfying instance of poetic justice: Guido deserves, not heaven or hell, but to be eternally himself, frustrated and defeated, maddened and raving, as a perfect example of the "use" of a "mood" like his.

If, then, in addition to its character as the *apologia* of a play-actor who cannot tell the truth even when he tries, Guido's second monologue is to be seen as the self-destructive struggle of a man determined at all costs to resist the one influence in his life experience that might have brought about his metamorphosis—thus remaining the dogmatic male supremacist inevitably bringing about his own defeat—how do Guido's ardent espousals of several currents of modern thought fit into the picture?

There are fragmentary outcroppings of modern philosophy throughout his monologue, scientific or historical points of view that were rooted in the Renaissance and produced lush harvests in the centuries following. Guido gives elaborate exposition to three of these points of view which, though all of a piece, can be separated out and identified as currents of thought that were conspicuous from the seventeenth century onward and were particularly dominant in the era in which Browning wrote *The Ring and the Book*. All three work from naturalist rather than supernaturalist assumptions, all have the general character of what is called scientific rationalism, and the raw effect of each is materialistic.

Guido's first excursus into the broad field of modern ethical and political theory is his reconstruction and endorsement of the theory of the "social contract" as developed by Hobbes and popularly known as utilitarianism, a theory that was given its peculiar nineteenth-century orientation by Jeremy Bentham and its most popular exposition by John Stuart Mill.

> I say that, long ago, when things began,
> All the world made agreement, such and such
> Were pleasure-giving profit-bearing acts,
> But henceforth extra-legal, nor to be:
> You must not kill the man whose death would please
> And profit you, unless his life stop yours
> Plainly, and need so be put aside:
> Get the thing by a public course, by law,
> Only no private bloodshed as of old!
> All of us, for the good of every one,
> Renounced such licence and conformed to law:
> Who breaks law, breaks pact, therefore, helps himself
> To pleasure and profit over and above the due,
> And must pay forfeit,—pain beyond his share:
> For pleasure is the sole good in the world,
> Any one's pleasure turns to someone's pain,
> So, let law watch for every one,—say we,
> Who call things wicked that give too much joy,
> And nickname the reprisal, envy makes,
> Punishment: quite right! thus the world goes round.
>   (XI, 515–534)

Guido accepts this as game theory: he broke the rules that on other occasions had protected him and hence must pay the price—"wherefore, here's my head,/Flung with a flourish!" (XI, 544–545). If there were genuine sincerity in Guido's dramatic gesture, we could forgive him a good deal on the strength of it. But even his Hobbesianism is calculated. He is using it to give a patina of philosophical respectability to his wolf-eat-dog approach to life and to torture his auditors as much as, under the circumstances, he possibly can. He has both despaired of getting free and failed fully to internalize the devastation with which the night will end; therefore, he is reckless, bullying, and unnaturally bold. It is repentance that Guido is afraid of—what he pushes to a distance as an "unmanly appetite for truth" (XI, 171) but what, in truth, he fears would draw him into an existential chaos in which he would simply disintegrate. So, on the one hand, he sets up a moral philosophy with a neat, impersonal pleasure-pain, reward-punishment calculus in which Man and Nature are the only factors, and, on the other, he debunks Christianity as the creation of "a crazy land/At a fabulous epoch" (XI, 565–566) which has, in these latter centuries, become the pretense of hypocritical knaves and the hocus-pocus of self-deluded fools.

Why, then, does the invisible poet link utilitarianism so closely with the character of Guido? Is Browning suggesting, even so obliquely, that the philosophy of Hobbes's *Leviathan* is rotten at the core, a codification of moral and political evil so systemic in the modern world that it falls into the Pope's category of "no hope/Except" (X, 2116–2117)—that is, that only "a suddenness of fate," a violent social apocalypse, can cleanse the system of this all-pervasive disease? Probably not, although such a fire-storm view of modern man's plague-struck situation had been held by one of Browning's most sympathetic contemporaries, John Ruskin; moreover, the working out of the myth of *The Ring and the Book* appears to have drawn Browning toward views that were not otherwise characteristic of him. But without peremptorily foreclosing that extreme interpretation of the linkage, it can perhaps be more fairly argued that Hobbes's assumption of a "State of Nature," his dependence on the sanctions of a pleasure-pain, reward-punishment ethical calculus to sustain the social contract, his thoroughgoing, freewheeling secularism, and his lack of provision for an inward-acting repentance, whether of a classical or a Judeo-Christian kind, makes the modern world a convenient hunting ground for such roving, cunning, ill-natured buccaneers as Guido, who prey upon the innocent, claim factitious historical privilege, exploit the basest self-interest in themselves and others, represent their motives in the falsest of ways, reduce morality to a contest of ingenious contrivance, and very often win. In an all-enveloping sense, it freezes male dominance into the moral and political system, and, through its emphasis on so-called free, natural competition, it makes the battle of the historically weak against the historically strong harder, more prolonged, and seemingly hopeless.

Neopaganism[13] is Guido's second modern excursus.

> So, the living truth
> Revealed to strike Pan dead, ducks low at last,
> Prays leave to hold its own and live good days
> Provided it go masque grotesquely, called
> Christian not Pagan? Oh, you purged the sky
> Of all gods save the One, the great and good,
> Clapped hands and triumphed! But the change came fast:
> The inexorable need in man for life—
> Life,—you may mulct and minish to a grain
> Out of the lump, so the grain left but live,—
> Laughed at your substituting death for life,
> And bade you do your worst,—which worst was done
> —Pass that age styled the primitive and pure
> When Saint this, Saint that, dutifully starved,
> Froze, fought with beasts, was beaten and abused
> And finally ridded of his flesh by fire,
> Keeping the while unspotted from the world!—
> Good: but next age, how goes the game, who gives
> His life and emulates Saint that and this?
> They mutiny, mutter who knows what excuse?
> In fine make up their minds to leave the new,
> Stick to the old,—enjoy old liberty,
> No prejudice, all the same, if so it please,
> To the new profession: sin o' the sly, henceforth!
> Let the law stand: the letter kills, what then?
> The spirit saves as unmistakeably.
> Omniscience sees, Omnipotence could stop,
> All-mercifulness pardons,—it must be,
> Frown law its fiercest, there's a wink somewhere.
>   (XI, 1973–2001)

Guido's version of neopaganism reads like a vulgarized revision of Julian the Apostate's nostalgic swan song as represented by Swinburne in his *Hymn to Proserpine*.[14] He begins with a sarcastic reference to the conceit, traditional in art and poetry, of the death of Pan and his age of pagan naturalism with the birth of Christ and the era of supernaturalism that that symbolic birth ushered in. Then he goes on to assert the unnatural rather than the supernatural character of Christianity, which, he says, yielded again to the "inexorable need in man for life" after a period of primitive and macabre enthusiasm for Christianity's cult of death, man having decided to enjoy the natural liberty of the old dispensation while making a formal profession of the new. The conclusion Guido derives from this scenario is that the Pope condemned him, not for the thing he did, but for his failure to observe the customary Roman formality of confessing his error and making an "act" of contrition. It is one of Guido's cleverest hits at Roman practice as observed by a Tuscan heathen, striking not at the fundamental idea of confession (recognition) and contrition (acceptance), though Guido has other reasons for rejecting that idea, but at the symbolic form that the idea must inevitably take, which just as inevitably deteriorates into empty ritual for routine-minded people and looks like the rankest sort of hypocritical formality to the alien-minded foreigner.

But even Guido's cleverness has a vulgar character, analogous to the difference between Sophocles' *Oedipus Tyrannus* and Seneca's *Oedipus Rex* or to the difference between the Greek tragedic prototype and the Roman revenge tragedy. Vulgarity is an innate dimension of Guido's character as a Tuscan. He has his counterpart in Lycaon, who was changed into a wolf for sacrificing a child on the altar of Zeus, and Tuscany is a mirror of the remote and savage Arcadia of an antiquity earlier than that of Theocritus's pastorals or of Virgil's conversion of it into "the land of love, song, and rustic simplicity."[15] The transformation he longs for, as his references to two stories from Ovid's *Metamorphoses* show (XI, 2048–2074), is backward, not forward. Let Pompilia become the daisied stream of the pastoral poets; let him become the prehuman wolf unhindered by the human half into which the wolfman has grown. Then, when he grows "Into the man again, be man indeed/And all man" (XI, 2054–2060), not that "other kind" of man, half woman instead of half wolf.

There is no fine logic to Guido's arguments, as there is no

refined legitimacy to his identification with the utilitarians or the neopagans. He makes an occasional hit that is stunningly on the mark, but he shoots at almost every target. What comes across clearest and strongest is that he does not know who he is, is desperately fearful of finding out, moves with centrifugal velocity away from a center that he cannot bear to look at, and creates an endless number of fabricated selves that provide momentary illusions, but which he can throw away without any serious sense of loss. He is the most dangerous of human types—one who ultimately has nothing to lose but a gnawing sense of pain that needs to be perpetually and futilely assuaged.

Guido's third modern excursus—into natural selection—is consistent with the first two; indeed, its terms, like Darwin's own, could have been drawn from political economy.

> My lamblike wife could neither bark nor bite,
> She bleated, bleated, till for pity pure,
> The village roused it, ran with pole and prong
> To the rescue, and behold the wolf's at bay!
> Shall he try bleating?—or take turn or two,
> Since the wolf owns to kinship with the fox,
> And failing to escape the foe by these,
> Give up attempt, die fighting quietly?
> The last bad blow that strikes fire in at eye
> And on to brain, and so out, life and all,
> How can it but be cheated of a pang
> While, fighting quietly, the jaws enjoy
> Their re-embrace in mid back-bone they break,
> After their weary work thro' the foes' flesh?
> That's the wolf-nature.
>
> (XI, 2302–2316)

Guido is both less informed and less sophisticated on this subject than on the other two, and that is appropriate. It would have been a rank anachronism had he known things about evolutionary theory wholly unfamiliar to the seventeenth century. "Nature red in tooth and claw" is a nineteenth-century metaphor, but the idea behind it is very old; it simply became more terrifying as faith in a superintending benevolent power weakened, and Guido can easily be acknowledged as ahead of his time in the virulence of his disbelief without being seen as anachronistic. Even his failure to use such terms as "the struggle for existence" and "the survival of the fittest" through "natural selection" is right: it would take another century for the first two terms to get into the book in which, more than half a century after that, Darwin would find them and, through them, the basis for his evolutionary hypothesis.

Guido's theatrical determination to *be* a wolf accounts for the virulent way he uses this idea; it accounts, too, for the deceptive high that he induces in himself by means of it. "My fight is figurative," he says to Cardinal Acciaiuoli soothingly, "blows i' the air,/Brain-war with powers and principalities,/Spirit-bravado, no real fisticuffs!" (XI, 2318–2320), seeing that his act has been so effective that his auditors fear bodily harm to themselves. But the strutting self-image will not last. Though in his state of self-inflation he assures them that he "shall not, . . . when the knock comes,/Cling to this bench nor flee the hangman's face" (XI, 2321–2322), he does much worse, cravenly attempting to erase all that he has said, begging piteously to be chained a madman, forever, to the dungeon floor, and praying hysterically to her on whom he had vowed to avenge himself even through eternity, Francesca Camilla Vittoria Angela Pompilia Comparini.

Notes

1. For a discussion of the overall structure of the poem, see Boyd Litzinger, "The Structural Logic of *The Ring and the Book*," in *Nineteenth-Century Literary Perspectives: Essays in Honor of Lionel Stevenson*, ed. Clyde de L. Ryals (Durham: Duke University Press, 1974), pp. 105–114.
2. See Robert Langbaum, "Is Guido Saved? The Meaning of Browning's Conclusion to *The Ring and the Book*," *Victorian Poetry*, 10 (1972), 289–305.
3. Despite the fact that even the Pope calls it "babble" (X, 1317), commentators still solemnly debate whether or not Browning believed in a literal hell. For a witty and graceful treatment of the issue, see Boyd Litzinger,

"The New Vision of Judgment: The Case of St. Guido," *Tennessee Studies in Literature,* XX (1975), 69–75.

4. The critical literature does not yet contain a sufficiently detailed, aesthetically adequate, historically informed comparative study of these two poems, though it seems likely that the passage of poetry from Romantic to Victorian and from Victorian to modern could be studied there with more specific and rewarding results than through any other model.

5. Quoted in *The Poems of Tennyson,* ed. Christopher Ricks (New York: W. W. Norton, 1969), p. 1463.

6. See *The Poems of Tennyson,* ed. Ricks, p. 860.

7. No suggestion is being made that the Arthurian chronology would have allowed a literal reversal, but that, had the classical tragedy of *Guinevere* been followed by a double-barreled revenge tragedy like that of *The Last Tournament,* the impact on the reader's perception of the poet's overall theme would have been enormous.

8. This is Langbaum's position. See note 2, above.

9. The relevance of a passage in the Preface to Newman's *Apologia,* which appeared in the year (1864) in which Browning started vigorously to work on *The Ring and the Book,* is inescapable:

> Yes, I said to myself, his very question is about my *meaning;* "What does Dr. Newman mean?" It pointed in the very same direction as that into which my musings had turned me already. He asks what I *mean;* not about my words, not about my arguments, not about my actions, as his ultimate point, but about that living intelligence, by which I write, and argue, and act. He asks about my Mind and its Beliefs and its sentiments. . . . (*Apologia pro Vita Sua,* ed. A. Dwight Culler [Boston: Houghton Mifflin, 1956], p. 16.)

10. See *The Poems of Tennyson,* ed. Ricks, p. 1464.

11. Other passages that might have been cited include XI, 162–176 (discussed earlier), 1311–1312, 1323–1324, 1342–1343, 1680–1687, 1688–1701, 2049–2061, 2128–2136, 2302–2316.

12. The terms *tragic redemption* and *pathetic damnation* are used here to establish a crucial distinction between poetics and theology. *The Ring and the Book* is an innovative *poem* in a long *literary* tradition, and though its subject matter, especially that aspect of its subject matter reflected in the Pope's monologue, has a theological dimension, Browning is not presuming to play a theologian's role. While redemption and damnation have theological connotations, they are not exclusively theological terms, and the issue of Guido's salvation should not be allowed to slip silently into a theological frame of reference. *Tragedy* and *pathos* are classical literary terms, and they establish the imaginative as distinct from the mystical touchstones appropriate to criticism of the poem and, carefully used, are safeguards against allowing the peculiarities of the poem's myth to draw the critic's thinking about it into a parochialism that, to many readers,

is alienating. Whether Guido "goes to heaven" or "goes to hell," if "speech must babble thus!" (X, 1317), is neither the critic's literary concern nor within his capacity to determine. That, gratefully, can be left to other seers. For the student of poetry, tragedy and pathos are sufficiently rich and pointed issues.

13. Neohellenism would be its finer, more cultivated Greek-rooted form.
14. Swinburne's Julian (*Hymn to Proserpine*, ll. 35–36) says, "Thou hast conquered, O pale Galilean; the world has grown grey from thy breath;/We have drunken of things Lethean, and fed on the fulness of death." Julian the Apostate, Roman Emperor after Constantine, is said to have uttered on his deathbed, "Thou hast conquered, Galilean."
15. See Philip Mayerson, *Classical Mythology in Literature, Art, and Music* (Waltham, Mass.: Xerox College Publishing, 1971), pp. 153–154.

10.

"Here were an end, had anything an end": A Final Note

For a poet in an age of ever shorter poems to take some 21,000 lines and 150,000 words to "teach" us the "one lesson" that "our human speech is naught" is, on the very face of it, a contradiction so outrageous that we must believe that he believed that the most constructive part of what he was trying to do could be finally discovered by contemplating the contradiction itself. *The Ring and the Book* is one of our language's longest, most complex testimonials to the idea that "Our human testimony [is] false"; it leads us through a labyrinth of representative estimations of the fame of certain characters to the conclusion that "our fame/And human estimation [are] words and wind, (XII, 832–836). The poet-speaker then insists that this is "the artistic way" of telling the truth, perhaps even the only way of telling it. So bold a cluster of contradictions lays a particularly heavy and precarious burden on "the artistic way" and demands that we search the poet-speaker's brief characterization of the way art works for much more content than is usually found there:

Art,—wherein man nowise speaks to men,
Only to mankind,—Art may tell a truth
Obliquely, do the thing shall breed the thought,
Nor wrong the thought, missing the mediate word.
So may you paint your picture, twice show truth,
Beyond mere imagery on the wall,—
So, note by note, bring music from your mind,
Deeper than ever the Andante dived,—
So write a book shall mean, beyond the facts,
Suffice the eye and save the soul beside.

(XII, 854–863)

The commentators on *The Ring and the Book* have customarily subjected the poet-speaker's characterization of "the artistic way" to their reading of the poem rather than subjecting
their reading of the poem to the poet-speaker's *ars poetica*. Thus
Langbaum: "Art, then, is truer than philosophical discourse
because it is closer to the facts, taking into account more com-
plexities, breeding the thought precisely. It shows the truth twice
in that it shows the physical facts and the metaphysical meaning behind them—opening out an extra dimension 'beyond . . .
the wall' because it brings to the business of understanding the
mind's deepest resource, imagination, what Wordsworth called
'Reason in her most exalted mood.' Above all, art is more convincing than philosophical discourse because, confronting false
formulations with facts, it causes us to start again with the facts
and construct the truth for ourselves."[1] Thus Altick and Loucks:
"With the events of the Franceschini case, as with the events
narrated of Christ, it is incumbent upon men to look behind
appearances and contested motives, to find the symbolic, transcendental meaning behind deeds. . . . *The Ring and the Book*
is the memorial of Browning's four years' dedication to his ideal
of art as a religious exercise."[2] Thus Sullivan: "The creative
process, then, does not involve a presentation of truth directly
to man, but a gradual revelation, indirectly, by the poet-agent
working through the medium of other human voices. In the
process, through his special gifts of insight and '*outsight*' and
extraordinary will-power, the poet gives to the final revelation
a spiritual and eternal value: this poem will '*Suffice the eye and
save the soul beside.*'"[3]

What these glosses on the passage under discussion share is a tendency to overliteralize the poet's meaning. Browning is not saying, in the literal sense in which Sullivan asserts it, that *The Ring and the Book*, by its "final revelation of a spiritual and eternal value," will "save the soul." Nor is it as literally true that Browning's "ideal of art" was "as a religious exercise" as it is that his ideal of religion was as an artistic exercise. Moreover, he was not so much urging his readers to "find the symbolic, transcendental meaning behind deeds," as Altick and Loucks assert, as showing them how marvelous an experience it is for the human spirit to discover in itself resources it had almost despaired of and to rise above an overwhelming infinity of death-dealing details to a vision of the clear midday sun. Christ is relevant essentially because Christ thought, taught, and acted like that; what poets and other people may have in common with Christ is a hieratic imagination and a will to *believe* that is a way to *become.* And the proper antithesis to art is not philosophical discourse, as Langbaum suggests, but unimaginative dullness. We may, as philosophers or nonphilosophers, "start again [and again] with the facts" and never "construct the truth for ourselves" unless we take "the artistic way"—that is, perceive reality, according to our capacity, *sub specie aeternitatis,* see "life steadily and see it whole" (Arnold), find "a way to the Better" by taking "a full look at the Worst" (Hardy). Browning certainly saw much modern philosophical discourse as having lost touch with the human situation in its wholeness and thus as inadequate to mankind's whole need, its elegant partiality actually contributing to man's growing sense of existential despair, but the corrective metaphor he applied to it was Pompilia, not the Pope: she rather than he exemplifies "Reason in her most exalted mood."

A whole human person in a whole universe is "the thought" that *The Ring and the Book,* like all art, may or should "breed." That is what makes *how* so much more imperative than *what;* it is why the poet speaks "nowise to men,/Only to mankind." To become a whole person in a whole universe is an endless, mysterious process of becoming for which one sometimes has, like Pompilia, to pay an awful price, to have "undue experience how much crime/A heart can hatch" (III, 107–108). But against the background of all the other men and women in the poem, in the context of all the *dramatis personae* that constitute its "image of the mighty world," its vale of tears, hers surely is the best consummation of our saddest, wisest, most honest, and most imaginative possibilities.

Everyone else is more privileged, and everyone else is slighter, shallower, less admirable, more terrified. Guido is her countervailing metaphor, not because he is so morally repugnant, but because he is such an ugly, failed, shrunken, self-imprisoned and self-tortured, unimaginative and hopeless human being. Caponsacchi and the Pope are drawn to her so magnetically because of a hidden germ of heroism in themselves that enables them to perceive the magnificence of her life in comparison with their own hopes and failures. Each of them is moved at such an existential level that he spends lavishly the whole treasury of angry thoughts and hieratic metaphors to give her human glory a heavenly habitation and a sacred name. In her is chiefly centered the imagery of the eye, the ear, and the heart—painting, symphony, lyric-epic poem—that stirs in them the thoughts that overleap the ramparts of the physical world and the feelings that cleanse them of their compacted earthly glooms and enable them to do their duty and save their souls. They are our aids to reflection, and through them, indirectly and partially, the poet lends his mind out to us. But as they are they, we are we, and thus the ultimate judgment, like the ultimate conversion, must be our own. Otherwise, even Paradise would be a world of fairy-tale magic in which we could not hope to be more than eternal strangers.

Pompilia also converts our initial contradiction into a tentative insight. She, too, uses "human speech," gives "human testimony," contributes to the "fame/And human estimation" of various characters. However, what she says is kept as close as possible to what, *in her personal experience,* was, is, and will be. She is "endeavour[ing] to explain her life," not creating verbal models of moral, epistemological, metaphysical existences external to her own knowledge, her own understanding, and her own imagination. She exonerates Violante insofar as generosity and realism will allow; she takes upon herself the responsibility of having acted on the Archbishop's evil counsel; she finds extenuation in her own naïveté for the virulence of Guido's early response to her and suspends judgment as to why his campaign against her was so relentless and fatal; the paeans of praise she sings for Caponsacchi are all firmly rooted in the limitless rush of gratitude she feels for his part in her own freedom, growth, and final fulfillment. Thus language and reality are kept in a simple, mutually creative relationship by Pompilia. The only "testimony" she gives is the testimony of a heart that has been hard at bay; her "speech" is not borrowed fabrication, but the language of personal experience and the perceptions that derive from it; the only contribution she makes to "fame/And human estimation" is offered in explanation of her own life and of those who, in quite contrary ways, made its ultimate outcome possible. So while she cannot redeem the essential falseness of "human speech," its tendency to detach itself from events and become a disguise rather than a revelation, she does show how, in a world in which man can hardly hope to do more than approximate the truth, we may get to love what we may get to know only hereafter.

Pompilia is a representative of all those countless, uncelebrated persons who succeed in avoiding the relentless pressures, transparently malignant or seemingly benign, to yield their identity to some regimen, institution, system, habit, expectation, or theory of their culture that unselfs them, often before they even know what they have lost. Instead, she stays as close as she can to the reality she knows and makes a philosophy out of her own experience. She not only knows what she believes; she also believes what she is. If there is that about her that deserves the epithet *miraculous,* it is the gift of temperament. She has a disposition to believe; she has the capacity to convert one order of experience into another order of experience; and when the opportunity comes—her pregnancy, her deliverance, her flowering into personal grandeur—she makes the conversion and saves her soul. But that is potentially so universal a characteristic of the human spirit that to call it miraculous is to call human nature itself a miracle. With that, *The Ring and the Book* has no quarrel.

Notes

1. Robert Langbaum, *The Poetry of Experience* (New York: Random House, 1957), p. 110. This commentary is offered as a gloss on XII, 854–863 (in the Kenyon edition, 859–867).
2. Richard D. Altick and James F. Loucks II, *Browning's Roman Murder Story* (Chicago: University of Chicago Press, 1968), p. 361. This is the authors' final sentence, after which they quote XII, 854–863.
3. Mary Rose Sullivan, *Browning's Voices in "The Ring and the Book"* (Toronto: University of Toronto Press, 1969), pp. 172–173.

Index

Books of The Ring and the Book *Cited*

Books of The Ring and the Book *Quoted*